Educational Leadership and the Community

SCHOOL LEADERSHIP AND MANAGEMENT SERIES

Series Editors: Brent Davies and John West-Burnham

Other titles in the series:

Effective Learning in Schools
Christopher Bowring-Carr and John West-Burnham

Effective School Leaders
John MacBeath and Kate Myers

From Bursar to School Business Manager
Reengineering leadership for resource management
Fergus O'Sullivan, Angela Thody and Elizabeth Wood

Leadership and Professional Development in Schools
How to promote techniques for effective professional learning
John West-Burnham and Fergus O'Sullivan

Managing Learning for Achievement
Strategies for raising achievement through effective learning
Edited by Christopher Bowring-Carr and John West-Burnham

Managing Quality in Schools (2nd edition)
John West-Burnham

Middle Management in Schools
How to harmonise managing and teaching for an effective school
Sonia Blandford

Reengineering and Total Quality in Schools
Brent Davies and John West-Burnham

Resource Management in Schools
Effective and practical strategies for the self-managing school
Sonia Blandford

Strategic Marketing for Schools
How to integrate marketing and strategic development for an effective school
Brent Davies and Linda Ellison

Inviting Educational Leadership
John Novak

Heads in Partnership
Joan Sallis

Schools for the 21st Century
Developing best practice
Irene Dalton, Richard Fawcett and John West-Burnham

Working with Support Staff
Trevor Kerry

Performance Management in Schools
How to lead and manage staff for school improvement
John West-Burnham, John O'Neill and Ingrid Bradbury

Educational Leadership and the Community

Strategies for School Improvement through Community Engagement

Edited by
Tony Gelsthorpe
John West-Burnham

An imprint of **Pearson Education**

London · New York · San Francisco · Toronto · Sydney · Tokyo · Singapore
Hong Kong · Cape Town · Madrid · Paris · Milan · Munich · Amsterdam

PEARSON EDUCATION LIMITED

Head Office:
Edinburgh Gate
Harlow CM20 2JE
Tel: +44 (0)1279 623623
Fax: +44 (0)1279 431059

London Office:
128 Long Acre
London WC2E 9AN
Tel: +44 (0)20 7447 2000
Fax: +44 (0)20 7447 2170
Website: www.educationminds.com

First published in Great Britain in 2003

The right of Tony Gelsthorpe and John West-Burnham to be
identified as authors of this work has been asserted by them in accordance
with the Copyright, Designs and Patents Act 1988.

ISBN 0 273 66164 7

British Library Cataloguing in Publication Data
A CIP catalogue record for this book can be obtained from the British Library.

10 9 8 7 6 5 4 3 2 1

Typeset by Pantek Arts Ltd, Maidstone, Kent.
Printed and bound in Great Britain by Bell and Bain Ltd, Glasgow

The Publishers' policy is to use paper manufactured from sustainable forests.

Contents

■　■　■

Preface

■　■　■

The relationship between schools and their communities is emerging as one of the significant themes in the debate about the reform of the education system in many countries. In this book we have sought to bring together a wide range of contributors to illuminate and extend the debate about the emerging issues in this important aspect of discussion about the nature of schools in the future.

As editors we have made a number of assumptions, notably that the status quo is not an option and that the concepts of education and community are inextricably entwined. We have therefore sought to balance theory and practice. Each contributor has been encouraged to write from their own perspective – there has been no attempt to create a consensus or new orthodoxy. The opening chapters make the case for a fundamental reappraisal of the relationship between schools and the communities they serve. There are then a number of phase-specific case studies of emerging practice. Then follows a number case studies which illustrate specific strategies and approaches. These are reinforced by a number of international examples. The collection ends with a discussion of possible ways forward.

We are very grateful to all the authors for their contributions to this project. We are particularly grateful to Penny Faust for her support in the editing of some chapters and to Ingrid Bradbury for her skill and tolerance in managing the production of the manuscript.

A book such as this inevitably reflects the interests and networks of the editors. We would welcome feedback and discussion on the issues raised.

Tony Gelsthorpe and John West-Burnham

Introduction

■ ■ ■

In the turbulent world of the twenty-first century we sometimes shun the word 'community'. Faced by the teeming multiplicities of inner city life and the division of the countryside between incomers and villagers born and bred, we are reluctant to talk of community without analysis, definition and explanation. Schools face a similar challenge in making sense of the chaotic complexity of the world in which they work. Yet successful schools have a strong sense of context: they understand the ambitions, aspirations and needs of those they educate and their families; they get to know their neighbours and seek to make them friends. They work to form a harmonious whole out of that which is fractured, disparate and diffuse.

In the last decade and a half, the task of schools has been the harder because of the rigidities of the system. The programme of reform has been driven by an agenda which has been more about uniformity than diversity. National strategies and government directives have been the engines of change. Much has been gained. Our primary schools, in particular, are recognised worldwide for the improvements they have wrought in literacy and numeracy standards and for narrowing the gap in achievement between the highest and lowest socio-economic groups. We have much to be proud of and tens of thousands of children have benefited.

But much has also been lost. The culture of too many of our schools has become managerial, driven by short-term plans, objectives and targets. The inspection regime, undoubtedly one of the key factors in raising standards, has nonetheless given rise to a mood of compliance. Those who look over their shoulders cannot see the horizon.

But since the general election of 2001, the government has begun to strike a new note. The Secretary of State has said repeatedly that the next wave of reform must come from within the schools, driven by teachers and their leaders. She calls this transformation. We have a new emphasis on innovation and creativity, a respect for the inventiveness and imagination of professionals rather than an instinct to suppress any initiative which deviates from the norm.

Of course, the profession does not believe it yet and government ministers must expect to be judged by their actions over the long term, not the words of last week's press release. And it will take time, years rather than months, to transform a culture which has become passive, bureaucratic and risk averse into one which is vibrant, creative and bold. But what an opportunity there now is for school leaders to seize.

Their task is riven with paradox. They must maintain standards within the core subjects and yet inject into the curriculum the verve, imagination and spirit which have been threatened by over-prescription. They must give teachers the opportunity for invention, creativity and the exercise of professional judgement, while taking action to reduce the heavy workload which is driving too many of them out of the profession. They must expand the vision, values and ambitions of their pupils as international citizens, while continuing to meet the needs of the local community of which they are part.

But perhaps the school's relationship with the local community is less a source of paradox than a means of resolving it. The local community is, in a real sense, the gateway to the world. In developing a deep and mutual relationship with the people and organisations among which it is embedded, the school gains not only information, knowledge and support. Its sense of moral purpose is enhanced as its impact extends beyond the young to the community as a whole. The interplay of different value sets, the conflict of competing priorities, the need to find agreed solutions offer a rich educational opportunity. The school is stronger for subjecting its aspirations to the scrutiny of community expectation.

The shape of the English education system will change, perhaps dramatically, over the next decade. There will be more specialist schools. There will be closer working relationships with the independent sector. There is likely to be considerable encouragement to schools to work federally, sharing resources and expert staff, using technology and more flexible patterns of work the better to differentiate teaching to meet pupils' needs. All of these things will both challenge traditional relationships between school and community and offer massive opportunities to rethink, revive and renew. This book offers a reconsideration of the principles and purposes of schools' roles in community education and leadership. It is timely indeed.

Heather Du Quesnay
Director and Chief Executive
National College for School Leadership
July 2002

About the contributors

■ ■ ■

Michelle Anderson was the inaugural Executive Manager of the Royal Children's Hospital Education Institute (RCHEI), Melbourne, Australia. The institute is a unique model of intersecting practice, research and training with a particular focus on innovative uses of technology. Previous to this position, Michelle has worked extensively in education in service, leadership, training and policy roles in, for example, drug education and health curriculum development. She has a Masters of Education from the University of Melbourne; her thesis examined multiple leadership in schools. Awarded a prestigious Winston Churchill Fellowship, Michelle travelled to the UK and Canada to investigate the development and leadership of collaborative initiatives in strengthening the health and education interface for children and young people with health and associated needs. Michelle's current consultancy work focuses on proactive evaluations of programmes across health and education.

Pat Bagshaw has taught for 33 years, in a variety of schools, in different London Boroughs, but leaving London for the interesting challenge of being the 4th Principal of Countesthorpe Community College in Leicestershire., between 1989 and 1995. Pat has had a long interest and involvement in community education, starting as a student in Toxteth. She started teaching in Newham in 1969, undertaking various jobs, becoming a Senior Teacher in one of ILEA's 4 'community education projects' at Quintin Kynaston, in Westminster. Deputy Headship in Newham, from 1987–1989, led to a first headship at Countesthorpe. Pat returned to Newham in 1989, as Head of a school to be replaced by a new school, built for the community of Custom House, in the 'Docks' area. This opened in 1999 and currently is being established as a community school serving the area, raising expectations and promoting educational opportunity in a developing community.

C.J. Gerda Bender is a senior lecturer in the Department of Teaching and Training Studies. Her research concerns adult and community education for community building; school–community–university collaboration (service learning) and community programme development and evaluation. She is co-author of five books and has published various articles on community education and development. Gerda teaches adult learning; adult and community education; lifelong learning; education for community building; community programme development and evaluation; and learning theories. Gerda is an active community developer and presents various courses on community development and does consultancy on programme development and evaluation (impact assessment). She has significant research experience in the fields of adult and community education and community development/building. She is a counselling psychologist, registered at the Health Professions Council of South Africa, and social worker, registered at the SA Interim Council for Social Work.

Frances Bowring-Carr has a long experience of teaching in secondary schools, mainly in west Belfast. During the late 70's and early 80's she was involved in extensive school-based staff and curriculum development with a range of schools across Northern Ireland, working from the Department of Further Professional Studies in Education at Queen's University Belfast. Until her recent retirement, she was an inspector of schools with the NI Department of Education for sixteen years.

Christopher Bowring-Carr has taught at secondary and tertiary levels in the UK, the Middle East and the United States. He was, for some 15 years, an HMI, as an English and a secondary specialist. He resigned from the Inspectorate in 1988 and now lives in Northern Ireland. He works as an independent consultant and as a tutor for the Open University and the Universities of Leicester and of Hull. He first became interested in community education when he was an AEO with Leicestershire in the early 70's, a county that was innovative in this area, as in so many others. His other interests are in the ethics of educational leadership, and in seeing how the curriculum offered by our schools and colleges can shed the assumptions and organisation of the 19th century in order to meet the needs of the children of the 21st.

Bernard Clarke attended grammar school in Redditch, Worcestershire. There followed periods of work in a bank, lorry driving, teaching with VSO in India and in residential social work. His degree from Bradford University in Social Sciences and Psychiatric Social Work was followed by a PGCE at Bristol University. He worked for ten years at Filton High School before being apprenticed to Joan Gregory, followed by Keith Foreman, as Vice Principal at Burleigh Community College, Loughborough. He was headteacher of Peers School, Oxford from 1988 until he joined King Alfred's, Wantage in January 1998. Bernard is married to Anthea, a health visitor, and they have four children who have all attended the schools he has worked at, providing excellent professional development for the headteacher!

Heather Du Quesnay is the Director and Chief Executive of the National College for School Leadership. She started her career as a Latin teacher and taught in Birmingham for 11 years, the last five years as a deputy head of a comprehensive school. She went on to become Director of Education in Hertfordshire and the London Borough of Lambeth. Before taking up her post at NCSL, she was responsible for major improvements and restructuring in several local education authorities.

Tony Gelsthorpe, recently Principal of a Community College in the UK, is now an independent consultant. He has worked in secondary schools, community colleges and the education department and advisory service of a local education authority. University tutoring and international consultancies in Germany, Sweden, the Middle East and South East Asia have contributed to his professional life. He currently works with various organisations including the Department for Education and Skills, the Learning and Skills Council, schools, local authorities and non-profit organisations. A practising community learner, he helps to manage a co-operative and friendly society promoting arts training through performance for young people in the community locally and internationally. For the Secondary Heads Association, he is the author of *Managing Community Education*; with Christopher Bowring-Carr and John West-Burnham, *Transforming Schools through Community Education*, published by the Community Education Development Centre.

Jean Gledhill is Principal of John Kitto Community College in Plymouth. She was born in Blackpool but lived and was educated in Sheffield. She trained at St Mary's College of Education Cheltenham. For 15 years, at Oakbank School, Keighley, she led the Expressive Arts Department and was part of a team running the Modular Curriculum. During that time, she listened to Harry Ree, who had retired to settle in North Yorkshire. This opened up the beginning of an understanding of the real joys and benefits comprehensive community education can bring. After leadership experience in Leicestershire schools she became head of North Manchester High School for Girls from 1993–2001. The school moved from 18% 5 or more A–Cs at GCSE to 40% and from 714 students to over 1400 and Beacon status. More importantly, it became a true community school. The opportunity came to move again and a chance to run a fully designated Community College John Kitto in Plymouth.

John Grainger is Director of Education and Lifelong Learning at the Community Education Development Centre; his team specialises in community based solutions to reaching 'hard-to-reach' groups and extending learning opportunities to those who have both benefited least from education and who least understand the value of learning for transforming lives. This message is communicated to providers of learning and to potential learners directly. Particular aspects of that work are the development and nurturing of community schools (schools that work in and with their communities), assisting schools with community plans that are required as part of funding bids, and working with Local Education Authorities and Education Action Zones and their schools in developing parental and community involvement. They work closely with teams at DfES, with schools, local authorities and regional government agencies and departments, and the voluntary sector. Previously John worked for more than thirty years in local government roles involved with youth work, adult learning, community development, play, community schools, giving learners a voice, and capacity building with the voluntary/community sector. John also taught for three years in a Leicestershire middle school. He has also had the useful and interesting experience of chairing a national charity for three years.

Peter Hall Jones has been the head teacher at Little London Community Primary school and Nursery since September 1994. Prior to this, he worked as an advisory Teacher for Leeds City council and in schools in Leeds, Hackney and Tower Hamlets after leaving Charlotte Mason College in Ambleside with his teaching degree in applied Education. Peter has continued to work with what he regards as 'the best team of teachers, support staff and out side agencies, parents/carers and children' at Little London whilst enjoying secondments, speaking engagements and other 'outside school' activities with Lea's, the DfES and most recently The Cabinet Office Women and Equality Unit. Little London Community Primary School and Nursery has been identified as both Visionary and an example of Excellence. Peter and all the staff and friends of Little London continue to strive for innovative and continuous improvement.

Yardena Harpaz is Director General of the Israel Association of Community Centres. After wide experience in school teaching and youth work in Israel and the USA she became involved in community school projects in Israel. She is involved in a wide range of national and international bodies concerned with educational and community development. She has published widely on topics related to community and education.

Jan Heystek was a deputy principal in a secondary school before he joined the University of Pretoria. At the moment he is senior lecturer in the Department of Education Management, lecturing at all levels from diploma to doctoral students. He is the secretary of the South African Education Law and Policy Association, as well as the chair of the Education Management interest group of the Education Association of South Africa. Some of the research projects that he has completed include the management problems and the related in-service training of school managers in South Africa, the partnership between parents and schools to improve education in schools, and the role of learners in the governing body in secondary schools. He is the study leader of several doctoral and master degree students and the author or co-author of several publications.

Tony Hinkley is Director of the 21st Century Education Project in Dudley. Previously he taught for 30 years, 16 years as deputy headteacher of a large comprehensive school. He also has experience in industry and management training. He is a member of the Executive Committee and National Council for the Secondary Heads Association and leads their work on 'Schools of the Future'. This has led to the creation of his current post as Director of a new project, putting SHA's vision into practice as a pilot scheme. Currently he is working to create a 'Classroom of the Future' centrepiece at Farnborough International Airshow 2002. He is also an adviser on projects including developing parent partnerships in primary schools and learning-centred leadership. He is a member of the 'Thinking and Learning' Advisory Group for NFER-Nelson and the 14–19 Black Country Partnership Group. Recently he led a 'Learning to Learn' pilot research project in his school in conjunction with the Campaign for Learning and has contributed to the RSA's Competence-based Curriculum.

Javed Khan is Assistant Director, Head of Lifelong Learning, Birmingham City Council, which he joined after working for over 15 years in schools, sixth form and further education colleges. He leads a division that is responsible for the UK's largest Adult Education and Youth Services, Birmingham's Family Learning provision, the Excellence Challenge programme and Education's International Development Unit. He also leads on the city's drive towards becoming a major Learning City. Javed has vast experience of working in large urban areas whilst leading initiatives that widen participation and reduce social exclusion. He has worked extensively with the voluntary/community sector and local business, developing strategic partnerships to tackle inner city deprivation. He is a member of the Basic Skills National Advisory Committee and a Board Member of the Learning Communities Network (LCN). Javed was highlighted by *The Guardian* newspaper (September 2001) as one of 12 'rising stars' in UK local government.

Marianne Lundholm has a background as a teacher and after graduate studies in linguistics taught Swedish as a second language to immigrants. She the worked as a vice principal in adult education and was responsible for staff and curriculum development. During the 1990s she worked as a teacher educator. At the same time she worked 'in the field' on school improvement and team development. Now she is involved in a project run by the Swedish Institute for Public Health, National Board of Immigration and the Board of Education. The aim is to support seven schools in immigration areas to 'open the school'. The project is called 'The school in the middle of the suburb' and is a network of seven schools meeting at conferences with different themes connected issues arising in community education. Since 1983 she has been the Swedish representative of ICEA Europe and has initiated exchanges between Sweden, England, Germany and Canada about community education. She has been involved in planning several conferences and has also been active as a workshop leader. She has also worked with a small group within ICEA working on standards for community schools.

Neil McKechnie is Head of Educational Development for West-Dunbartonshire Council working with the new community schools project. He has professional qualifications both in social work and education and associated management experience. From 1986 he was involved from the beginning in integrating pre-5 year old children's services as part of Strathclyde Region Council's policy of integrating these services. He is leading the Integrated Children's Services Approach between education, social services and health and this is a key policy of the Scottish Executive. In a voluntary capacity he works as a Justice of the Peace.

Julian Piper has been Community Schools Network Manager for Community Education Development Centre in Coventry since May 2001. He has also worked on the Schools Plus Teams Project for DfES jointly with Education Extra and organises the regular briefings for LEA Governor Services Managers. Julian was involved in youth work and outdoor education whilst completing a chemistry degree and training to be a chemistry teacher in the early 1970's and then taught in Oxford for 10 years before gaining a secondment to open the school to the community with help and support from CEDC and the then Oxford Polytechnic. He became area youth worker for the same area of the City and continued to develop a substantial provision for outdoor and residential activities for mixed age groups (including adults and young people). In 1989, after gaining the Advanced Diploma in Community Education with Warwick University and CEDC, he became Vice Principal at Babington Community College in Leicester where he was responsible for the management of a large adult education programme, a full day-care nursery and youth work provision.

Nick Thornton has been CEO of the Australian Principals Centre Ltd for three years coming tithe position after seven years as General Manager of Children's Services at the Spastic Society of Victoria. Before that Nick was a secondary teacher, curriculum developer, Principal of Altona Secondary College (seven years) and a senior public servant. His last position in the Education department of Victoria was General Manager of the Barwon South Western Region in country Victoria. In an earlier life, he was President of a large subject teacher association for ten years and is the author of several school textbooks. He has presented at a range of leadership conferences at national and international level and has worked as a consultant to UNESCO. Other sins include being a certified practising accountant and enjoying travel, good food and wine.

Sue Wedgwood is the head teacher of Summerbank Primary School, Tunstall, Stoke-on-Trent. It is a large inner city school with 400 children on roll, 43% of who are from the ethnic minority community. She was seconded to the LEA working with neighbouring schools to develop and enhance Personal, Social and Health Education. Studying at Manchester Metropolitan University, she gained an MSc in Education Management. The focus of her research was Ethnic Minority Achievement. A long-term partner of CEDC, Sue has developed many community initiatives at the school and recently won the West Midlands Regional Teacher of the Year Award for school and community involvement.

John West-Burnham is Director of Professional Research and Development at the London Leadership Centre, Institute of Education, University of London. He was previously Professor of Educational Leadership, International Leadership Centre, University of Hull. John worked in schools, further and adult education for 15 years before moving into higher education. He was a part-time Open University tutor for 15 years. He has worked at Crewe and Alsager College, the University of Leicester and the University of Lincolnshire and Humberside. He was also Development Officer for Teacher Performance for Cheshire LEA. John is author of *Managing Quality in Schools*, co-author of *Effective Learning in Schools, Leadership and Professional Development in Schools* and co-editor of *Performance Management in Schools*, plus 12 other books and over 30 articles and chapters. John has worked in Australia, Israel, New Zealand, Republic of Ireland, Singapore, South Africa, UAE and USA. He is co-ordinator of the European School Leadership Project and is a consultant to the National College for School Leadership in England. John's current research and writing interests include transformational leadership, leadership learning and development and educational leadership in the community.

1

▪ ▪ ▪

Education, Leadership and the Community

John West-Burnham

The purpose of this chapter is to explore the prevailing definitions of education, the relationship between schools and the community and emerging
models of educational leadership.

The central proposition of this chapter is that the concept of school improvement
is essentially redundant and that the focus of the education system in the future
will have to be on the community – the key determinant of educational success.
This means that the definition of educational leadership has to switch from institutional improvement to community regeneration. The technical aspects of
schooling can only go so far in enhancing educational achievement – to achieve
maximum potential, fundamental change in the community is necessary.

The nature and purpose of education

A discussion of the nature and purpose of education is an essential prelim-
inary to any discussion of the relationship between schools and the
community they serve. One of the most significant features of education in
most societies in the twentieth century, especially in its final decades, was the
increasingly technical nature of schooling. The curriculum became much nar-
rower and more technically focused, notably through the emphasis on literacy
and numeracy. This reductionist approach has had the effect, in combination
with prevailing models of accountability, of raising standards. However the
definition of standards is so narrow and instrumental that there is a danger
that success in schooling has marginalised a broader concept of educating.

The dominant purpose of education in many national systems is economic; the creation of an employable workforce. The key measure of such employability has been seen as literacy and numeracy. Parallel with this growing emphasis has been increasing concern about the implications of this approach.

> [These results] suggest strongly that more attention might be paid to the non-academic behaviour and development of children … It also suggests that schooling ought not to be assessed solely on the basis of the production of reading and maths ability.

> (Feinstein, L. in Mulford and Silius, 2001)

What was seen historically as one constituent of education, academic success, has now become the dominant force which, because of its links with accountability, has tended to drive out the other dimensions. The practical results of this, in England, are to be found in the marginalisation of the humanities, the arts and the engagement of schools in a broader range of activities usually classified as the extra-curricular. Thus, in England and similar education systems, education has in effect become academic schooling. Recognition of the problems this might cause has resulted, in England, in the introduction of citizenship to the curriculum. However, it has been introduced as a subject – it has been commodified. What should be a set of social activities and behaviours has been rendered an artificial construct – a subject rather than a way of life.

It is dangerous, and over-ambitious, to try and produce the definitive definition of what education should be. But in the context of this book certain fundamental propositions can be advanced; the most basic statement is found in article 26 of the Universal Declaration of Human Rights:

> Education shall be directed to the full development of the human personality and to the strengthening of respect for human rights and fundamental freedoms. It shall promote understanding, tolerance and friendship.

This statement can be elaborated into a number of specific propositions about the purpose of education:

- to enhance the personal, social, cultural, ethical and spiritual development of every individual;
- to prepare people to play an active part in their communities as citizens in a democracy;
- to develop the potential to be employable and to play a full economic role in society;
- to maximise life chances through academic success;
- to create a society founded in acceptance and tolerance.

If these fundamental propositions are accepted as a benchmark, education is essentially a social process. How strange then that education in most so-called advanced societies is usually expressed through a system of schooling. Schools are essentially artificial constructs; they bureaucratise the education process through time, place and content. Education is commodified into packages –

terms, subjects, schemes of work, etc. The twentieth century saw the increasing divorce of schools from the realities of life in community, society and work. This is in sharp distinction to the view of Henry Morris, arguably one of the key figures in the theory and practice of community approaches in education, who stated that:

> We should abolish the barriers which separate education from all those activities which make up adult living … It should be the first duty of education to concern itself with the ultimate goals of education.

(Bowring-Carr et al., 2000: 6)

The dominant trends in most English-speaking education systems in recent decades have been to reinforce the bureaucratic infrastructure of schools; to narrow the definition of academic success and to promulgate the view that the primary purpose of education is economic – in both personal and national terms. In the context of a narrow and constraining model of accountability, the effect has been to reinforce the institutional insularity of schools and to exacerbate the impact of social and economic factors on organisational success.

The net result of these trends has been, paradoxically, to weaken the links between schools and their communities while demonstrating the importance and significance of such links.

Schools and their social context

While social disadvantage may not be an excuse for poor achievement in academic terms it certainly is an explanation. As Power et al. (2002: 26) conclude in their study:

> [Educational] outcomes in deprived areas are worse than those in non-deprived areas, whether they are measured in terms of qualification, attendance, exclusions or 'staying on' rates. Inner-city areas in particular feature as having low outcomes.

They go on to point out that in England in the 1990s 'the gap in outcomes grew rather than narrowed' (p.64). They also point to the need to reduce the 'compositional effects that appear to result from high concentrations of disadvantaged students' (p.65). A significant issue emerges in their conclusion that:

> … schools serving deprived populations could do more to ensure better home–school relations, which appear to be less facilitative than those in schools serving non-deprived areas. (p.66)

Schools in deprived areas have a great deal in common with schools in non-deprived areas – the same curriculum, assessment regimes, inspection and accountability models, etc. There are significant differences in funding, teacher supply and access to resources but these are not consistent as causal factors. What is consistent is the notion of deprivation.

This raises the question of the nature of the relationship between schools and their communities. Mulford and Silius (2001: 5) found that there was not a direct causal relationship between high community involvement and improving student outcomes:

> On the basis of our results, and if a choice needs to be made between working with and being sensitive to the community and improving home educational environments, then the latter will have more direct and immediate 'payoff' for student outcomes ... Of course, having a strong community focus may be important for other reasons such as for the development of social capital in the community, especially in poor inner city and rural communities.

The distinction between family and community is a valid one – the impact of the family is more direct, immediate and sustainable. However the family is a classic manifestation of community. The status, significance and value attached to the family will often be a product of broader, community-based values. The resilience and potency of the family will be a function of generic factors – most significantly social capital.

In their study of the factors influencing the development of young people in the USA, the Search Institute (2000) found what they describe as a 'crumbling infrastructure' which has a number of key manifestations:

1 Most adults no longer consider it their responsibility to play a role in the lives of their children outside the family.

2 Parents are less available for their children because of demands outside the home.

3 Adults and institutions have become more uncomfortable articulating values.

4 Society has become more and more age segregated.

5 Socialising systems (e.g. families, schools and congregations) have become more isolated, competitive and suspicious of each other.

6 The mass media have become influential shapers of young people's attitudes, norms and values.

7 As problems and solutions have become more complex, more of the responsibility for young people has been turned over to professionals.

These symptoms are in stark contradistinction to what would normally be regarded as criteria for an effective community. Amit (2002: 18) offers criteria to describe a community:

> People care because they associate the idea of community with people they know, with whom they have shared experiences, activities, places and/or histories. Community arises out of an interaction between the imagination of solidarity and its realisation through social relations.

If there are not the 'shared experiences' and the 'realisation through social relations' then community cannot be said to exist and the factors identified by the Search Institute can be said to be both cause and effect. What is being described is a paucity of social capital – the lower the level of engagement in a community, the lower the level of social capital, and so the more likely it is that an area will be deprived – not just in economic terms but also in social terms. Social poverty is as negative and destructive as economic poverty.

For Putnam (2000: 296–7) there is an absolute link between levels of social capital and success in the education system:

> *States that score high on the Social Capital Index – that is, states whose residents trust other people, join organisations, volunteer, vote and socialise with friends – are the same states where children flourish: where babies are born healthy and where teenagers tend not to become parents, drop out of school, get involved in violent crime, or die prematurely due to suicide or homicide. Statistically, the correlation between high social capital and positive child development is as close to perfect as social scientists ever find in data analysis of this sort.*

Social Capital is essentially about networks, trust, engagement, communication, shared values, aspirations and interconnectedness. High social capital produces the benefits that Putnam describes above. He also points out that 'social capital appears to be a complement, if not a substitute, for Prozac, sleeping pills, antacids' (p.289). Social capital appears to be the panacea for the social, psychological and physiological ills of society, and it might even extend to education.

What is clear is that high social capital enhances academic success. Therefore one answer to academic under-achievement might be not just to strive to improve the efficiency of schools but rather to increase social capital.

Education improvement and the community

The last decade of the twentieth century was the decade of school improvement. Vast amounts of energy were expended in improving the outcomes of schooling – and they were generally successful. By a range of criteria schools were much better at schooling; literacy and numeracy scores rose and there was significant improvement against a range of criteria. This was largely achieved through the implementation of national strategies at institutional level. One effect of this was to make principals and headteachers the managers of externally imposed policy initiatives. What was referred to as leadership was in fact 'super-management' as the key areas of leadership activity were removed to the centre and implementation became the criterion for success. However this success criterion is that of a previous generation – the success of schools may not be appropriate for a world in which:

Entirely new points of departure will be required in order to significantly improve the capacity of all segments of society, including enterprises and local communities, to break with the rigid and hierarchical methods of the past and embrace solutions based on greater personal accountability, internal motivation and uniqueness.

(Stevens et al., 2000: 22)

Most government policies fail to address the issues of 'personal accountability, internal motivation and uniqueness'; rather they emphasise consistency, conformity and compliance. According to Mulgan (2000: 184):

Too much was imposed top-down rather than involving communities themselves; too many initiatives were short-term; too many focused on one or two problems rather than tackling the cluster of related problems in the round.

For Mulgan two of the key themes in the 'emerging agenda' for learning are:

- Policies for knowledge go wider than formal education: diet, housing and poverty bear directly on cognitive development and educational performance.
- Education and learning will increasingly take place beyond educational institutions. (Mulgan, 2000: 151–2)

If a fundamental distinction between school management and educational leadership is accepted, then a radical reconceptualisation of the nature and purpose of such leadership is required. In essence the shift is from institutional improvement to community transformation. It is very doubtful as to how much more capacity to improve there is in the school system. A football team does not improve its league position by setting its players to run faster or pass more balls. It has to score more goals; running and passing are necessary but not sufficient factors in winning matches. Improving schools is a necessary but not sufficient component of educating a society.

If educational success is a function of high social capital, then educational leadership has to make capital development a high priority. The change is from an emphasis on the school as an institution to the school as an agency:

Some forms of social capital are, by choice or necessity, inward looking and tend to reinforce exclusive identities and homogeneous groups ... Other networks are outward looking and encompass people across diverse social cleavages.

(Putnam, 2000: 22)

School improvement leads to bonding, introspection and detachment. While this creates institutional integrity it compromises engagement and networking – the basis of the creation of social capital. If academic standards are to be raised in a sustainable way and broader educational aspirations achieved, then educationists will have to see their role in terms of creating social capital rather than just improving classroom practice.

The Search Institute (1998: 8) talks about 'asset building' rather than social capital but the principles are the same:

The answer doesn't lie primarily in creating new programs or in hiring in more professionals. The primary answer lies in bringing into reality a fundamental shift in thinking – from a problem focus to a positive vision.

The Institute goes on to identify the characteristics of asset-building communities which include:

- All residents take personal responsibility for building assets in children and adolescents.
- The community thinks and acts intergenerationally.
- The community builds a consensus on values and beliefs, which it seeks to articulate and model.
- Families are supported, educated, and equipped to elevate asset building to top priority.
- The community-wide commitment to asset building is long term and sustained.

(Search Institute, 1998: 9)

These points (and others not quoted) reinforce the model of a rich network with high interdependence and, perhaps the crucial component, a shared vision within the community as a whole. Writing in 1915, Dewey argued:

The role of the community in making the schools vital is just as important as the role of the school itself. For in a community where schools are looked upon as isolated institutions, as a necessary convention, the school will remain largely so in spite of the most skilful methods of teaching. But a community that demands something visible from its schools, that recognises the part they play in the welfare of the whole… Such a community will have social schools, and whatever its resources, it will have schools that develop community spirit and interests.

(Skilbeck, 1970: 125)

'Social schools' is a very powerful image in this context, as is the notion of a school being 'visible'; both reinforce the notion of schools being *of* their communities, not just in their communities.

An alternative, but reinforcing, perspective is found in the work of Paulo Friere. He argues for education as dialogue – the shared creation of meaning and the movement to action. For Friere dialogue is a co-operative activity based in respect which can serve to enhance community through the building of social capital. Although Friere's methods are not directly transferable to school systems, his emphasis on collegiality and consensual governance offers a model for community action.

An example of how this approach might work in practice is found in the New Mexico Community Conversations Project – a project funded by the Mott Foundation in eight school communities in New Mexico, USA. The project centres on 'public conversations' involving common interest groups (for example, all parents or all teachers) which are trained and facilitated in public conversations skills and then moved into mixed interest groups. The project, currently in its early stages, is designed:

- to enhance diliberative and civic skills;
- to promote community involvement in education and collaborative problem solving;
- to focus on teaching and learning;
- to generate new understanding of and commitment to education;
- to use public conversations as a means to improve education.

Dialogue is seen as having a number of positive attributes – it creates positive and sophisticated networks, it enhances the communication skills in the community and it can help secure involvement and sustain motivation. The conversations about education are of themselves educative. The process is also fundamentally democratic in that it encourages participation and builds capability in communities traditionally disenfranchised.

The project has a number of transformational features:

- It focuses on educational improvement and reform through the active involvement of all stakeholders.
- It creates a common skill base to support interaction.
- It reinforces and enhances engagement.
- It creates rich and sophisticated networks.

The project has the potential to inform policy, develop social capital, strengthen engagement and release human potential (information provided by Dr George Otero).

These perspectives on education in the community have significant implications for our understanding of the nature of leadership. The focus has to shift from improving the school as an institution, measured by very limited criteria, to developing social capacity in the community – still measurable but using very different criteria. It is reasonable to argue that the development of social capital would be a major factor in facilitating school improvement.

The management of an institution is specific, focused and controllable; leadership of the community is diffuse and complex. Educational leaders are very well placed to provide leadership in the community – schools as institutions usually have very high social capital. Educational leadership is fundamentally concerned with values and essentially aspirational in nature. In many communities, schools represent the biggest single public investment and are the best-resourced organisations – yet many only function for 15 per cent of the year. Most importantly there is a symbiotic link between schools and their communities – children. Schools need to be successful with their communities, not in spite of them. The other chapters in this book provide numerous examples of the strategies available to schools to work towards higher engagement with the communities they serve. On the basis of the evidence in those chapters it is possible to offer a model of the characteristics of educational leaders in the community.

Educational leadership for community development

Values

There is a profound ethical base to such leadership. At its heart are the principles of equity and entitlement. This is extended into the belief that a crucial component of the educational process is the fight for social justice. Economic, social and cultural poverty is a major barrier to educational opportunity. Leadership in this context is about more than fighting discrimination – it is about the active promotion of a society based on positive acceptance and engagement. Many schools have a distinguished record of promoting equity, but the strategy has to be actively promulgated in the community if it is to be sustainable.

When individuals (students, teachers, parents) are bound to shared ideas, values, beliefs, and frameworking, bonds of fellowship emerge which empower the membership as a whole.

(Sergiovanni, 2001: 66)

The school becomes a microcosm, a model, of the ideal for the community – but this has to be extended if it is to be sustainable. While the moral foundations give a community authenticity, it is in the extension into the broader community that it becomes sustainable:

The system of shared values and beliefs creates an identity among the members of a social network, based on a sense of belonging. Thus the social network is engaged in communication within a cultural boundary which its members continually recreate and renegotiate. Social boundaries ... are ... boundaries of meaning and expectations.

(Capra, 2002: 76)

It is a key function of leadership to extend the boundaries of shared meaning and expectations.

Vision

School leaders have become increasingly familiar with the concept of having a vision as to how the school should be in the future. This has to be extended into the whole community. Indeed it is difficult to see how a vision for an institution could be developed without reference to the wider community. Such a vision might include reference to:

- shared values and vision
- social cohesion
- economic growth
- the development of a learning community
- inclusiveness
- safety and security.

Such a vision will be subject to regular review and change – the speed of social, economic and technological change requires regular, fundamental review of the vision:

> *Leadership consists in facilitating the emergence of novelty. This means creating conditions rather than giving directions, and giving the power of authority to empower others ... Being a leader means creating a vision: it means going where nobody has gone before. It also means enabling the community as a whole to create something new.*

(Capra, 2000: 106)

Relationships

Relationships are the life-blood of the community; they translate aspirations into experience and are the single most powerful signifiers of communication and culture. Our judgements about almost all social interactions, membership of organisations and communities are usually expressed in terms of our perceptions of the quality of relationships. The value of a friendship is not measured in terms of its technical efficiency but rather in terms of the level of emotional engagement. Although Goleman (2002: 192) is discussing organisations in the following extract, the principles can be readily applied to communities; the purpose is:

> *... to foster emotionally intelligent leadership widely and deeply at every level, and to systematically create norms and a culture that support truth and transparency, integrity, empathy, and healthy relationships.*

For Goleman the powerful leadership style is the authoritative or visionary which is expressed and described through relational behaviours – self-confidence, self-awareness and empathy. Relationships are fundamental to the creation of social capital – in fact it is not exaggerating to say that social capital is found in relationships and networks and the level of engagement in a community is directly proportional to the quality of interpersonal interaction. It is a primary responsibility of the leader both to model and facilitate such relationships.

An example of the importance of this institutional level is found in Bryte and Schneider's (2002) study of trust in schools. They regard trust as the 'connective tissue' which enables schools to work effectively. Trust is defined in their study as having four components:

- respect
- competence
- personal regard
- integrity.

In their research, Bryte and Schneider found that schools with high levels of trust have a one in two chance of making significant improvements. Schools with low levels of trust have only a one in seven chance of improving. In this group only schools that made improvements in trust made improvements in academic performance. The research showed that the integrity of social relationships was an essential precursor to any form of improved performance by the school.

It is not unreasonable to postulate that the evidence from Chicago schools in this study, coupled with the example from New Mexico cited above, points to the quality of human relationships in the institution *and* the community as vital prerequisites to change and growth.

Learning

Communities are healthy when they are learning; in fact a definition of a community would have to include a capacity to grow and develop in an organic way. Again, it is a significant component of leadership both to model and facilitate effective learning at individual and community level. Wenger (1998) develops a social theory of learning around the concept of communities of practice which are to be found in every domain of human activity – in fact they are a way of explaining human activity. Significantly, in the context of the critique of schools earlier in this book, he argues:

> *In spite of curriculum, discipline and exhortation, the learning that is most personally transformative turns out to be the learning that involves membership of communities of practice.*

> (Wenger, 1998: 6)

For Wenger learning 'is part of our participation in our communities' (p.8). He argues that a community develops coherence through the relationship between three dimensions:

- mutual engagement – people engage in actions whose meanings they negotiate with each other (p.73);
- a joint enterprise – negotiation and mutual accountability (p.77);
- a shared repertoire – shared stories, tools, discourses, styles, concepts and artefacts (p.82).

It is the function of the teacher to allow this to happen and to actively promote these dimensions. The most successful leadership teams, project groups, classrooms, drama and musical performances in schools share high coherence in these three elements. It might be thought of as another manifestation of high social capital. All the traditional taxonomies of leadership can be subsumed into the notions of the creation of communities of practice; not in the sense of structural or organisational interventions, but creating the supportive infrastructure that recognises the dynamic, interactive and complex nature of community learning:

> *The aliveness of an organisation – its flexibility, creative potential and learning capability – resides in its informal communities of practice.*

> (Capra, 2002: 97)

Resources

The development of social capital is contingent, to a significant degree, on the availability of economic capital. The availability of resources is a fundamental component of community regeneration and sustainability. Equally the process of social change is a function of economic security and well-being. Economic and social entrepreneurship are in a symbiotic relationship. This is not to argue that poverty precludes the existence of social capital. High social capital can exist in poor communities and wealth is no guarantee of high social capital. What is significant is the level of social engagement and poverty does tend to minimise the motivation to engage.

Long-term poverty is socially debilitating – it creates a vicious downward spiral which can become self-reinforcing across the generations. Loss of hope leads to loss of aspirations and expectations. There is increasing evidence of the neurological and psychological implications of poverty, especially on children's capacity to learn.

It may well be therefore that one dimension of educational leadership for community renewal is engagement in economic entrepreneurship. This seems far beyond historic expectations of school management – and it is. Educationalists do not necessarily make good capitalists, but in many communities the schools are reservoirs of very high leadership and management expertise. Schools are major resources in their own right – just think of the ICT resources in most schools, inadequate by most criteria but often lying idle for 85 per cent of the year.

Too often education has seen business as a source of handouts and business has seen education as a means of marketing to the young. There are, perhaps, opportunities to see schools not as venture capitalists but as key partners in creating employment and injecting resources into the community. Schools are one of the most powerful sources of networking in the communities – and networks are powerful precursors to economic success. Putnam (2000: 325) cautiously argues that:

> *... social capital of the right sort boosts economic efficiency, so that if our networks of reciprocity deepen, we will all benefit, and if they atrophy, we will all pay dearly.*

There appears to be a clear equation linking economic, social and academic success, with education contributing to all three and schooling only directly to the latter.

Conclusion

There is a demonstrable link between social capital and academic success; the success of a school is directly correlated with its social and economic environment. The capacity of schools in challenging environments to sustain improvement indefinitely has to be questioned. Schooling as a process can only ever achieve a certain level of success without a broader view being taken of the factors that contribute to educational success.

This means a shift in our perception of leadership in education: away from the successful management of institutions into the creation of communities that have high social capital – an important by-product of which is academic success. From this perspective, leadership is a moral process firmly rooted in the viability and sustainability of communities. Leadership is thus an agency for social change, for community renewal and the creation of communities of learning – both formal and informal.

This does not require a radical reappraisal of our understanding of what the requisite knowledge, skills and qualities of leadership are. The difference is one of scale – changing the perspective of leaders from the school as an end in itself to the school as a pivotal economic and social multiplier in the community. Time and time again the senior staff in schools have demonstrated their abilities as creators of social capital, facilitators of networks and promoters of change. In focusing on the creation of social capital they will be transforming schools by transforming communities.

References

Amit, V. (2002) *Realising Community*. London: Routledge.

Bowring-Carr, C., Gelsthorpe, T. and West-Burnham, J. (2000) *Transforming Schools through Community Education*. Coventry: CEDC.

Bryte, A.S. and Schneider B. (2002) *Trust in Schools: A Core Resource for Improvement*. New York: Russell Sage.

Capra, F. (2002) *The Hidden Connections*. London: HarperCollins.

Feinstein, L. (2001) 'The relative economic importance of academic, psychological and behavioural attitudes developed in childhood', in B. Mulford and H. Silius, *Leadership for Organisational Learning and Improved Student Outcomes*, Research Matters No. 15. London: Institute of Education.

Goeman, D. (2002) *The New Leaders*, London, Little Brown.

Mulford, B. and Silius, H. (2001) *Leadership for Organisational Learning and Improved Student Outcomes*, Research Matters No. 15. London: Institute of Education.

Mulgan, G. (2000) 'The prospect for social renewal', in OECD, *The Creative Society of the 21st Century*. Paris: OECD.

OECD (2000) *The Creative Society of the 21st Century*. Paris: OECD.

Powers, S., Warren, S., Gillborn, D., Clark, A., Thomas, S. and Code, K. (2002) *Education in Deprived Areas: Outcomes, Inputs and Processes*. London: Institute of Education.

Putnam, R.D. (2000) *Bowling Alone*. New York: Simon & Schuster.

Search Institute (2000) *Asset Building*. www.search-institute.org

Sergiovanni, T.J. (2001) *Leadership, What's In It For Schools?* London: Routledge Falmer.

Skilbeck, M. (1970) *Dewey*. London: Collier Macmillan.

Stevens, B., Miller, R. and Michelski, W. (2000) 'Social diversity and the creative society of the 21st century', in OECD, *The Creative Society and the 21st Century*. Paris: OECD.

Wenger, E. (1998) *Communities of Practice*. Cambridge: Cambridge University Press.

2

■ ■ ■

Engaging Communities and Schools

Tony Gelsthorpe

Community engagement in schools lies at the heart of the processes of educational leadership. It is the key measure of success to mutual community benefit and achievement where shared vision promotes commonly agreed aims for individuals, groups and organisations. The dimensions and facets of this engagement are many and varied, ranging from equality of opportunity to social and economic regeneration; from widening learning access and participation to school improvement and transformation. Community leadership is an essential element of educational progress towards social justice. It provides the foundation for individual and collective well-being and the enhancement of life chances. In a democratic society, without community engagement, there is no vision or purpose to educational leadership.

The need for a wide social and economic and, hence, community context in which to set, analyse and develop educational provision is well documented not least in the seminal work last century by Midwinter (1975), in his challenging critique, proposals for and practice of community education:

> *People get, therefore, the social provision they deserve, and that includes education. Their type of society governs, that is, the type of social treatment meted out to them. We have probably, in education, been long in error about this, viewing the problem in isolation as a puristic and academic consideration. Of course there have been administrative and other practical devices envisaged, but have they always investigated, deliberately and consciously, their valid and proper relationship with their social and economic surrounds?*

> (Midwinter, 1975: p.17)

Hence there is the significance of educational development within overall social and economic policy, not least in terms of, for example, a democratic society, social justice, inclusion and well-being, and wealth creation from a successful economy and strong economic renewal and regeneration.

Against this background and crucial to a clarity in the purpose, direction and practice of educational leadership is, of course, a view on the prime aims of the service and, as the main organisation of delivery for most people, specifically, of schooling. Discussion and literature on the aims of schools are extensive and wide ranging. Not least, with the priority given to the raising of standards in recent years, comes a preoccupation with the quantitative rather than qualitative measurement of school success and improvement. Nowhere is this more clearly seen than in the centralist tendencies of the national curriculum and its assessment in the UK, government provision of teaching, learning and other professional strategies required to be adopted by schools and the practice of target setting with the publication of league tables of examination and assessment results. The evidence suggests a significant narrowing both of provision and performance of schools, especially in the curriculum. In the context of the longer term and more robust measures of educational achievement and improvement, some of which will be derived from the practice of community education, the gains may well be short term and limited, certainly not fulfilling the wider aims of the education service.

Hence achievement needs to be defined in much broader terms for society, communities and individuals. It is necessary to reassert the key purpose of producing individuals who can manage their own learning, who are active citizens, enjoy academic success and are employable, enterprising and entrepreneurial. In order to achieve this, the practice of educational and community engagement together is paramount, with consequent leadership, organisational and pedagogical transformation. The experience described in many of the chapters of this book exemplify this at an early stage of development and further reflect the proposition made by Bentley (1998: p.178–179):

> The answer, at the most general level, is that we need to reconceptualise education as an open, living system, whose intelligence is distributed and shared across all its participants and whose aims and applications go far beyond the achievement of formal, standardised qualifications, numerical targets and occupational grades. Schools and colleges must become network organisations, not in the fullest sense of collapsing their structures and rules into formless, over-connected webs, but by establishing themselves as hubs at the centre of diverse, overlapping networks of learning which reach out to the fullest possible range of institutions, sources of information, social groups and physical facilities.

Thus, whilst the development of learning communities is not the focus of this particular chapter or whole book, there exist significant, practical concepts in application and experience which are helpful and of importance and relevance (National Advisory Group for Continuing Education and Lifelong Learning, 1999; Department for Education and Employment, 2000; Yarnit, 2000). Moreover, many of the ideas are dealt with in individual contributions throughout this text.

More specifically, in order to identify, define and articulate the line of educational leadership envisaged here, it is helpful and practically useful to map and exemplify the pattern of relationships between education and the community. This chapter uses examples from community schools to illustrate both the context and the potential of education in the community for the processes of educational leadership.

Towards a values framework

For the purposes of investigating the relationship between education and the community, it is possible to begin to identify a basis of values and principles that underpin a comprehensive community education service which can be drawn from the range and variety of existing practice and some literature (see, for example, Hargreaves, 1982).

In practical terms, for educational leadership in the community, it is obviously essential that these values and principles are drawn from the interface between education and the community. With the case of schooling, they must be explicit, shared and understood across the school and its wider community. They then frame and guide planning, prioritisation, decision making and resource allocation in managing the community service.

The very processes of establishing, articulating and agreeing these values and principles thus lie at the centre of community education practice. These values might include the following:

1 Access to high quality learning is the right of all.
2 Learning is a lifelong, life-enhancing process.
3 Involvement with the wider community enriches the curriculum and the teaching and learning enrich community life.
4 Learning to enable all to develop as informed, responsible, confident, caring members of society.
5 Democratic structures and processes which empower individuals and communities to identify their needs and participate in decision making.
6 Collaborative partnerships between services, agencies and institutions to respond to people's needs and aspirations.
7 Quality development and assurance with the planning, delivery, evaluation and review of learning involving all participants
8 Improving the quality of life for the greatest number of people through the recognition and development of individual worth and common effect.

From this values base, some of the developing benefits of educational provision and practice rooted in the community can be realised (see e.g., DfES, 1995, 1998, 1999, 2000). These include:

1 Good practice in opening up and sharing the provisions and opportunities of the education service with clients and communities.

2 Good communication and links between school and community to improve the management of the school and the effectiveness of its prime purpose of enriching and improving learning.

3 Social and economic regeneration in the community stimulated by the operation of the school through, for example, neighbourhood renewal.

4 A contribution to the further development of the school's positive public image.

5 Acknowledgement of a school's responsibility to foster partnerships with other services and agencies, not least in support of lifelong learning.

Towards community curriculum practice

Historically the curriculum practice of schools in the community, as illustrated and explored by Hargreaves (1982), has been varied and variable in terms of genuine engagement with the community. Nonetheless, in building for the future, sound foundations do exist. It is common to identify and define a range of activity including the following elements. These can and do overlap as they are related to each other. They can and need to be led and managed in a mutually supportive and coherent manner.

The community curriculum, including teaching and learning

Content

1 Learning about the community, including local studies, case studies and fieldwork.

2 Using the community as a resource, including parents and members of the community, sharing skills and expertise, community service, work experience, industry and business links.

3 Citizenship education aimed at:
   - helping pupils to acquire and understand essential information so that as adults they will be able to take on an informed active role in the community
   - providing pupils with opportunities and incentives to participate in the life of the wider community.

Teaching and learning

1 Styles and approaches which use the wider community and its members to contribute to teaching and learning and curriculum review.

2 Often characterised by features such as access, involvement, participation, collaboration and flexibility, e.g. the accreditation of prior learning.

The school as a centre of learning for the community

1 A base for the youth service and its youth work curriculum covering, for example:
   - decision-making skills and political education and social skills
   - life and social skills
   - self-awareness and personal relationships
   - current issues
   - health education

2 Facilities for further, adult and continuing education covering, for example:
   - daytime and evening classes
   - adult basic education services
   - recreational courses and programmes
   - vocational and non-vocational classes
   - certifies courses for GCSE, GNVQ, GCE and VCE

3 Provision of the local library and/or health centre and/or citizens advice bureau
   - in partnership with the local authority and/or health authority and/or national organisations

4 Pre-school provision
   - playgroup
   - crèche
   - toy library
   - toddler groups
   - children's classes

Community use of premises

1 Dual/joint use/provision of sports/leisure/arts facilities. These are, under current local government arrangements, subject to agreements between different local authorities including district and county councils where there are two tiers of local government or unitary local education authorities.

2 Community rooms or areas, partly funded by local donation and contributions, within a school and community centre available for community use.

3 Use by groups, clubs and societies of rooms and facilities for meetings, activities and events for which they pay a hire charge.

4 Often these activities are undertaken in partnership with agencies and organisations in the voluntary sector to include work with, for example, volunteer bureaus, pre-school groups, senior citizens and youth organisations.

Community development and action

1 A range of initiatives from family learning (e.g. home start, school nursing service, local area health authority), through schooling initiatives (e.g. school attendance, home/school contracts, learning agreements) to community action (e.g. traffic improvements, securing community facilities, acting as a base for programmes of positive discrimination).

2 Involvement at times in partnership and collaboration with voluntary sector organisations and agencies.

3 Focus on key educational concepts and practices of access, opportunity, entitlement and empowerment.

Community regeneration

It is increasingly recognised that, as major plant, facilities and resource centres in the community, schools can act as engines for regeneration, building from much recent and current practice (Rennie, 1999) and the strengths that they can contribute to local communities. These include:

1 A well-established community of interest of parents who can contribute significantly to skill sharing and development, learning and other partnerships.

2 Existing alliances across the local community through families and clusters of primary and secondary schools; in combination, these have even greater potential.

3 Strong practice in many but not all schools in adult and continuing education which can provide substantial access to and participation in lifelong learning – a powerful tool for regeneration.

4 The learning community of the school itself, with staff and students contributing to a variety of community focused activities including daytime and evening classes, peer learning, family learning programmes and community service and action.

Where educational, social, health, library and recreational facilities are brought together at a site such as a village or community college, the added value is enormous, with shared opportunities and activities which provide good access, greater participation and excellent value for money. Increasingly in both the UK and elsewhere (OECD, 1998), this co-location of children's, family and community services is a provision created for new and developing communities.

Policy development

Whatever the practice of community school engagement, its leadership and management need to be set within a clear framework of values, principles and policy. In exploring these policy developments, access, participation and democratic involvement between schools and their local communities in the processes are crucial. Such developmental partnership activities must, therefore, be seen as part of an approach of mutual trust and confidence to delivering a service of quality. Activities are likely to cover a vast range of practical applications including for example:

- community service
- community use of premises
- co-location of services
- customer care
- social inclusion
- work experience
- home–school liaison
- parental involvement
- citizenship education
- inter-agency partnerships.

Governance is obviously one of the key frameworks for leading and managing community focused education. Access to and participation in educational governance is a fundamental characteristic of a public education service based in a democratic society. The defined role of the local education authority in the UK system (Audit Commission, 1998, 1999; DfES, 2000) and the role of governing bodies in schools in England are attempts to encourage such local involvement and management. Whether these practices are effective or otherwise (Woods and Cribb, 2001) is not the subject of this chapter. Suffice to say that in terms of, for example, local education authorities, the agenda of school improvement, whilst creating enhanced demands and expectations of poorly performing local authorities in England, does really focus only on challenging schools in difficult circumstances, education development planning and target setting. As such, it is rather insubstantial. Nonetheless, some of the features of practice at a neighbourhood, village, estate, suburb or community scale have been developed in innovative approaches such as village and community colleges (see Chapter 3).

Some of these features are illustrated and extended on a larger scale and more recently developed example from a whole city in Sweden, Örebro.

The Citizens' Örebro in Sweden

'All public power emanates from the people' is the opening statement of the Swedish constitution. This fundamental principle is the foundation of an innovative community regeneration programme in Örebro, a vibrant city of 124, 250 inhabitants in southern Sweden.

The programme, called 'The Citizens' Örebro', is the result of extensive discussion and consultation over ideas and proposals generated by neighbourhood committees, with contributions from individuals, citizens' groups, user groups and local societies. The programme, which incorporates the 2025 vision of Örebro under Agenda 21, is supported by the municipal council and fosters the development of seven communities, each with a cultural centre based around a neighbourhood school. Each centre:

- is owned or administered by local residents who have a common responsibility for the premises;
- is open throughout the day and in the evenings;
- acts as a focal point and a catalyst for school development in the community;
- enables local people with different backgrounds to meet and relax together, to engage in educational and cultural activities, to develop their creative skills, to participate in community and environmental regeneration and to become actively involved in the democratic process;
- supports the municipal community organisation to empower local residents;
- enhances the quality of life for all those involved.

The Citizens' Örebro programme is underpinned by a number of key principles:

1 Citizens can make a significant contribution in their local community to enhance the quality of life.
2 The neighbourhood school is where residents can meet friends, attend evening classes, use the library, enjoy leisure activities, or just meet for a chat over coffee.
3 The school is a centre for local project work on sustainable development and changing lifestyle.
4 The school plays an important part in encouraging the democratic process. All schools are self-managed and run by a board where the users and staff decide on most of the issues.
5 Municipal planning involves local residents, tenants, local politicians and municipal employees, together with builders and property owners.
6 Members of the neighbourhood committees participate in decision making, acting as representatives of other citizens or associations. Voluntary and non-profit organisations have helped the community to become more self sufficient.
7 These new ideas have encouraged the community to re-evaluate priorities, roles and tasks. Local decisions which used to be made centrally by elected representatives and staff are now being made by local user committees, associations and other elected groups.

Such strongly idealistic, almost utopian and, at times, paternalistic ideas and practices raise significant questions about the nature of society and representative democracy. Many of the features are far removed from the day-to-day context and life experiences of, for example, people in disadvantaged and challenging communities. Sufficient here to note this essential point and to recognise that, in practice, much community education across the world is directed at challenging deprivation and disadvantage and to establishing a fairer distribution of learning for all citizens. Subsequent chapters illustrate this very strong theme both in the UK and internationally.

In the UK, alternative approaches to local government, democracy, participation and active citizenship are being encouraged, with community schools becoming more involved in neighbourhood renewal and regeneration and given an emphasis on developing schools as community learning hubs and cultural centres.

As West-Burnham argues, however, in the previous chapter, questions about improvement in educational achievement remain to be addressed. In turn, a step change in approaches to the synergy between educational and community leadership may well be demanded.

What is of value to school–community engagement? What makes a positive difference?

In the context of community, in terms of the role of education in society, some of the current practice and examples described imply questions about value, quality, effectiveness and performance. These issues may arise from the establishment and organisation, leadership and management, working practices and agreed outcomes of community education. Whatever, rigorous analysis and evaluation of practice are necessary. This is not easy when the evidence base has not traditionally been a strong one and the causal relationships may well be diverse and complex.

The Australian project Leadership for Organisation Learning and Students Outcomes (LOLSO) illustrates precisely and clearly from an extensive longitudinal study the nature of some of the features of this complexity (National School Improvement Network, 2001; Silius and Mulford, 2000). Though a direct causal relationship between high community involvement and, for example, improving student outcomes, was not established in direct terms, community focus was identified clearly in its influence not only on the socioeconomic circumstances of the schools, but also upon the various measures of leadership variables. High correlations, very close to 0.8, were evident in this analysis. In the context of a study concerned with teacher leadership, organisational learning and student engagement, the interpolation of leadership processes between community focus and these positive outcomes is of considerable significance. In many examples in this book, such interrelated features and practices are clearly evident and crucial to successful outcomes.

Paramount for better or for worse are questions about any clear relationship between community perspectives and the achievement of pupils in community schools. In their study of national inspection reports and school transformation in the UK, Bowring-Carr et al. (2000: p.15) comment that 'the inspectors do not make any explicit linkage between a community perspective and the academic

23

attainment of pupils', noting, however, that significantly 'this is the result of the nature of the inspection process'. It also relates to the nature of the performance outcomes of the community schools and the way in which these are exemplified and investigated or otherwise through the inspection arrangements. Thus:

> It is well established that there is a correlation between the level of self-esteem that students possess and their subsequent achievement in academic work and in general behaviour. It is clear from these inspection reports that, whatever the level of academic achievement prior to entry to the school, and whatever the level of socio-economic advantage or disadvantage, in those cases in which the school has deliberately set out to involve itself in the community and involve the parents and community in its day to day life, then the self-confidence, articulacy, willingness to take responsibility and self esteem of the students has been of markedly high quality. It would appear that a symbiotic relationship is set up between the outward-looking school and its community, in which both parties benefit. The confident school is able to welcome its community, and the community helps the school to grow in confidence.

(Bowring-Carr et al., 2000: p.15)

Collaborative partnership working, though attempted across the public sector and particularly extensively in the education service and community renewal (Social Exclusion Unit, 1998), remains a challenging approach to effective practice (Taylor, 2000). Such is fundamental to the bringing together of community and educational leadership. Partnerships have rightly been seen as an effective solution to dealing with issues that involve cross-policy development and initiatives and also a way of ensuring that policy and intentions are delivered in practice. A whole host of partnerships have been set up across a range of activities that cover community, neighbourhood and local authority, sub-regional, regional and national issues. There is a tendency to favour and support especially those partnerships where it is necessary to bring together the main power broker and stakeholders, not least when these typically come from very different contexts, organisational cultures and ways of working. There is a risk, however, that partnerships are seen as a panacea for appropriate application to solution seeking and resolution at local levels linking school and community. This may not be the case. One considerable cost in such partnership approaches is the leadership, management and executive time needed to support the activity or programme and, in particular, the need for more than adequate information gathering, dissemination and communication. Furthermore, there are long-term implications for unsuccessful partnerships:

> Too many partnerships are unsuccessful, mostly unnecessarily. The consequence of a failed partnership in the area concerned can be long-term in respect of the damage done to trust between the organisations involved and hence the prospect for future joint working. A proliferation of partnerships in the same area also results in even the most necessary and successful partnerships achieving less than they otherwise could as a result of the critical people on the ground being spread too thinly.

(HM Treasury, 2002: p.3)

Experience and research within the education service and other public services provide clear evidence regarding many of the essential determinants of successful partnerships. Recently and specifically in relation to schools and the youth service, which have a long history of working together, a research study by colleagues at the Community Education Development Centre (2000) takes this particularly rich context for analysis and review. More widely but similarly valuable in terms of developing good practice, a report from the Public Services Productivity Panel of HM Treasury (2002) looks at a range of public sector work on the ground and establishes some essential features for partnership working:

1 *A balanced team.* Partnerships need to consist of a balanced team involving all relevant bodies.

2 *Trust.* Before people are prepared to implement the partnership's decisions in their own organisation, they need a high level of trust in each other and hence confidence in the collective decisions they take.

3 *Motivation.* To ask people and organisations to work in partnership is to ask them to adopt new ways of working and to accept a degree of collective control over their activities.

4 *Conflict resolution mechanisms.* Bringing people together in partnership, often with divergent views on issues, leads to conflicts within the group.

5 *Collaboration.* The ability to work collaboratively and take collective responsibility for decisions reached is vital for effective partnership working.

6 *Clarity of objectives and responsibilities.* If the people working in partnership are to be well motivated and able to work well together, they need to be clear about what they are trying to achieve, how they are going to achieve it and where their individual and group accountabilities lie.

7 *Appropriate funding.* Funding for partnerships needs to be pursuant to the task.

8 *Continued sponsorship.* Successful partnerships enjoy the continued support of their key sponsors, helping them to address critical blockages.

9 *Room for manoeuvre.* The organisations that make up the partnerships need sufficient freedoms and flexibilities, for example, in the use of budgets, in order to contribute effectively to the partnership.

It is clear, not least from the early developing experience described in this book, that the potential for achievement and improvement in the whole community from developing educational and community regeneration is immense. The school is a vital organisation in the economic and social fabric of any community and, as such, the educational leadership provided, supported and sustained in both directions between community and school needs to be visionary, innovative, imaginative, flexible and empowering. Driscoll and Kerchner (1999), drawing from considerable research into social capital capacity building in communities in the USA, describe this as 'public schooling … rediscovering its sense of place'. They go on to assert that a focus on economic regeneration in particular:

> *... is just as important to educational administration as the developmental, peda-gogical, and social-service theorizing that long has described the institution of the individual school.*

The implications of this are, obviously, hugely significant for leadership development. Whilst the health of school leadership in the UK is good (Hay McBer, 2000; HM Inspectorate of Education, 2000), the range, breadth and innovation of school–community engagement to which we might aspire is challenged and restricted by some inadequate vision, limited expectations and over-prescriptive, limiting national and local government policies and practices. Mere service and curriculum delivery from the school to the community will not do for the demands of meeting these high expectations and attainable outcomes. Education and community relationships are inadequately and inappropriately described in terms of traditional provider–recipient structures and processes. Alas, some of the problems associated with these activities emanate simply from current, naive approaches to school improvement arising from bolt-on community involvement. Even the terminology is suspect with vocabulary such as 'plus', 'extra', 'additional' and 'extended'. Such words are a poor reflection of the scale, extent and degree of transformation required and possible. Often they are cosmetic and short term, with a distinct ceiling on achievement and improvement. They inadequately promote the success which is possible from communities which rightly raise and articulate demands and expectations from the educational community. In short, the reforms are weakly led, often on a single institutional basis, rather than being embedded in processes, partnerships and strong relationships. Thus, as Crowson (2001: p.15) describes:

> *The community-reaching-in side is now an additionally recognised key to potential-ities for school reform. Sharing and reciprocity rather than bridging and buffering; partners in community growth and development; 'opening one's soul' to commu-nity examination and embracing the community's culture; joining other community institutions in both empowerment and investment; merging school, community, and workplace in an expanded domain of developmental activity; part-nering with community institutions in school-to-work; and, finally, in school administration, moving effectively toward the doing-it-together construction of 'civic capacity' and 'civic engagement'.*

In attempting to secure a rigorous, developmental and practical conceptual framework for educational leadership and the community, there is strong and effective work in related contexts (for example, White, 2001 in promoting non-profit leadership) and the community as a whole. Particularly well-evidenced insight into the features of social and economic capital which are vulnerable and at risk in our communities is provided by Putnam (2000). In describing what he summarises as the collapse and revival of American community, he uses notions of 'bonding' and 'bridging' to provide the basis of a possible framework. Such would entail a clear analysis of school and community engagement and connection, some aspects of which are outlined in Table 2.1.

Table 2.1 School–community engagement, connection and integration: a possible framework for development

Level 4	Fully inclusive	BEYOND BRIDGING

- Democratic, reciprocal, transformational leadership with educational and community connection and integration.
- Families contributing to the use and provision of all activities.
- Fully open and responsive curriculum meets demands and expectations.
- Shared planning, resourcing and prioritisation of agencies and partners.
- Community and school facilities and resources are shared.
- Teachers recognise and acknowledge their participation in the venture.
- The school as part of the community is a major engine for social and economic entrepreneurship, renewal and capacity building.
- School and community are democratically empowered together in terms of planning, resourcing, prioritisation and decision making.

Level 3	Inclusive	BRIDGING

- Leadership focused on community renewal and social activism.
- Families as partners in education.
- Negotiated and relevant curriculum.
- Integration with other agencies.
- School as a community resource.
- Teachers as social educators.
- The school as a centre for social and economic enterprise.

Level 2	Theoretically inclusive	BRIDGING

- Leadership involvement with community initiatives.
- Active contributions sought by parents.
- Inclusive curriculum involving 'knowledge-creators'.
- Positive co-operation with other agencies.
- Controlled access to school resources.
- Teachers engaged with parents and community initiatives.

Level 1	Exclusive	BONDING

- Leadership focused on school improvement and management.
- Parents involved by invitation.
- Restricted definition of the curriculum.
- Functional activity with other agencies.
- Minimal alternative use of resources.
- Teachers' role limited to effective pedagogy.

Conclusion

Extensive and sophisticated notions of truly open reciprocity in the leadership of education and community are obviously some way away from the current, day-to-day practice of community schools and colleges. However, there is a growing body of evidence, much of which is well illustrated in later chapters of this book, that good practice is developing and that the confidence now present in the enormous contribution to raising achievement and improvement across whole communities is growing and increasingly recognised and acknowledged by policy makers.

Whilst it is absolutely right to prioritise the application of these ideas and activities to target challenging communities in terms of disadvantage, not least in terms of opening up communities for learning, development and renewal, their potential for transformation is universal. Hence it is important to cover the full range of social and economic circumstances in which to take advantage for society as a whole. Nonetheless, when and where resources are limited, whether in the UK in its areas of deprivation or internationally, particularly in 'the South', then those resources have to be appropriately targeted and prioritised to meet community needs.

Overall, as indicated here and from the examples given throughout, there is an immediate need to review and reconsider the fundamentals of leadership in this regenerated engagement and commitment to the relationship between education and the community. Existing models, approaches, skills and qualities sought in training and development programmes (recently surveyed in Office for Standards in Education, 2002) are inadequate to develop the already existing practice and to establish a new order for transforming the service and communities. Mere improvement is insufficient in both our educational organisations and their very leadership.

There is the need to inspire and aspire to a culture and climate for leadership which is more experimental, risk taking, innovative and creative and not to train, for example, school leaders who then become marooned and isolated in their individual institutions, reacting to central authorities and policy determination with a passive or, at best, token and restricted responsiveness and performance targets. Hence, performance and achievement of education for the whole community requires transformational styles of leadership as part of that very community. Much of this is about attitudinal change, but the key broad goals and shared understandings of practice need to be strong and clear, not least drawn from a fully proactive community base. Midwinter (1975) describes 'the educative community' as such a framework in which 'sharing and reciprocity' are indeed replaced by 'bridging and buffering' (Crowson, 2001).

This is a sustainable future of constant community capacity, building where leadership styles and approaches are rooted in mutually beneficial principles and activities for a more democratic and empowered, educative learning society for all.

References

Audit Commission (1998) *Changing Partners: A Discussion Paper on the Role of the LEA*. London: Audit Commission.

Audit Commission (1999) *Held in Trust: The LEA of the Future*. London: Audit Commission.

Bentley, T. (1998) *Learning Beyond the Classroom*. London: Routledge.

Bowring-Carr, C., Gelsthorpe, T. and West-Burnham, J. (2000) *Transforming Schools through Community Education*. Coventry: CEDC/University of Hull.

Community Education Development Centre (CEDC) (2000) *Better All Together*. Coventry: CEDC.

Crowson, R. L. (ed.) (2001) *Community Development and School Reform*. Oxford: Elsevier Science.

Department for Education and Employment (DfEE) (1995) *Our School – Your School: Community Use of After School Activities*. London: DfEE.

Department for Education and Employment (DfEE) (1998) *Extending Opportunity: A National Framework for Study Support*. London: DfEE.

Department for Education and Employment (DfEE) (1999) *Raising Standards: Opening Doors – Developing Links between Schools and their Communities*. London: DfEE.

Department for Education and Employment (DfEE) (2000a) *Schools Plus: Building Learning Communities*. London: DfEE.

Department for Education and Employment (DfEE) (2000b) *The Role of the Local Education Authority in School Education*, London: DfEE. www.dfes.gsi.gov.uk/learole/policypaper/

Driscoll, M. E. and Kerchner, C. T. (1999) 'The implications of social capital for schools, communities and cities', in J. Murphy, and K. Louis (eds), *Handbook of Research on Educational Administration*. San Francisco: Jossey-Bass.

Hargreaves, D. H. (1982) *The Challenge for the Comprehensive School: Culture, Curriculum and Community*. London: Routledge & Kegan Paul.

Hay McBer (2000) *The Lessons of Leadership*. London: Hay McBer Management Consultants.

HM Inspectorate of Education (2000) *Improving Leadership in Scottish Schools*. Edinburgh: TSO for the Scottish Executive.

HM Treasury (2002) *Working Together: Effective Partnership Working on the Ground*. London: HM Treasury. www.hm-treasury.gov.uk/pspp

Midwinter, E. (1975) *Education and the Community*. London: George Allen & Unwin.

National Advisory Group for Continuing Education and Lifelong Learning (1999) *Creating Learning Cultures: Next steps in Archiving the Learning Age*. Sheffield: NAGCULL.

National School Improvement Network (2001) *Leadership for Organisational Learning and Improved Student Outcomes – What Do We Know?* Research Matters No. 15. London: Institute of Education.

Office for Standards in Education (2002) *Leadership and Management Training for Headteachers.* London: Office for Standards in Education (HMI 457). www.ofsted.gov.uk

Organisation for Economic Co-operation and Development (OECD) (1998) *Under One Roof – The Integration of Schools and Community Services in OECD Countries.* Paris: OECD.

Putnam, R. (2000) *Bowling Alone.* New York: Simon & Schuster.

Rennie, J. (1999) *Branching Out: Schools as Community Regenerators.* Coventry: CEDC.

Silius, H. and Mulford, B. (2000) 'Towards an optimistic future: schools as learning organisations – effects on teacher leadership and student outcomes'. Paper presented at the annual AARE-NZARE Conference, Sydney, December.

Social Exclusion Unit (1998) *Bringing Britain Together: A National Strategy for Neighbourhood Renewal.* London: Cabinet Office.

Taylor, M. (2000) *Top Down Meets Bottom Up: Neighbourhood Management.* York: Joseph Rowntree Foundation.

White, W. S. (2001) *The Challenge of Nonprofit Leadership.* Flint, Michigan: Charles Stewart Mott Foundation.

Woods, D. and Cribb, M. (2001) *Effective LEAs and School Improvement.* London: Routledge Falmer.

Yarnit, M. (2000) *Towns, Cities and Regions in the Learning Age: A Survey of Learning Communities.* London: Local Government Association Publications.

3

■ ■ ■

Schools and the Community

John Grainger

'We're not just a school that offers a curriculum; we're a centre of learning for the whole family.'

'The Early Years Centre is a great place to learn. The Mums and Toddlers Group is a great place to find things out in a comfortable way over a cup of coffee. It's also a natural way to get information.'

Schools' community involvement has reached the mainstream of educational policy making at last! The evidence from an internal Neighbourhood Renewal Unit briefing document suggests that:

- extended school models produce academic and social gains for the children in those schools;
- the social gains include positive attitudes to learning, improved behaviour, better school attendance, reduced truancy;
- the gains tend to be sustained over a period, not just short term;
- extended school models are popular with pupils, teachers and parents;
- individual services located in schools yield comparable benefits (e.g. adult and family learning, child care, health services);
- there are multiplier benefits from co-location of several services on site.

These trends are based on growing experience both in the UK and the USA.

What initiatives reflect this growth of interest in schools and the community? All secondary schools in England applying for specialist status have to submit a Community Plan that demonstrates how it will extend the learning opportunities to its family of primary schools, at least one other secondary school in the locality, and all the parents, made possible by the additional investment the status attracts. If this plan is not judged to be satisfactory the school cannot gain the status and it loses out on the extra money associated with that. Taken at its face value, it's a limited notion of community, but community has to start somewhere. There is evidence that schools embarking on the provision of learning opportunities for parents very often find those opportunities extend to include grandparents, the neighbours of those parents and other members of their communities. The best schools take the brief far beyond the minimum and some have really taken it very seriously and have used the opportunity to be very innovative in their approach.

Schools involved in the Excellence in Cities initiative are encouraged to generate new partnerships in the delivery of learning for their pupils and the wider community, not least in the recruitment and training of mentors to work alongside the very bright and those who need most help to achieve their potential. Those with additional capital facilities are also required to develop extended opening hours so that the local community can benefit from the investment.

In Scotland the Executive is funding New Community Schools – enabling all the agencies that work with children and their families to offer co-ordinated services, preferably on the site of the school since that's where the children have to be. This 'Full Service' model, pioneered in New York state, has proved that when all of a child's needs are met in the context of ensuring that all the family's needs are met, their achievement rises. Concentrating on a child's educational needs in isolation is generally less effective.

Belfast schools are involved in a pilot project – Communities in Schools. This initiative will create vital links between schools, social services, community groups, health services, the business community and other relevant agencies to deliver services to young people in a personalised, co-ordinated and accountable manner in the school environment. Through the scheme services will be delivered to young people in a familiar environment. The scheme, which draws on the well-established American Full Service Schools model, will be piloted in six schools in North and West Belfast over a three-year period.

'Schools Plus' schools are benefiting from the expertise made available from a range of external sources that have identified and made accessible local resources, local expertise and local opportunities in the community. These existing but largely untapped partners have begun to work together to raise achievement in those schools. Partnership working is demonstrated as central to the delivery of quality education and sustainable improvement. This project is an outcome of the report of the Schools Plus Policy Action Team established by the Social Exclusion Unit in 1997 and reporting in 2000.

Family education is now accepted as an effective means of raising achievement: children who learn alongside their parents do better at school than comparable children who do not. The teachers find those children are better motivated and the parents learn useful skills and have that learning accredited – going on to undertake further learning they had never contemplated before.

The Community Education Development Centre (CEDC) has 2,000 schools in its Community Schools Network – representing all types and phases – that define themselves as community schools. They share a commitment to working with their communities; they understand that school improvement is maintained through community engagement. The proof, for them, is in their everyday experience. They (and many of the schools participating in the initiatives highlighted above) are schools in their communities.

The Education Act of 2002 includes reference to 'Extended Schools'; schools that offer complementary activities to both children and families, and to the wider community. It is an acknowledgement that many schools already take this approach but do so without the full legislative support they need to back their initiatives; it is enabling rather than compulsory, designed to ensure services are provided and activity happens.

But this picture, although it reflects a movement towards acceptance in the mainstream of education practice of a school's involvement with its community, lacks consistency. In particular there is:

- *no* clarity explicit in these initiatives about what is a community school;
- *no* consensus about what community schools do;
- *no* universal acceptance that community schools are effective at raising achievement (let alone better than other schools that do not share this philosophy);
- *no* quantifiable evidence that community schools increase levels of achievement of their pupils through community interaction;
- *little* independent analysis of what makes a successful community school (although what does exist (for example, Bowring-Carr et al., 2000) highlights key aspects of this approach that contribute to higher achievement).

Are 'real' community schools only in education authorities that are committed to this approach – Cambridgeshire and Leicestershire, to name but two? Not any longer: even education authorities with a long tradition of schools in their communities no longer advocate this as the most desirable model. There are many other driving forces (especially those of control of different services, finance and management) that influence the nature of provision on the ground that govern whether a school is a community school or not.

This chapter will attempt to ease readers into the psyche of advocates of community schools – schools working in partnership with their community – by offering a working definition and by outlining the journey in schools leading to the initiatives mentioned earlier that have, in turn, provided a real sense of acceptance that this way of working has legitimacy in the context of the 'schools effectiveness agenda'.

In effect, this chapter describes a process of transition for schools from '*introverted schools*' to '*extroverted schools*': there have been points of innovation along the way, usually ascribed to an innovator working in schools that have needed to find a real way of responding to the circumstances of the communities they serve, and it is these important initiatives that are highlighted. So, a working definition:

> *A community school is one that meets both the learning needs of its pupils through utilisation of the learning resources available in the community and also attempts to meet the learning needs of the wider community.*

It is a two-way relationship that benefits both (and by benefit one expects the pupils' levels of achievement to rise because there is a shared sense of the value of learning, whilst others locally are also engaging in learning when they otherwise would not or could not). Such schools are clear about their place in their community. They do not separate any learners from their circumstances and, as such, can be agents of change within the community, ensuring that issues are highlighted and addressed by the appropriate bodies. Often, they see the community as the *solution* to issues that arise in the school rather than the problem that causes them. Community schools work in partnership with their learners: they also create partnerships with other organisations that can contribute to meeting learning needs both in the school and outside. The potential of everyone to contribute to the provision of learning opportunities is recognised. It is not only teachers who teach; and learning takes place at a variety of appropriate venues, not only at the school or college. Ensuring access to learning is a key priority along with overcoming the barriers to participation in learning. Community schools are at the heart of a 'Learning Community', often created by them.

Community schools are not only secondary schools. Primary head teachers, in particular, often say quite rightly: 'What about us? We've always worked with the community. It's the way we are.' Yet a lot of the attention is centred on the secondary sector. Primary and special schools manifest the same characteristics. Indeed, some primary school head teachers argue that their schools are natural community schools because parents find it easier to get involved in their children's learning, local people are more relaxed about contributing to the learning of younger children and, particularly in rural locations, the community is more likely to view the school as a community resource. All of this can be true – but this chapter is not about arguing that one phase is better able to deliver than another. Ultimately, whether a school is a community school or not rests upon what it (i.e. the head teacher, governors, teaching and non-teaching staff, and parents) believes in. The practice is driven by the values.

There is no right or wrong way for schools to develop this relationship with their community. There are no longer local authority preferred models imposed on community schools. Each individual school has to work out for itself the most effective way of meeting the learning needs of its community, both internal and external. And this creates a whole lot of interest because there is always scope for sharing good practice, always potential for developing new practice, and always scope for cross-sector stimulation about what works.

Some schools have been designed to be community schools: the physical space is designed to be used flexibly to meet a range of needs and often includes bases for allied agencies (at Pen Pych Community Primary School in Rhonda Cynon Taff, for example, the local police have their office in the school); the values of the school and its staff are known.

Other schools have devised and adopted an approach to working with the community over time. Their buildings were probably not designed to complement this type of approach to learning but, nevertheless, it works because of the 'can-do' attitude of everyone involved.

There are examples of schools offering learning in a variety of appropriate locations in the community – a community centre, an online centre, a shopping mall, a leisure centre, the youth club, and so on. There are also examples of schools sponsoring learning activities, taking some responsibility for quality standards without necessarily retaining direct control – e.g. out of school activities taking place locally.

Yet other schools 'add on' an interest in the wider learning needs of the community through classes provided in their premises by other departments of the local education authority (i.e. adult or community education) or other agencies (e.g. Workers Educational Association or the Women's Institute). Some schools use lettings as a means of signalling that their school is part of the community and demonstrate their belief in sharing their valuable but public resources.

Parents are increasingly part of day-to-day learning in schools. They are the primary educators of their children – and the school enables them to take on this responsibility. They become voluntary classroom helpers and are first in the queue when a paid position becomes available. Parents' rooms are a significant resource in schools where they exist. In some schools the specific learning needs of parents are taken into account and met in many different ways. It is no longer very rare to find adults learning in the classroom alongside teenagers, especially for GCSEs and A or A/S levels.

Schools work together in groups or 'families' to ensure a co-ordinated approach for the children across all phases. The achievement levels of fewer children fall after they transfer from one phase to another, especially from primary to secondary. Learning resources are extended for all schools working in their communities: the skills, talents and experiences of local people are available to enrich those of the teaching staff. Other professionals – e.g. youth workers – are able to contribute complementary approaches to learning. Learning can be given a 'reality check' by taking the learners to locations where the result of the learning is in practical use. Individual pupil needs can be given greater attention through co-operation between agencies and the involvement of others (as mentors, for instance). The school's resources become available to a wider learning audience – this is especially true of IT resources.

These few examples convey a richness of learning, a collegiate approach to learning, a sharing of responsibility for learners. They are the results of achieving a shared understanding of the importance of learning; teachers, parents, learners of all ages all accept that learning is the route to full personal potential.

Development of community schools

So, community schools are all different. Schools find their own solutions in order to engage with the learning needs of their communities. Given that this wasn't always the case, how did we get here, to this point in time? What has been the journey over, say, the last 25 or so years? The names of the luminaries are well known – Morris, Midwinter, Fairbairn and company – but what did they do and why? How does the contribution of each fit into the overall process? There is not the space to go into detail about each of the key contributors, but some of the main points of innovation follow.

Henry Morris saw society changing rapidly with many people experiencing great difficulty in adapting to the changes. He was particularly worried about changing attitudes towards religion and the need to develop new skills in the workplace. However, he also decided that if issues such as these were to be addressed it had to be achieved in the normal context in which people lived. Morris saw learning as the solution and designed the so-called *village colleges* as the solution.

He believed that all aspects of society would benefit from planning – the village college was, for him, an integral aspect of that planning process. The newly planned environment should serve social and cultural as well as educational and economic ends. However, significantly, he believed that education would only be meaningful if the barriers created between it and the remainder of people's lives were removed (Reé, 1985). Thus, village colleges were designed as open systems where the learning needs of the whole community would be met in as fluid a way as possible, combining learning activity for different groups within one community-based resource.

Morris's particular understanding that lifelong learning is of the greatest importance and that learning is an integral part of day-to-day living still provides us with a basis for developing schools in their communities. In addition, although fashions in architecture change as much as anything else and the original design of village colleges has been superseded by new materials and techniques, nevertheless his basic approach to creating a learning resource that can be used to deliver a range of different types of learning to more than one group of learners can be seen in the most recently completed community schools.

Sawston Village College was the first purpose-built manifestation of Henry Morris' philosophy – in 2002 it was still serving its community.

Twenty-five years after Morris, in 1949, Stewart Mason made a series of proposals for community colleges in Leicestershire that were implemented by his successor, Andrew Fairbairn. One of Mason's main beliefs was that local people should decide what learning activities these colleges should provide. This democratic approach to the provision of learning has, since that time, been masked by initiatives and debates deriving largely from differing political ideologies – local government of schools, the changes of role of the local education authority, the proportion of school budgets fully in the control of schools, the role and composition of governing bodies. Overall, schools have gained more control over their budgets and there is an acceptance that local people should be encouraged as far as possible to get involved with the governance of their schools. Where schools offer a range of learning opportunities to the wider community, the exact nature of those is locally determined. However, there is still no real possibility of combining the two management functions – of learning provided by the school to its pupils and to the whole learning community. The Extended Schools proposals in the new Act will, at last, bring this nearer to reality for those schools that want to adopt a comprehensive approach.

Geoff Cooksey, Director of Stantonbury Campus in Milton Keynes, welded together the best of both Morris and Fairbairn by emphasising 'shared partnership': a central governing board, delegating as much decision-making responsibility as possible to specialist sub-committees, and representatives of all contributing partners and users; a single management team of principal officers, both within and without the teaching profession; staff involvement with the policy of the whole campus, regardless of sectional interests; relationships which were non-authoritarian, open and welcoming and an interweaving of community concern and support through all facets of the campus, together with a shared view of the combined local and district function of the campus as a whole (Poster, 1982).

The campus comprised two secondary schools, a theatre, a leisure centre, a youth centre, an ecumenical church, shops, a playschool and a base for other agencies to operate. Teaching staff worked flexibly across the sectors to ensure a co-ordinated approach to learning provision for people of all ages. Staff from the constituent parts of the campus collaborated to provide new learning opportunities and special events. The campus was open 20 hours a day every day of the week.

Geoff Cooksey was central to the way Stantonbury worked in the 1980s; he took risks and had his share of disappointments. However, he brought together at that time the best practice from Derbyshire and Nottinghamshire, Leicestershire and Cambridgeshire into one learning community. In many ways Stantonbury Campus under Geoff's leadership, and continuing in 2001 as a specialist media and arts college, is a forerunner of much that is *schools in the community* today.

Its particular emphasis on partnership working was, at that time, fairly unique. I was Youth Officer in Milton Keynes and accustomed to inter-agency breakfast meetings in Geoff's office comprising representatives of many different organisations called by him to discuss particular pupils or to develop a new strategy for meeting a specific learning need in the community. It was also noticeable how involved the young learners were in the development of his approach to delivering learning and how committed they were to the concept as well as the man.

Eric Midwinter was the director of the national centre for urban community education, set up as a continuation of the Liverpool Educational Priority Area Project to widen the perspective and co-ordinate the movement for the improvement of education in urban areas in the 1970s. He argued that we should not be so terrified of the intangible, the immeasurable and the visionary. To Eric a community school is 'one that welcomes in and ventures out into the community', a concept building on the utilisation of premises for community involvement and also on home–school interrelationships. This form of education:

> ... should be an enthusiastic and committed search for the truth about community life and the pleasurable and devoted development of the requisite skills to cope with community issues. The school should be a projection of home and community ... It also offers the starting point for the examination and possible reform of the community.

(Midwinter, 1973: 76)

Midwinter believed that a school should have a community curriculum. It should not be inward looking nor inhibiting:

> The community school is a relevant school, which directs children to an immersion in the community and which, in so doing, attempts to co-identify education and life. This is the particular concomitant of blurring the physical borders between school and community; this curriculum is not about one teacher teaching thirty children; it is about thirty-one human beings experiencing life together.

(Midwinter, 1973: 76)

There are connections here to the Schools Plus Policy Action Team report (sub-titled Building Learning Communities) which advocates flexible approaches to learning that can be offered in locations outside school, utilising resources made available in the locality and managed by teachers and others – further details later in the chapter. The 14–19 Green Paper of 2002 has taken up and further developed this theme, arguing for choice to be available for all students in order that they pursue an appropriate learning path to their needs, and that learning in the community be part of that scenario.

Today there is growing recognition of the contribution that schools can make to tackling issues in the community – e.g. campaigning on key issues such as road safety, housing conditions, the treatment of offenders; taking the lead in attracting resources for regeneration, bringing agencies together; supporting tenants' associations – reinforced by an understanding that the resolution of such matters is an integral part of ensuring that learners can concentrate on their learning and realise their potential, and that this will likely as not be reinvested back into that community in some way. Such schools are the projection of home and community: they do not impose values that contradict those prevalent in the home, due to their closeness to local residents; they are also leaders of the community.

Paulo Freire was a Brazilian who lived and worked in Chile. He believed that effective learning could only take place in context. In today's sense that would take learning out of the schoolroom and, conversely, turn many workplaces, social settings and homes into places for learning. Freire also argued that learning was always two way: the roles of educator and learner are not helpful because both play both roles in relation to each other.

In practice, Freire's model complements that of Midwinter; both believe in an egalitarian approach that is based on a sharing of learning resources. No one group of people has a monopoly over knowledge and there are different types of knowledge that together create what all people should know if they are to be rounded individuals playing a full part in society. Lastly, both believe that learning takes place in a variety of settings and, again, schools should recognise the importance of this fact.

It is true, of course, that Freire has had a particular influence on the education system in Scotland where his teachings form much of the basis of community education. He probably would not appreciate this (structural and philosophical) division between learning in schools and other learning opportunities.

Another point of innovation comes with the publication by Hargreaves (1982) of his book *The Challenge for the Comprehensive School*. He asserts: 'The concept of the community school, like the concept of community itself, is a flabby and sometimes vacuous one.' He goes on to describe four changes that he saw at that time occurring within community schools:

1 *The promotion of a community within the school*: increased democratisation, especially between teachers and pupils. However, in my own view, the limits to this imposed by teachers have on the whole prevented pupils from truly participating in decision making about the important aspects of life in school.

2 *The increase of participation in school by the outside community*: representation of parents on governing bodies was at that time an innovation (1977).

3 *The school as a community centre*: new schools were being built to match the rapid increase in the school population and sometimes shared the site with other facilities; many schools offered their premises for use by the community for 'non-educational' activities.

4 *The development of the community-centred curriculum*: reform is focused on the curriculum itself rather than on the structure of the school as an institution and its relationship with the community. This was before the national curriculum, although that shouldn't be seen as an excuse to remove the community as a learning resource.

Hargreaves and Midwinter both address the attitude held by some that a community-based curriculum is 'second best', appropriate for less able students but not those who are gifted and talented. At their time of contribution 'public examinations' were sat by a minority of students, were centred on traditional subjects and were taught formally. Other subjects were regarded with some disdain but experimentation was acceptable. As Hargreaves puts it: 'academic education is to be contrasted with "learning about the community" which is for pupils who are "thick" and who waste teachers' time and efforts. The hidden-curriculum message being transmitted to *both* groups of pupils is a disastrous one.' This situation was overridden by issues of class and by levels of disadvantage. Again, a community-centred curriculum was accepted for those who were not expected to do well at school. In referring to the work in Educational Priority Areas led by A. H. Halsey, however, Hargreaves notes that the curriculum must relate to the environment of the learner:

> *The school curriculum must be based on the community and its objective must be the development in children of an understanding of the environment in which they live. A change of emphasis was essential ... from the learning of information to the acquisition of skills.*

(Hargreaves, 1982: p.57)

The report produced by Halsey concluded:

> *The schools in most urgent need of help served communities where the sense of community and community resources were most depleted. It is natural, therefore, that they should assign to the school an important task in the regeneration of those communities.*

Only schools in such disadvantaged communities were encouraged to develop this approach. In 1997, therefore, the Community Education Development Centre found the financial backing to offer a project to schools entitled 'Schools as Community Regenerators' (Rennie, 1999). Eight schools took part, each identifying a partner involved in local regeneration and focusing on sustainable development. The spectrum of ideas that emerged was not only imaginative and creative, but also surprisingly wide, ranging from outreach initiatives for parents with young children and mobile IT training for women to specialised training for young people wanting to work in the tourist industry. All of these ideas already seem to be part of mainstream provision in schools around the country – it's amazing how quickly innovation becomes the accepted norm!

Phil Street, Chief Executive Officer of CEDC, offers an apparently simple exercise for schools to use to judge whether they are committed to the operational principles of community schools:

1 *To what extent does your school extend access to educational, recreational, social or cultural activities to the wider community? List the provision and the activities.*

2 *Are you offering lifelong learning educational opportunities? List the provision and the activities.*

3 *Is the community being involved and used in the delivery of the National Curriculum? List examples of involvement.*

4 *Which other agencies is your school collaborating with to meet community needs? List the agencies and purpose for collaboration.*

5 *What are the opportunities for the community to be involved in the governance or management of community school activities?*

(Street, 1997: p.10)

I would ask, in addition,

6 What measures have been put in place to join these operational principles together in practice? List the measures in place.

7 How are these aspects of school life integrated into its 'mainstream' activities? Provide evidence of the integration to maximise the advantage to all learners.

In 1997 a series of Policy Action Teams was established by the Social Exclusion Unit of the newly elected Government. Policy Action Team (PAT) 11 was entitled Schools Plus with a remit to:

Identify the most cost-effective Schools Plus approaches to using schools as a focus for other community services, reducing failure at school, and to develop an action plan with targets to take these forward.

For several years schools had been the subject of intense external judgements and internal scrutiny with a focus on achievement levels. With the publication of PAT 11's Report (DfES, 2000), school achievement became part of the same agenda as involving the school in its community, rather than the two remaining entirely separate.

The question was, how could schools be encouraged to embrace this approach to learning – especially when the criticism for failing to raise achievement levels was so professionally damaging for school managers? How could head teachers be convinced that working with the community, building partnerships, developing a learning community, would actually contribute to, not detract from, raising achievement levels?

Whilst the DfES worked internally to line up its policies behind the Schools Plus approach, it commissioned CEDC to produce a toolkit (DfES, 2000b) that illustrates the many approaches to working in the community current in schools around England. It saw this publication as a resource both for schools considering adopting such methods and for those already working in this way but, perhaps, seeking to extend their work.

The 2002 Education Act provides the legislative framework for schools that wish to pursue the Schools Plus approach. It removes the artificial barriers previously placed between the governance and financial management of the school and its community activities. It promotes the notion of an 'Extended School'; a newly minted, neutral term that has no history, to encompass all the activity this chapter has summarised.

The best community schools have positive characteristics that help to meet high standards and expectations. On the specific issue of achievement (including attainment, access, entitlement, opportunity and participation), the following were identified as particularly significant factors:

- a rich curriculum and variety of relevant and appropriate learning styles
- access to learning opportunities by a range of people
- integrated provision
- partnerships with other agencies and services
- coherent curriculum provision
- positive attitudes towards learning
- value for money and best value
- behaviour management and improvement
- greater diversity.

Additionally, community schools are social and community regenerators – building capacity, positive expectations and motivation, championing social inclusion, investing in social capital and active citizenship.

The innovators I have mentioned in the past few pages have been largely responsible for enabling schools that wish to look outwards rather than inwards to do so. By implication, that old saying (applied in this context) about the sum of the parts available to schools on their own being exceeded by the creativity and extension of opportunity generated by working with others is absolutely true. But it goes further than schools into society itself.

The core idea of social capital theory (like its conceptual cousin 'community'), says Putnam (2000: p.19), is that social networks have value:

> Just as a screwdriver (physical capital) or a college education (human capital) can increase productivity (both individual and collective) so too [can] social contacts affect the productivity of individuals and groups.

Not all the benefits of social connections accrue to the individual making the contact; it can have 'externalities' that affect the wider community.

This theory speaks to the school that invests in its relationships with the community: the value accrues to both the school (i.e. pupils, teachers, parents, etc.) and to local residents and the organisations and groups that operate locally. But its effectiveness is dependent over time on building individual relationships between people, getting to know and trust each other so that all contribute to the learning community. Putnam refers to 'bonding' or exclusive social capital (introvert) and, by contrast, to 'bridging' or inclusive social capital (extrovert). Some forms of social capital are, by choice or necessity, inward looking and tend to reinforce exclusive identities and homogeneous groups; an example might be an exclusive club or movement where membership is strictly regulated and members defend their values aggressively. Bonding is good for reciprocity and for mobilising solidarity; it is also a necessary criterion for embattled communities. Bridging networks, by contrast, are outward looking and encompass people across diverse social groupings; youth clubs and the civil rights movement, for example. These networks are good for linking external assets and for sharing and fully utilising information. Recruitment agencies operate within the various networks of staff, creating links between them in order to identify potential best fits with a person specification, manipulating who they know in order to find the right candidate for a position. Putnam proposes that 'bonding social capital is good for "getting by", but bridging social capital is crucial for "getting ahead"'.

How might these models illustrate the notion put forward here about introvert and extrovert schools? Clearly there is a direct link between introvert and bonding, between extrovert and bridging. So, schools that feel overwhelmed by initiatives, on the receiving end of criticism of examination results, suffering falling roles or staff shortages, and which respond by developing internal bonds as part of a strategy against 'the enemy', could be described as introvert. Schools that see the community as the solution and not the problem, at the other extreme, could be described as extrovert. Colonisation of external resources along with the utilisation of the enthusiasm and expertise of local people can be used to generate collaborative approaches that are successful in managing initiative overload, in reducing disadvantage, in raising attainment levels and in creating a can-do environment for teachers and learners alike.

It is this mind picture that encapsulates for me the approach of schools working as part of their communities. They are inclusive of all learners, they embrace the contributions of others, they nurture and foster learning opportunities wherever it is possible to offer them, they prioritise those others who have benefited least from learning – and their students' achievement is high, stays high and gets higher!

References

Bowring-Carr, C., Gelsthorpe, T. and West-Burnham, J. (2000) *Transforming Schools Through Community Education*. Coventry: CEDC.

Department for Education and Employment (DfES) (2000a) *Schools Plus: Building Learning Communities*. London: DfES.

Department for Education and Employment (DfES) (2000b) *Building Learning Communities*, London: DfEE.

Hargreaves, D.H. (1982) *The Challenge for the Comprehensive School*. London: Routledge & Kegan Paul.

Midwinter, E. (1973) *Patterns of Community Education*. Cambridge: Advisory Centre for Education.

Poster, C. (1982) *Community Education*. London: Heinemann.

Putnam, R.D. (2000) *Bowling Alone*. New York: Simon and Schuster.

Reé, H. (1985) *Educator Extraordinary – The Life and Achievement of Henry Morris*. London: Peter Owen.

Rennie, J. (1999) *Branching Out: Schools as Community Regnerators*. Coventry: CEDC.

Street, P. (1997) *Managing Schools in the Community*. London Arena.

4

. . .

Managing a Community Primary School

Peter Hall Jones

I suppose, to be honest, I would have to say that we've managed the Little London Community Primary School and Nursery, on 'a wing and a prayer'.

I'm not sure that I'm proud of this admission. It doesn't sound particularly impressive or dynamic or actually very professional, but it is honest. And it's perhaps a supportive statement for all those who fit uneasily into the modern myth of a supposedly hyper-efficient, development planned, milestone marked, costed, targeted, focused approach to everything in life.

We've been called maverick, trendy, hippy, misguided, mad, radical and indeed 'right' to do what we have done and continue to try to achieve. Indeed sometimes, though not often, all or more of these compliments, or accusations depending on your point of view, have been offered by the same person in a single conversation or soliloquy.

However we seem to have had some success. Neither I nor my teachers at secondary modern, sixth form or teaching college ever thought for a moment that I'd contribute to a book on education. Yet here we are, very aware of all our failings, taking a moment to talk about our journey to date: a journey of seizing creative positive opportunities, uniting and including people, treasuring people, valuing people, saying 'yes, no problem' rather than 'no you can't do that'; seeking forgiveness rather than permission, informing people in suits on a 'needs to know basis', and holding true to our vision, wheeling and dealing where necessary, treating praise and criticism with equal suspicion.

I believe it was Stephen Spender who said, 'There is nothing we imagine we don't already know.' We've merely tried to be honest with ourselves about what we really know to be true, and what we really know to be dogma and racist and tosh. We've tried to challenge suspicion and cynicism with openness and compassion and to adopt the principle offered to me when I took my St John Ambulance first aid course: 'If someone comes along who reckons they know more about it than you, let them do it and you direct traffic instead.'

As head of Little London Community Primary School and Nursery I've directed plenty of traffic over the past seven years. I've cried a little and laughed a lot; I've taught little that was new to anyone but learnt a lot that I always knew to be true.

We've enjoyed a renaissance of collaboration and friendship with so many groups and individuals, sat back and enjoyed the mutual burgeoning relationships between and amongst them, seen and benefited from mutual support and kinship and seen at times, I honestly believe, the weaving of community, trust and optimism.

Of course there have been the other days when it felt like everything had gone horribly wrong, and we've all just wanted to resign and take up an easier job running the UN or explaining cricket to an American. These have been few and far between fortunately (and officially!) – sustained as we have been by our vision, enthusiasm and belief.

Who are 'we'? It would be fair to say that 'we' exist on a continuum as long and as broad as any continuum that relates to any group of people. Whilst some of us are committed to the central importance of community involvement, others are less so and would settle for community respect or acceptance. Whilst some of us see community involvement helpful in as much as 'it' can help support children's achievement, others of us see 'it' as the core function of 'a school'. Whilst some see community involvement as the inevitable sharing of certain limited resources, others of us see 'it' as a regenerative, community building, world order changing ideal.

Whilst I would wish for the community concept to be shared and 'owned' equally by all, I have grown to accept that at the very least those who are not actively against us are with us.

Desperate not to become an imperial raja of our community, a despotic, omnipotent dictator of people, I have been disappointed and disillusioned at times by my failing completely and utterly to sell the concept to all members of the community. To sell the concept so sublimely well that all are equally able, willing and enthusiastic to take on the leadership and development of the vision and practices that support and underpin and derive from our drive.

There is a role for leadership and, by definition, if some people are leaders, then others must be followers; for if there are no followers, the leaders are merely sad fools talking to themselves and the wind. Community is a continuum, a range, a breadth of thought, opinion, ability, commitment and need and we should not berate ourselves for achieving something short of complete compliance, for when we are wrong this lack of complete compliance will be what saves us (Socrates and his argument with Thraceamachus on the right of might).

As my wife so eloquently put it as I indulged in a shortlived despair one evening on my frustration that some didn't share my conviction or willingness to continue and extend the community concept in their own way, 'You love to eat good food and delicious meals but you can't/won't cook, almost literally, to save your own life.' Allowing for the specifics of this particular matrimonial issue, the point is of course completely sound. We all need to eat but we aren't all great creative cooks. Likewise not everyone in the community, school-based staff, parents/carers, partner groups and services, will be able, willing or want to steer the ship or choose the destination. They are content and committed to enjoying the journey and helping out along the way.

We may believe that 'community is good for you', but we'd be hard pressed to make it compulsory – you know what I mean?!

Earlier on I referred unashamedly to 'vision' and 'belief', words I much prefer to 'plan' and 'objective'. Of course both vision and belief are profoundly difficult to capture and describe without waffling off into a world of, well, waffle. I'm further inhibited by a distant memory of Basil Bernstein whom I believe partly defined the restricted linguistic code as one that constantly used metaphor and colloquialism. This is the language I shall find myself resorting to in order to describe a picture rather than explain it, with a greater if still pathetically small chance of the reader being inspired rather than informed.

As you will no doubt have gathered from the liberal use of phrases such as 'wing and a prayer', 'wheel and deal' and so on, there wasn't ever really a master plan – rather a wishy-washy, namby-pamby, abstract picture from the Impressionist era. That picture would have been one based around the worth and value of each and every individual: the belief that there is no such thing as a bad child, parent/carer, estate, organisation or institution – just frustrated, dormant, oppressed, unloved, unrealised potential or resource; the belief that the world is basically symbiotic – half the world wants or needs to give and the other half needs or deserves to receive; that negotiation and the Solomonic middle way can satisfy; that teachers like me aren't the sole solution or surely we wouldn't have the problem by now; that education occurs when the right teacher says or does the right thing in the right way at the right time for the right learner and that this teacher may not be 'a teacher'.

Given such missionary mantras it will again come as no surprise, and as mentioned earlier, that we never actually started off with a development plan with appropriate mileposts, action columns or budgets, let alone monitoring and evaluation boxes. (Am I the only person who thought Monitoringandevaluation was all one word? It always reminds me of the joke about Lillian Thompson being an Australian fast bowler in the 1980s.)

Indeed here would be a good point to acclaim the virtue of retrospective planning, a form of planning I have always found more accurate and efficient than the old-fashioned forward planning concept. Has the naturally beautiful ever been so as the result of a plan: the sunrises, the Dales, falling in love, the smile on a child's face, the wag of a dog's tail? What would the development plans for any of these look like? What would be a milepost? How would you budget for one? Who would ever read the plan? Would you rather read the plan or giggle with the child?

Have you ever seen a plan for the renaissance period? Well there hasn't been one for us either and I believe it's an inappropriate syllogism to assume you need a plan to ensure or to promote the probability of success of community, people-based activity. The best and perhaps only workable, flexible, responsive, sustaining and sustainable plan to have is a plan to work with able, flexible, responsive and optimistic people.

A lot is made of flexible teaching and flexible management structures and personalities. For us it is a principle best defined by yin and yang, best described by t'ai chi.

For the creative individual responding to the pressures of challenge, the potential of opportunity is simply a matter of turning the coin over, seeing the other side. Teachers do it all the time. We meet need. By identifying and understanding the problem, the solution invariably hits you in the face. As Kurt Rowland, I believe, put it, 'Listen and Hear. Look and See.' Flexible management is at base as simple as that.

Within a community school context, identify what isn't happening, really refine down the issue and there is the solution. And yet still we seem programmed to continue down the wrong path.

We didn't have much parental involvement or engagement with school based activities. We sent out letters and news-sheets seeking to engage them. We sent out lots. We sent them out frequently. We changed the font. We put borders around the page. We sent them out on the same day every week. We sent them out on different days of the week. We posted them in the windows.

'Parents and carers just don't read the letters we send out' was still the constant cry. So why carry on sending them out?

'They only respond when you get hold of them and talk face to face.' Well let's do that then. The yin and yang says they don't read letters, therefore don't send them out. They do respond to one-to-one conversations so let's create more of those. But when you attempt to look and see, listen and hear, a different level of awareness or consciousness is revealed. Why don't they read the letters?

- Well, some of them can't read.
- Often the letters don't get home because the children don't have bags to put them in.
- Some parents aren't interested (allegedly).
- There's too much writing on the letter (victims of our desire to communicate, we said too much).

- Parents and carers assume it won't be of interest or relevance to them.
- They'd rather talk at the gate with their mates than read my letter.
- If it's important the school phones or they grab you in the morning and tell you.

Parents and carers had it sussed. I find it hard to disagree with any of the above, they're all slightly obvious. So if we listen and hear, look and see the problem, raise our awareness and consciousness, we respond with the yang to the yin presented:

- Embark upon a wide variety of adult education to promote the reading skills of adults in the community.
- Get school reading bags for letters to go home in.
- Put interesting things in the letter, use children to demand parents/carers read letters, competitions, rewards, offers, etc.
- Break writing up into tabloid style, use desktop publishing techniques, entice and excite the reader.
- Every parent/ carer who comes in to see the head teacher has his or her comment, request, idea, complaint put anonymously into the weekly letter.
- Identify the lead gate expert and suck her into the system. She's obviously a natural and respected news broadcaster so she may as well work for the 'state' owned media!
- Don't phone. Don't remind verbally. The mantra will be 'As you saw in the letter.' 'Pity you didn't get the letter we sent, you missed out on…'
- Stop sending letters and release staff to communicate verbally, back up letters verbally, translate, etc.

But still we send out letters and complain that they don't work. We never seem to learn. Of course each of the above responses to identified needs can then be further broken down because we need to be fully conscious of the issues our quick yang responses raise:

- Adult education for parents/carers to learn to read.
- Where?
- In school with their own child?
- In school with other children in a different class?
- With young children using simple books?
- With older children using more adult friendly content?
- In parent groups specifically for the purpose?
- Individual tuition in school?
- Individual tuition at home?
- Classes outside school in other venues?

But how do we advertise this service – send out a letter to find out who cannot read? I don't think so. Do we approach specific people/suspects? Of course we should do all of the above at one and the same time and repeatedly and differentially, through every individual and opportunity.

- What about equal opportunities?
- How do we make sure everyone has had the chance to learn to read?
- What about the Data Protection Act?
- Can we pass people's information on to the colleges? Well, we're not informants, we're trying to help. You can take a horse to water ... you can't make them read.
- Can we make them want to read?
- What might they want to be able to read? Shall we ask them? Maybe they want to be able to read all the blooming letters the damn school keeps sending out?

The challenge isn't a problem, it's an opportunity. What about getting the non-reading parents/carers to come and talk to our staff about what prevented them learning to read, what their teachers did wrong? What about getting the reading parents to 'read' with our non-readers in a new and collaborative way, modelling learning and motivation?

As manager all you then have to do is organise all this. The process is made more efficient obviously by knowing your parents/carers. Of course by doing all of the above you get to know your parents really well and they get to know and trust you really well as well. Win-win and 'the third way' aren't just political constructs and mantras of the late 1990s.

All the provision and activities here represent the warp and all the conversations, jokes, apologies and digressions in talking *with* as opposed *to* parents and carers provide the weft. A strong fabric is commenced, one that will withstand the odd disagreement or fall-out. The odd cock-up, the odd misunderstanding is all that is required for the conversations and relationships to be formed that can recreate society and community, trust and optimism.

Half the world wants and needs to give and the other half needs and/or deserves to receive seems a plaintive truth. From the wildebeest roaming across the plain to the refugee on the axle of the Euro express, we are constantly and painfully reminded of need. The bread and butter waste mountains, the lorries that pass lorries travelling in the other direction on motorways, the children's Christmas shoeboxes of toys bizarrely and at times touchingly remind us of those needing to receive and the need for giving.

The management of a successful community school requires the role of brokerage to be formed between these two groups. The local college of further education, the locally funded group, the early retired, the bored, the well meaning, all need clients, people to rescue, people to work with. In a school we have pupils in need. It should really be quite a straightforward exercise to match the two together.

Having matched them together sit back and enjoy. Refocus the management job. Get back to fostering the ethos and culture whereby all these new participants in the education process can express their creativity and observations. Support them and develop their ability to 'Listen and Hear. Look and See.' For then in an atomic reaction of creativity and goodwill the school can generate enough energy to transform the most dense of matters.

Some will take more than others, some will give more than others. Well, that's the way of the world and appropriate to the needs and abilities of us all at different times in different ways. Some will no doubt have a problem with this apparent individual inequality whilst choosing to ignore the community balance. The most obvious response to this concern is use of the twin and completely compatible models of equality. Everyone gets the same access; everybody gets what he or she needs. People low in security, self-esteem, optimism and self-belief find it hard to accept the wisdom of the compatibility of these two concepts. I have found a medical analogy the best to offer in these situations.

When sitting in the doctor's waiting room one is rarely envious when a patient comes out clutching a huge bag of medication. One rarely says to oneself, 'I want to have that much too.' Rather one feels sorry for the patient. We hope we won't need as much, if anything to make us better. It's important to know that if you need as much medicine, if not more medicine, it will always be available to you.

Rather like love, community support needs to be inexhaustible. My personal view is that people who can't accept the concept of equality are people who have found the love they have known to be exhaustible and thus they can't afford to trust. This is the role of the community school: to show inexhaustible love and service; to give to those of need when it is needed.

Clearly this love is channelled through activity and provision as identified by the analysis of need. However the mere provision of need is quite simply not enough. Provision of need alone fails for at least two reasons. First, if you offer any individual or group a lot of help the immediate effect upon them may well be negative.

A patient in hospital stirs on hearing the soothing footsteps of a nurse. The patient feels less lonely, safe and cared for. The nurse leans over and whispers to the patient, 'We're just taking you up to intensive care.' Immediately the patient feels worse, scared and worried. Second, when you celebrate your fortieth birthday with friends and family, life begins again. A few months later, when the trousers won't fit, the muscles ache and you get puffed out after the shortest run to the car, when the parking ticket is about to run out, you realise the passing of time. At this point the proliferation of young, fit people in tracksuits and sports clothing all around you and the proliferation of gyms, health farms and weight loss treatments rarely inspires a get fit regime, but rather makes you feel worse, less able and worthy and more likely to succumb to the slouch position of acceptance and the unavoidability of middle-aged spread.

Likewise in a community school, provision of every life-enhancing opportunity can backfire. Faced with a plethora of support and opportunity, the effect can be to magnify one's own inability and depression, to make one feel more inadequate and unworthy of any self-respect.

So a range of provision is certainly necessary, but the management of these facilities when done most effectively is to provide only some of them some of the time. People may miss out on an opportunity, kick themselves gently and then grab that same opportunity next time with far greater determination. People missing out on fleeting provision in this way then also create a waiting list and some new people will thus be attracted to the provision when it reappears, if only because they see others queuing for it – by definition if they are all queuing it must be worth having.

This plethora of support also needs to be the support that's wanted when it's wanted. So much talk and so many earnest meetings of people in suits are focused on the holy grail of 'joined up thinking'. All too often, having taken part in so many of these meetings myself, the 'joined-upness' only exists at the level of corporate plans or in order to promote yet more damn meetings. Rarely have I seen evidence of this joined up thinking actually affecting the lives of the people we seek to serve.

Joined up thinking only needs to exist at the point of delivery. The provision we make for our communities has to make sense to them, *now*. There's no room for fanciful thoughts or plans because in this context the plan may well appear to the participant as manipulation. Courses and classes and opportunities for community engagement need to be what the community members want, when they want it. The clever manager has a back-up, a room full of provision, a diary of connections and providers who hopefully owe the manager a favour and thus can provide what is needed when it is needed.

This may not sound hyper-efficient, but plans and programmes only purport to be efficient. Real community work relates to real people and the most needy of people will not always fit into a plan.

Provision of opportunity also needs to be within the community. City-wide plans that show depth and breadth of provision across a wide geographic area are for politicians, auditors and personal glorification alone, because so many of the neediest fear to travel or do not have the means to travel. Travel is for the confident, the affluent, the free and the inquisitive – not necessarily for the mums in my school or the senior citizens on our estate.

We have sought to develop the model of the 'training pool' in all our provision. The training pool works for those swimmers for whom the 'chuck 'em in at the deep end' will never work. The training pool allows the nervous swimmer to keep one foot on the floor at all times and for the side of the pool never to be more than a couple of strokes away at any point. Having grown comfortable in the small pool, two things happen. One either becomes dissatisfied with the small pool and wants to swim further for longer, or the small pool becomes crowded by new non-swimmers and one is forced into the big pool.

So how does one get continued success in the big pool? Well, a quick scan around the big pool soon affords the more confident new swimmer the realisation that once again if I stick in the shallow end I can keep one foot on the floor all the time. Similarly I can ensure that I am always only a few strokes from either the shallow end or the poolside.

Other swimmers might wish to use the big pool to swim longer distances, jump in more safely or make more of a splash. These swimmers will demand of themselves the confidence to go deeper and further. Yet others will agree to the shallow end only, to be drawn deeper and further through games with friends and they're in at the deep end without knowing or caring.

Community provision, we believe from our experiences, must be planned and managed similarly. All such community provision must be at the local level – the very local level – for the insecure, the dispossessed and the unsure do not naturally make the best explorers. They need a training pool. So all provision must be at the local level, in the school, in the community centre, in the village hall, in the home. *Local*.

These facilities, providers and resources must not be too sophisticated. Indeed I think there is a serious argument for this provision to be flawed and imperfect in order to remove the gloss of sophistication and to prevent the 'not for the likes of me' mentality that we all recognise in ourselves. The imperfect provision also often acts as the unifying issue that leads the disparate group of individuals to work collectively to improve their lot.

The other important factor about providing the imperfect training pool is that we can build in obsolescence. We can build in ultimate frustration and this is good insofar as individuals learning to swim in the perfect, luxurious, all-singing, all-dancing training pool would never leave. If we provide clients with slightly imperfect soon to be frustrating provision, at the same time we build in the opportunity and need for such clients to move on to the big pool, the local college, the centre or group down the road.

In this context surely one of the best things a member of our community ever said to me was, 'I'm sorry Pete but I need to go to the college because your facilities won't let me do what I need to do.'

I see two axes. One is horizontal, the development of skill. The other axis, joining the first one in the bottom left-hand corner of my mind's eye, goes up to the right at an angle of about 45 degrees. This line is the confidence line. As skill improves so does confidence and self-esteem. When these axes go far to the right and far up the page, then is the point to move on – a different point for each individual.

So local provision of what I want, when I want it. Provision that is flawed or limited to move me on to the next level when and if I am ready.

In order to make all this work there is the final and consequently most important piece in the jigsaw. As in the pool, most of us poor swimmers learn best when there is someone at our side; not necessarily the greatest teacher or the strongest swimmer in the world, but someone we trust. Similarly in community work, allowing for all the plans, joined up thinking and strategies, it is the person holding hands, supporting, smiling, cajoling and driving the participant on that is crucial to the success of the venture. By definition this is rarely the leader.

Many schools have such people on their staff. Many city schools have learning mentors who can be used in this way. We are blessed to have had a community co-ordinator, Margaret, who has organised and communicated, encouraged and held hands, moved furniture and calmed babies, run people home and made coffees, rescued me and supported others.

Absolutely crucial to any success of anything we have done has been the time and effort and wisdom and love of Margaret. Every school about to embark upon a community role needs a Margaret. The rest is all talk. Margaret has met and discovered so many great people, people with extraordinary talents, people so willing to give of their time. People driven by politics, religion and/or their love of people, their guilt of fortuity. So many people that simply want to give. We have met so many people dealt a poor hand; so many people who manage such extraordinary lives against the most amazing odds; so many people with low self-esteem and degrees of depression and indeed self-hate and loathing who have such immense potential. It has been in essence really quite simple to put these two groups together for the benefit and service of both.

We have a model of society as a circle, not a hierarchical pyramid of meritocracy or class – a circle where we all stand looking at the back of the person in front who in turn is looking at the back of the person in front of them. Of course if you follow this circle around then someone is looking at you.

When Nelson Mandela came to Leeds he told the children how excited he was to be sharing the stage with Lucas Radebe, the Leeds footballer. For so many of our children and indeed us as adults this was an amazing thought. Nelson Mandela has heroes too. He isn't just all our hero, he has a hero too. Of course when you speak to Lucas Radebe you find he has heroes too and so the circle goes on. I look at Nelson Mandela, he looks at Lucas Radebe, who looks at …

Our community is just like this. It's not a hierarchy. The local college needs students on seats. They look overseas and to untapped communities around the world with, quite rightly, targets for various under-represented groups. We have mums looking to find work, skill, time away from the house, an escape from poverty, looking at the colleges.

Harmony and contentment occur when two members of the circle I describe turn and face each other. As a community school we have in many senses encouraged the model of the symbiotic circle and then introduced people in this circle to each other.

I'm not sure if that's called managing a community primary school but it's the best way I've got of describing what we try and do each day along with all the usual school stuff.

5

■ ■ ■

John Kitto Community College

Jean Gledhill in conversation with Penny Faust

The challenge

Jean Gledhill came to John Kitto Community College as Principal at the beginning of the summer term 2001. Previously she had been Head of North Manchester High School for Girls, a comprehensive girls' school in North Manchester which had been failing when she arrived. Within seven years the roll had increased from 714 in 1993 to 1,400 in 2000; from 18 per cent achieving five or more GCSEs to more than 40 per cent. The school had become a Community School and had achieved Beacon Status.

This time Jean was taking over an already designated community college, but it was labelled as 'a school in challenging circumstances' and seemed to have lost the confidence of some of the people in the catchment area. In 1997 the OFSTED report had been good, but by the turn of the century the school roll had fallen from 270 to 220 per year and its reputation was, in Jean's words, as being 'very good with special needs pupils' and 'the school for thugs'.

The challenge was to turn John Kitto back into a Community College which genuinely reflected the needs and aspirations of the communities in the catchment area; to raise the level of attainment of all its users and to become a developing organisation integrated with its partners across the varying communities which it serves.

About the college

The John Kitto School came into existence in 1989 as a county 11–18 mixed comprehensive school to replace three secondary modern schools. The Community College designation was given from 1 April 1991 when the college took responsibility for community education over a large area. The college does not, however, directly touch any of the communities which it serves; its immediate neighbours are local industries and commercial organisations. The three local communities in the catchment area are all different, with their own specific demands on the facilities offered by the college.

The catchment area of the college includes parts of Plymouth which are characterised by a high degree of economic and social deprivation. In 2000 the three Plymouth grammar schools took 18 per cent of the potential pupils from the catchment area and a local Roman Catholic School took another 25 per cent, both Catholic and non-Catholic, for whom education at a Christian school was important. So the intake for John Kitto is skewed away from a normal distribution. The pupils are mainly white though there are a few asylum seekers and a number of pupils from ethnic minorities – Chinese, Greek, Turkish and two Roma families. In addition there is a substantial transient population from military families based in the area.

The college site is wonderful and well cared for. According to Jean, when she came for interview she 'thought she'd died and gone to heaven' in comparison with her experience in Manchester. The students were delightful; warm and friendly but lacking belief in themselves. The sixth form has its own buildings on site and is part of the Tamar Valley Consortium of three community colleges. The staff were subdued, beaten down by local and national issues and initiatives. They felt they were failures when judged by the government criteria relating to a large extent to the attainments of pupils in national testing regimes and the steeply falling roll. But there was a camaraderie amongst them and a commitment which Jean believed could become a powerful force for learning.

Across the road from the college, linked by a footbridge, is the local YMCA which was already working with the college in the areas of recreation and leisure. Also within the remit of the college are the activities of the Honicknowle Community Centre which cover a wide range of people in the community – from retired people through adult education to the very young. Youth workers at the centre also support disaffected youngsters from across the city who have been excluded from their local schools. In May 2000, pupils excluded from John Kitto were unable to use this local facility and were attending centres in other parts of the city.

The vision

Community colleges should reflect both the needs and aspirations of their own communities and where those communities are placed in their own context and history. Jean's vision was to develop a holistic educational experience for all the users of the John Kitto College facilities and resources. She believes that education cannot be slotted into particular sections – whatever is produced in one area affects everything else. What is needed is a strategic way of planning so that everything can fit together to produce a spider's web of educational experience. Her underpinning ethos is that learning is fun, a joyful experience that everyone can participate in.

The college budget incorporates the delivery not just of the statutory curriculum but also adult education, community work, community development work, youth work, family education and pre-school work – all under one umbrella which covers the different communities in the catchment area. What should be offered is a fully integrated service 'from cradle to grave'. In order to achieve this, Jean believes that there is a need to discover how people relate to each other and a fundamental requirement to take on board all the people who have an interest in the college in whatever is being planned and implemented.

The strategy

Extending the vision

Specifically, Jean looked at John Kitto College in relation to what was on offer educationally not just in the catchment area but in the whole of Plymouth, in order to enhance the college itself and the resources which would underpin future development. She came to believe that two major developments would bring real and lasting benefits to the college as a whole: application to become a Specialist College and designation as a voluntary aided or voluntary controlled Church of England school.

Specialist College status

Before her arrival, John Kitto College had steadfastly set its face against applying for Specialist College status. But with the advent of the new specialisms in 2001 and lured by the potential increase in resources of between £600–800,000, Jean suggested that becoming a Specialist College for Business and Enterprise would 'kick our culture along and turn our aspirations into one of 'I can'''. Business and Enterprise includes much more than excelling in business studies: it also includes ICT, a college strength, maths, which needed the impetus to become strong, and languages for business, which could be taken out into the community.

Voluntary aided/voluntary controlled status

The rationale for linking with the Church of England came both from Jean's experiences in Manchester and the situation in Plymouth. There is no Church of England secondary school in the city, so parents wanting a specifically Christian ethos for their children were sending them to the local Roman Catholic secondary school. The Church of England, however, was already an integral part of the various communities served by John Kitto, for example, there were thriving church-based groups for senior citizens, young people and pre-school children.

But it was more than that. In the latter part of her headship in Manchester, Jean had lost two of her students to suicide at a time when they were taking GCSEs. The families turned to both the school and the Church for support and comfort. Jean relied on her own strong roots in the Church to be able to meet their needs. But the young people had no such roots. The school provided strong moral education but had failed to tackle the spiritual aspects of life. When they went along to the funerals of their friends, students turned to Jean and asked her to teach them to pray. She found that immensely shocking and began to consider that in the drive to be non-dogmatic, tolerant and multicultural, the spiritual baby may have been thrown out with the bathwater.

That feeling was reinforced when she discovered that amongst other secondary schools in north Manchester the only ones which had not experienced any suicides amongst the pupils were those with religious links – the local Church of England, Jewish and Roman Catholic Schools. She visited those schools to discover what the difference was and found that they were openly teaching a religion, not in a dogmatic or intolerant way – there was enormous respect for other faiths – but in a way that supported the young people in their care. At that time she also learned that the Church of England included schools that did not have religious requirements based on a points system for entry, such as attendance at church. There were schools that had 25 per cent of pupils from families that were Anglicans, 25 per cent from other Christian denominations, 25 per cent from the local area and 25 per cent of other faiths.

Finally she discovered that John Kitto, for whom the college had been named, had been a Church of England missionary educator. It all seemed to hang together and she wanted the commitment and ethos of the Church to become part of the college. So in line with her resolve to take on board all the people who had an interest in the college in whatever was being planned and implemented, she determined to start the debate within the college as soon as it became appropriate.

Early days

On the ground

To become known and trusted

To begin with Jean made a point of putting herself out and about. 'I became very visible.' Within the college she walked the corridors, visited lessons and participated in dinner and playground duties. Her aim was to communicate that learning was fun and that John Kitto did have enormous potential. Beyond the immediate college site she also visited the partner organisations, Honicknowle Community Centre and the YMCA, 'to look, listen and learn' about their work, the challenges and where they wanted to go in the future.

To develop a culture of reward

In Manchester the head's office had been easily accessible for students and staff. The principal's office at John Kitto was away from the rest of the college at the end of a corridor. So the staff were enlisted to facilitate the celebration of student achievement; students were to be sent along whenever work had been done that deserved praise. Jean's PA was told that she wanted the kids in, whoever was in her office already. 'Whether it was the head of a local company or the mayor, everyone could and did share in and celebrate success.' She kept a prize box in her office, easily to hand. 'Some days kids were queuing up in that corridor to share their work.'

To develop a culture of learning

It became apparent that there was some really good work going on in college, but that there was disruption in some areas. Jean asked staff what they wanted to change. They thought that action in two particular areas would be helpful: consistency in enforcing uniform and banning the use of mobile phones in college. Most importantly, parents were consulted and agreed to help. The first week saw minor confrontations; the second week brought about a change in atmosphere which had to be sustained. Then there could be a change to a culture of learning in lessons.

To bring students excluded from the college back into the community

One of Jean's first actions as principal was to allow students who had been excluded from the college to use the provision for the disaffected at Honicknowle Community Centre. She felt that it was fundamentally wrong to send them out of their own area, thereby increasing their sense of isolation and alienation.

Management and governance

To restructure and enlarge the senior management team

Previously the college had been managed by two or three people. Jean not only wanted to open things up to enable people to use their talents, but also knew that she herself works best as part of a team 'through other people'. A number of roles were created and more women were included as part of the senior management team – 'good for girls and women staff'. There is now a team of four women and five men, including two vice principals, one with responsibility for the curriculum and the other with an overview of assessment and pastoral care and specific responsibility for finance. Other posts covered Key Stages 3, 4 and 5, assessment with respect to liaising with others and value added, and human resource management for both teaching and non-teaching staff.

To develop an effective conduit for change

Jean needed to pull together all the people involved with the college for a combined effort towards improvement. A meeting was arranged with key people from the college and its partners and she began by being provocative. 'John Kitto itself is struggling, designated 'a school in challenging circumstances'. If John Kitto goes down how will this impact on you?' As a result of the subsequent discussions, a strategy group was formed in order to initiate and sustain developments in a structured and planned way. This consisted of representatives of all the organisations which came under the college remit: the college itself, the YMCA and Honicknowle Community Centre.

To enable governors to work effectively

Jean believes that governors have to be informed properly in order to work effectively. The system was changed to ensure that all papers and reports were available before meetings, so that debate and decision making could be based on correct and appropriate information. In September 2001 a new governing body took shape with the chief executive of the YMCA taking the chair. Seven new sub-committees were set up and members of the senior management team began to attend all governors meetings and sub-committees, bringing benefits both to governor effectiveness and their own professional development. Using the governor training allocation and some professional development resources, the governing body and senior management team went to a hotel for the weekend with the specific aims of developing strategies for working together effectively and the development of the college.

To involve students more effectively in college planning and decision making

The School Council, consisting of members elected from the student body, was already in existence. Jean encouraged them to adopt a higher profile in the college and more active participation in decision making. She also appointed a new Student Executive, including a captain and vice-captain, from members of

Year 11. They represent the college on all important occasions and help market it. They are also her key advisory body from the students.

Perceptions and communication

To ensure effective communications across the college and with parents, and with the college's partners

An effective infrastructure for communication across the college was put into place so that developments were open and overt for students, staff, governors and parents. This consisted of: the strategy group which was the key vehicle for bringing together the YMCA, Honicknowle Community Centre and the College; the restructuring of the senior management team to enable more teams around the college to operate effectively; and the formation of the Inclusion Group from the heads of year, youth workers, the behaviour support centre staff, the attendance officer, the education welfare officer, the head of special needs and Connexions personal adviser, which meets twice every half term.

To change the atmosphere in the daily morning briefings for staff

Jean recognised that these meetings needed to be run with a lighter touch. She was determined that members of staff would leave with smiles on their faces and that the briefings would not, in any circumstances, be used for telling people off.

To change the external perceptions of the college

The first task of the strategy group was to begin to change the hearts and minds of the people in the city of Plymouth. In partnership with a local marketing firm, new (and glossy) information leaflets about the college were prepared and printed.

Planning for the future development of the college

Formally to include those who have a vested interest in the planning and decision-making process

Initially, early in the summer term 2001, parents were invited in to the college for sessions specifically to discuss various aspects of college life such as discipline, behaviour, uniform and the new initiatives of the Business and Enterprise College and becoming a Church School. Nothing was hidden. Jean commented, 'Some came to see who I was, but a lot wanted to engage and they soon got caught up in the business of the meetings.'

Jean's vision, however, extended to making the full development planning process a more inclusive activity. As a consequence, the strategy group worked together to organise two days for development planning at the end of the term. As many people/groups as possible were invited: teaching and non-teaching staff, governors, parents, members of the student council and executive, sixth formers, YMCA representatives, youth workers, community workers, community education staff, adult users, retired people, representatives of the diocese. 'On the day some pupils just turned up and asked if they could join in. The answer was of course "yes".'

In order to ensure that everyone felt welcome and included, the days began with 'ice-breakers' delivered by the youth and community workers who were specialists in the field. After that came information-giving about the work of all aspects of the college remit – explanations of Honicknowle, YMCA, community education, John Kitto curriculum, adult education, Further Education Funding Council (FEFC) funding changes and impact, etc. – followed by debate and development planning for the college, including the issues of Specialist College status and the proposed linkage with the Church.

The marketing exercise on behalf of the college was launched. The new leaflets were handed to everyone there with a brief to distribute them as widely as possible across Plymouth. As a result the leaflets turned up in places where John Kitto Community College had never before been considered.

To discover what people wanted from the college

Using the strengths of the people who specifically worked within the community – YMCA, community workers, youth workers, community education staff – a concerted effort was made to determine what the local communities thought about the college and what their needs were. It was important that people felt safe about articulating their requirements, so part of this consultation exercise consisted of work out in the field and part done on the development planning days. This consultation is ongoing, in Jean's words, 'using the people who have the skills to take down the barriers'. She says, 'I don't have those skills. I've been a teacher too long – I'm used to telling!'

Developments over the following year

Homework and breakfast clubs

One of the concerns articulated by parents and students during the consultation period was that of homework. Using the money allocated for being a 'school in challenging circumstances', Jean identified a teacher who was enthusiastic about working flexible hours so that a supervised Homework Club could be established for students who wanted to stay on after school hours. Working with a learning assistant, the teacher was able to give students appropriate support and assistance with their homework. The students themselves remarked that they needed something to eat in order to concentrate properly, so food was provided free for all those who stayed on. Now upwards of 30 pupils attend each day.

It also became apparent that both students and some staff would benefit from being able to have breakfast at college. After consultation with the canteen staff, a Breakfast Club was established, again drawing in students to discuss both their work and other issues with the staff who were there. In this case participants pay for their own breakfasts.

Provision of student space and 'alternative adults' in college

Discussions at the development days showed that not all students wanted to participate in sports or regulated activities during the school day. There was a need for students both to have space of their own to 'chill out' in and also opportunities to talk to people who were not teachers about their personal problems and wider issues. The youth workers from Honicknowle agreed to come up to the college to support students during break times and the lunch period. Defined areas were allocated for such discussions and/or students to play their own music or just relax. This in turn has had a knock-on effect, enabling the college pastoral team to work with the youth workers at Honicknowle, and then change the ways that they work with disaffected students who are still in college.

Extension of combined facilities offered by YMCA and John Kitto Community College

Although John Kitto and the YMCA had been working together effectively for some considerable time, both Jean and the Chief Executive of the YMCA, Carol Belton, recognised that there was plenty of potential for an extension of their joint activities in recreation and sports provision. To begin with there needed to be some ground clearing, the means by which some areas of dispute such as caretaking hours and duties could be resolved. Again, consultation with users of the facilities indicated preferences for what was needed by the college's pupils and surrounding communities. This resulted in the extension of the hours of use of the facilities and activities both at the college and YMCA.

Currently there is a community bid, including resources from John Kitto, to open a new Family Education Centre which will include full workplace nursery and crèche facilities on the YMCA site. This will not only involve looking after children but also include the support and education of families.

Reaching out into the community – Family Education Provision through WizzArt

Together with their feeder primary schools and supported by the Plymouth Family Education Team and Community Education Development Centre, John Kitto has been piloting an arts-based scheme to engage children and their families together in art-based projects. This brought families into primary schools that had never been seen before and began to turn relationships around. It culminated in a week of 'Take our Parents to Art School Day' in all the schools which made up the John Kitto Academic Council (the college and its feeder primaries). The timetable was collapsed in each of the schools on a particular day and various activities provided for parents and children together. Because John Kitto was big enough, the college was able to provide a variety of different activities from potting, painting and silk-screen printing to drama, singing and other musical activities. They all came together for a celebration at the end of the afternoon. Jean was enthusiastic, 'It was magic! If you'd seen all the mums in the middle of all these boys doing African drumming, counting like mad as they were going through all the different rhythms. Really good. And there were mums there we'd not seen before.'

Involvement of a local church in partnership with JK and YMCA

There was provision for local pre-school children to attend local nurseries, but some were expensive and none open to children with special needs. In a partnership between Rev. Angus Parker at St Pancras Church, John Kitto and the YMCA, a new nursery was opened for all local pre-school children, including those with special needs. St Pancras has now extended its activities into supporting other community initiatives, offering support for credit union and advice and guidance on debt relief.

Adult education

Adult education had always been a strong feature occurring in all the partner organisations: the College, YMCA and Honicknowle Community Centre. The various programmes included a really strong Basic Skills course and in the past year John Kitto achieved the Basic Skills Quality Mark. Recently, however, in one of its most exciting innovations, the college became a centre for Learn Direct: an online learning programme for adults. John Kitto provides the technology and tutors and people come into college to access the learning, which started with information technology but is now extending, at the instigation of the learners, into other areas.

Having other adults in college during the school day creates a profound impact. At best it makes students aware that learning can and does continue throughout their lives. There are other benefits too. At the moment lessons for adults occur concurrently with those of students, but they only learn together when the students are in the 16–19 age group. According to Jean, their presence in A-level classes really 'pushes the students along'.

Jean also emphasises that having them in and around the college premises also has a more general beneficial effect, for example, on behaviour. 'A group of lads can be going down a corridor doing what teenage lads usually do, pushing each other around with bags and arms and legs in all directions and I may tell them to stop – and they will. But if a woman is coming towards them with a pushchair, they'll stop by themselves. They move to the side, often speak to her and the child, and let them through. And then they'll carry on doing what lads usually do!'

Initiation of bid to become a Business and Enterprise College

The governors were enthusiastic and more general agreement was reached at the planning days that the college should apply to become a Specialist College for Business and Enterprise. This involved contacting businesses in the area, both commercial and industrial, to bring in sponsorship money. The college has to attract sponsorship of £50,000 for its application to be considered, so local business leaders were invited to a business breakfast at the college to hear about the bid and the benefits it might bring. As their contribution, the canteen staff gave their time free and staff and students were the hosts.

So far they have raised in excess of £20,000. Jean believes that the students were their greatest assets. 'They charmed the pants off the business people. It was good for the college and good for the kids to be with these business people, some of whom were the heads of quite large companies in the area.'

Initiation of application to become a Church School

Also discussed in depth on the planning days was the possibility of becoming a Church School. The governors had already decided in favour. They recognised that it would balance the catchment area, giving parents positive reasons for choosing John Kitto Community College for their children. They also wanted what Jean describes as 'a values based education that wraps around children to provide a very strong foundation from which to grow. That would be difficult to provide without the Church link.' Much discussion had also taken place throughout the summer term and in the end, on the planning days, nine out of ten discussion groups were positive about the initiative.

Initial contact had shown that John Kitto would be in competition with two other schools, one private and the other threatened with closure. In the end the Church decided to accept John Kitto's application and matters are now gradually proceeding to effect the change.

Professional development

The continuing professional development (CPD) of all the staff has become a priority for the college. It is part of the brief of one of the vice principals who provides information about courses and development programmes. Because there is a finite amount of money available, CPD links into the school development plan and departmental development plans. The college is currently leading on the development of middle managers and seeking ways of accrediting their learning with a local teacher training college. Within the parameters of college need and available resources, each member of staff, teaching and non-teaching, takes responsibility for their own professional development in the sense that they can put in for courses they think will enhance their careers.

Achievements

Looking back over the past four terms, what have been the achievements so far? At a fairly basic level the statistics are more than satisfying: a rising school roll and higher levels of attainment.

The college is winning back its roll; applications to the college this year have topped 270 and there is a waiting list for entry at Year 7. For the first time in the college's history, all Key Stage 3 results are above 50 per cent. These results will take John Kitto up the Plymouth league table as the college has outperformed several other schools in its part of the city. At the time of writing the GCSE results are awaited with some optimism.

Those, however, are only the quantitative results. At a qualitative level, the morale of the staff has lifted and the confidence of students has perceptibly grown. The external view of the college has shifted substantially. Its links with all of its partners and the communities in the catchment area have been enhanced and reinforced. Jean believes that they are doing good work which can be seen and appreciated. 'People are getting behind us now.'

The future

The college will soon be involved with another planning day to review the development plan for the coming year. They want to land the Business and Enterprise status, hopefully during 2003. The formal process for becoming a Church School will take a bit longer.

There are still some big challenges ahead. These include: raising GCSE results to bring the college out of the 'school in challenging circumstances' designation; the review of pastoral care across the college to seek improvements;

bringing the sixth form into the life of the college; the issue of attendance; the lessons of Learn Direct for 14–19 education; the changes that will come from FEFC and the challenges of the Learning and Skills Council. There are now mechanisms in place for communication, consultation and planning, but Jean does not believe that the infrastructure for the college is yet totally secure.

In the end what Jean wants is to see steady progress 'that lifts people up and makes them feel that they are going somewhere. In the long term, what is needed is that John Kitto Community College becomes strong and enduring so that it cannot be taken apart.'

6

■ ■ ■

Lifelong Learning Without Frontiers

Javed Khan

I'm going to take you on a journey of discovery. We're going to visit a fairly special place; a place that has become a melting pot of colours, cultures and creeds; where the history dates back centuries, as do many of the buildings. It should be described as a quiet, serene, picturesque and green part of the UK – a place that has more canals than Venice. We're going of course to Birmingham!

Birmingham is a place that for many people is significant only because it is difficult to travel from the south of the country to the north without at least passing road signs announcing its proximity. It's the 'city of a thousand trades' where the industrial revolution began, and is steeped in a history of manufacturing and trade, manual labour, smog and relentlessly underachieving football teams!

Well, things have changed – apart from the sporting results of course. Modern-day Birmingham is now, above all else, a major *learning city*; a city that is moving at warp speed to embed lifelong learning habits and practices across its multi-dimensionally complex and interconnected communities. If anything, Birmingham has been daring in its visions and prescriptions so that the city may be seen as a turning point in educational history. But before we arrive in Britain's largest local authority, let's put in context some of the transformational awareness that's led to Birmingham being at the leading edge of lifelong learning.

Lifelong learning opens the way to discussion of more than traditional ideals of education and the need for one-off training and qualifications in specific occupations. Whether communities stagnate and ossify or are able to meet the challenges of the future in an intellectually dynamic process depends on their readiness for continual learning – on their openness to what is new, their courage to try what is unusual and to adapt in unfamiliar territory.

The ability to innovate in the economy and in society is of fundamental importance not just for the UK. We need a new form of growth, growth based on knowledge. We need a new departure in educational policy in order to survive in our knowledge-based societies. This means not just the knowledge that has been accumulated by experts or can be called up at any time on the internet. Learning has to have a broader base, to embrace all age groups including those in their 'third age', and to be fully accepted in our communities.

Saying yes to continual learning, and social recognition of the value of all efforts to learn, will create a climate in which creativity is encouraged and a pyramid of creative achievements arises on a broad, lasting base. Arrogance and aversion to everything foreign will then lose their breeding grounds. It is of course easier to interest someone who is willing to learn and a community that is capable of learning in inter-dependent co-operation.

In moments of crisis – said Albert Einstein – *only imagination is more important than knowledge*. In education generally and lifelong learning in particular, we need to deploy greater imagination and more innovative approaches. We need to renew our commitment to education for all.

We live in a world that is rapidly changing. In the third millennium we are experiencing profound social and economic changes. We need to ensure that this transformation is both economically successful and socially and ecologically tolerable. In doing so, we must turn to our communities, who will give constructive shape, meaning and purpose to the transformation. By 2010, we expect that:

- Brighton will have a climate closer to that of the South of France today;
- the UK will have become a net importer of gas;
- the Jet Propulsion Lab in Pasadena, California could be launching a spacecraft with a huge sail, driven by the solar wind. Embarking on a journey in 2010, this interstellar probe will overtake Voyager 1 by 2018. Voyager 1 itself set off in 1977!

To be ready for tomorrow's world we will forget at our peril that nothing becomes outdated more quickly today than knowledge. It would be a reckless judgement indeed to regard the certificates gained in schools, vocational or tertiary colleges as the end of learning.

We must build human capacities through education adapted to local circumstances, provided with cultural sensitivity and rooted in intensive skills training. This – I would emphasise – does not require strategies conceived in ivory towers remote from the communities concerned. At the same time, we must address the problems that prevent people becoming learners. We must also always remember that illiteracy does not mean ignorance. Wisdom is more often found among those who lack knowledge than those who possess it. And lifelong learning can itself benefit from such wisdom in the process of empowering people to participate in the interest of development, democracy and peace.

To spread the message of the benefits of continual learning must be the prerogative of everyone in the community – from midwives, health visitors and doctors, to youth workers, librarians and those who attend mosques, temples, churches or chapels. It is also the business of newsagents, local firms, sports clubs and health clubs. It cannot be done *for* us but only *by* us. It requires a fundamental transformation in the way we perceive the world – a change that must come from within, through a process of lifelong education in the fullest and noblest sense of the term. We must reflect how adult and continuing education can contribute more effectively towards this goal.

The learning age – as the expansion of knowledge accelerates under the influence of the technologies – demands that we take lifelong learning seriously. Education is no longer a 'you only get one chance' activity endured between nursery and the age of 16. It is more a pleasurable habit acquired during and, if your parents help, before schooling. If you like, it is one incurable addiction worth having. The more we learn, the better our chances of a healthy and fruitful life.

Without an awareness of global citizenship, tomorrow's world will clearly not be prepared to meet the challenges that are taking shape. This is by first of all placing our confidence in people and by investing in creativity and the capacity for initiative that we will be able to face the problems of tomorrow. Our greatest strengths as human beings are courage and imagination. We must help these qualities to flourish by combining them with knowledge.

We also know that our inner city/urban schools today are characterised by low achievement, teacher shortages and subsequently a limited curriculum offer. Parents are keen to move their children out to where they see the grass as greener; in fact they are keen to move out themselves. The truth is, it could be argued, that communities are losing faith in their schools and increasingly schools and their communities are in conflict.

Our cities are also characterised by a plethora of regeneration programmes that where successful have created revitalised communities, where inward investment has made a difference. Multiplex cinemas rule OK! But this isn't enough. What we need alongside the regeneration of 'hope' is the creation of genuine learning communities – communities where the lifelong learning ladder is clearly available to all and is provided by a family of learning providers that are related only because they believe in inter-dependent collaborative practice as their daily sustenance. Then there may be hope.

Lifelong learning has developed rapidly over the past two decades. In some countries the number of adults enrolled annually in training courses is greater even than the number of young people receiving compulsory education. Nevertheless – and this cannot be said too often – not everyone has access to training, far from it. Education and vocational training for adults still remains the privilege of the most highly schooled populations, of men more often than women, of the wealthiest countries and of the best equipped urban areas. Too often training courses do not sufficiently acknowledge cultural diversity.

We must therefore reconsider the goal of equal opportunity and view it in the context of a pluralistic world where equality and diversity are recognised as complementary dimensions and acknowledged as such in education systems and plans. We need 'rainbow societies' where every citizen, throughout life, can find fulfilment, shape his or her identity and enter into dialogue with others.

Lifelong learning has a particularly important key function in the dialogue between cultures. The world is becoming smaller and we have to learn to live with one another in this world. We must therefore strengthen intercultural dialogue, not least as a way of helping to guarantee peace.

Ideally, lifelong learning can convey the value of cultural diversity and create openness towards different cultures, while allowing people to retain awareness of their own cultural identities. Mahatma Gandhi put it like this:

> My house is not to be surrounded by a wall and my windows are not to be locked. The cultures of all countries are to blow through my house with as little hindrance as possible. But I shall not let myself be blown away by anyone.

Lifelong learning can help us to learn to live together in our world by gaining an understanding of others and of their histories, traditions and values. Lifelong learning must and will become *as important as daily bread*.

Providers of learning need to place great value on the existing skills within their communities and celebrate the local culture, rather than what usually happens – reaching out with their own culture and agenda. The tokenistic multiculturalism of the 1980s – saris, samosas and steel bands, was not enough then and certainly isn't now. Our communities are more articulate, aware of their rights and more organised then they have ever been. They will not stand for second or sometimes third best. Before we dive into further community consultation meetings and seminars, let's take a breath and remember to be very wary of relying on community leaders who no longer have followers.

Politicians, practitioners and theoreticians of lifelong learning must stand by the message that continuing education is investment in the future. Investments cost money, but without them the edifice of social development will be threatened by decay and, in the longer term, collapse. The implosion of society must be prevented by the large-scale widening and deepening of lifelong learning, of learning that accompanies us throughout life. This must also be achieved for those communities in which the transition to the information society is still no more than rhetoric. We must break the digital divide, and do it quickly!

Only lifelong learning without frontiers – flexible, varied and available – can prepare us for the tasks before us. Adults learn everywhere and all the time. Phases of working and learning overlap. Lifelong learning is an integral part of development programmes, self-help programmes, health and environmental education programmes. In the 1,000 lifelong learning centres in Germany, for example, 15 million people take part in such programmes each year. Adult Learners' weeks now exist, for example, in South Africa, Slovenia, Switzerland, Australia, the

Czech Republic and Jamaica. Each event will differ but together they offer us one lesson – that promoting adult learning is a vital task across the world.

These are daunting agendas and in an era of unprecedented turbulence where the only truth we can be certain of is that 'continuous change is here to stay', let's take heart from history:

> In Italy, for thirty years under the Borgias, they had warfare, terror, murder, bloodshed – and they produced Michelangelo, Leonardo da Vinci and the Renaissance. In Switzerland they had brotherly love, five hundred years of democracy and peace. What did that produce? The cuckoo clock!

So let's return to Birmingham. Nowhere is learning more important than in Birmingham – a city that is truly international in character, whether in its economy, population or considerable ambition. Birmingham has always been a 'can-do' place that added value to things – the manufacturing heart of Britain's reputation as the 'workshop' of the world. While that brings an enviable legacy of wealth creation, there are undesirable side effects, since its people were once dependent on hundreds of thousands of unskilled and semi-skilled jobs. The technological revolution has changed all that. Jobs with prospects in the future demand higher levels of education and training and a commitment and ability to continually update. Unskilled jobs now lack security and are usually part time or short term.

Birmingham is a city rich in the number, range and quality of its educational institutions within the school and after school sectors, further and higher education establishments, libraries, museums, youth clubs and community venues. The city is also home to a multitude of well-established private, community and voluntary sector training providers.

The pace of change is accelerating, driven by technologies and economic pressures. So Birmingham needs to have the capacity to adopt change and prosper in the future. Its present and future citizens need, above all, the habits of continual learning to take advantage of and shape that changing world. The city's population is diverse and we know that very soon less than half of its residents will have an Anglo-Saxon/Mixed European origin. It has always offered the lure of economic and social warmth for the inward migrants, whether from the UK, Europe or a wider world. It continues to do so.

The drivers of information communication technology are not merely changing the job market. They provide the tantalising prospect, if harnessed cleverly, of acting as a catalyst to the learning process and, in particular, of cracking the cycle of deprivation and disadvantage. The city now needs to add value to people – Brummies – all of them who continue to arrive from all over the UK, Europe and the world in the hope of a better life for their families and themselves.

The scale of challenges for making lifelong learning meaningful in this city is immense. We know that Birmingham is a place where:

- 36 per cent of adults have no qualifications;
- only 5 per cent of these are attending a course to improve their basic skills;
- ward level unemployment ranges from 2.4 per cent to 26 per cent;
- 33 per cent of employers provide no training;
- we have young people who have never known a wage earner in their family;
- 10 per cent of young people are neither in education nor employment;
- one in four school children has a Pakistani origin;
- there are more black young people than white.

This is now. Where it must get to is the position where it begins to break the cycles of deprivation and exclusion that many of these communities are suffering.

That is why Birmingham City Council and the City Strategic Partnership (representing all the major institutions and sectors) have made the creation of a 'learning city' their top priority. The phrase itself implies more than individual learning. It encourages all institutions – hospitals, firms, the Police, the City Council, the voluntary sector – in being learning organisations that learn from experience. That is why 'improving on previous best' was the starting point of a campaign to transform educational aspirations, expectations and attainment. Less than a dozen years ago only 25 per cent of Birmingham 11 year olds had 'reading ages' at or above their age. Now 75 per cent do – and within a year or two it will be over 80 per cent. There has been a similar rise in maths. Over the same period the percentage gaining five or more higher grade GCSEs has risen from 23 per cent to 41 per cent. The aim is for 50 per cent – the national figure – by the summer of 2003. Fewer drop out of education at 16 and over 30 per cent go on to higher education – more than twice the number a decade ago.

Similar targets for adults are being established. Through the colleges, the voluntary sector and the city's adult education service they are ensuring that opportunities for learning surround adults in the library, supermarkets, clubs, places of worship and most prominently in schools. To acquire the learning habit in retirement is to sustain your health: and so they are working with the four new primary care trusts to play our part in making Birmingham a healthy city.

The city is determined to harness its collective energy to move beyond 'improving on previous best' to be 'at the leading edge of performance and practice'. In 2001 Birmingham posted its ambition to be a learning city and held its inaugural annual lifelong learning awards ceremony. This has been repeated in 2002 on a day designated as the Birmingham Learning Day – when people all over the city symbolised their personal learning aspirations by spending ten minutes to learn five phrases from one of the 22 major languages of our city. Over 28,000 people took part in 'Take 10 To Learn'. It is symbolic of mutual interest, respect and understanding of the many faiths, races and nationalities now proud to be Birmingham citizens – on all of whom the future peace and prosperity depends.

But we know that to make a city that is increasingly multi-faith, multi-racial and multi-lingual both peaceful and coherent is a formidable challenge. Not many places have done that. We need to take the issues of faith, race and language as positives – not issues to be ignored or regarded as too hot to handle. We ought to be alarmed that places of learning are increasingly mono-cultural and mono-faith. There needs to be upfront promotion, celebration and publicity of the wealth and strength that arises from diversity of race, faith and language. A true learning city, which is not the same as an educated city, is one that develops by learning from its experiences and those of others. So, what are the questions Birmingham as a learning city is facing:

1 What is the changed role to the traditional role of providers of learning, i.e. pre-school/primary/secondary schools, college and universities?

2 How is the issue of the different faiths to be promoted with sensitivity?

3 How do you link the different (segregated?) communities around a common agenda?

4 Can we find ways of digging really deep into communities and learning *from* them before we plan learning *for* them?

5 How do you ensure the unbroken learning routes to employment for 14–25 year olds?

6 What are the interventions that will reduce the 'skills gap' and prevent the 'brain drain' from the city?

So, what are the future specifics?

- sectoral employment growth?
- 'green' and 'health' issues?
- continued poverty? – i.e. cities will always be places that offer 'warmth' to economic migrants and how therefore do you catch their entrepreneurial spirit before they become apathetic?

But is this broad-brush analysis more or less correct? And does it mean that some institutional practices need to change? If so, which, what and how? What symbolic changes do you need to make *now*, in the next three years, in the next ten? Birmingham's response to these questions and more will clearly be the defining cornerstones that could help it win the race 'between education and catastrophe'. A successful twenty-first century city must take the issue of lifelong learning seriously. Birmingham is focusing on six aspects of this proposition.

A flying start

The most neglected aspect of our educational debate has been the period from birth to when school starts at age five or six. We now know that investment in coherent programmes affecting housing conditions, health and care support and education has a long-term pay off in the teenage years and beyond. The

UK government has recognised this and promoted a huge expansion of birth to age five programmes in the public, private and voluntary sectors. We need a focused service of support for families, especially first-time parents, or those with large families in challenging conditions, so that youngsters can receive 'good enough parenting' in the second year of their life when their increasing mobility offers challenges to the most appropriate (and usually diversionary) response from hard-pressed and uncertain parents.

Minding the gaps

Any analysis of 'risks' and 'resilience' will help to identify those most 'at risk' and with the least 'resilience'. We need to look in all the various stages – 'infancy', 'childhood', 'adolescence' and 'adolescence to young adulthood' – at those most at risk and institute proven intervention programmes (which usually involve more than one agency) in order to diminish the risks and increase the resilience. Some of these interventions will involve programmes designed to tackle the time outside school – the 85 per cent of waking time when children are not in school. So long summer holidays, weekends and after-school evenings are particularly hazardous times for the most vulnerable.

Beyond school

Birmingham has pioneered two ideas – the Children's University and the University of the First Age (UFA). The UFA is designed to promote the idea that secondary education equals belonging to school *plus* something else (in this case the UFA). The UFA can offer intensive accelerated learning for youngsters aged 10 to 14 and chances for older young people to work as tutors and mentors, thus providing a model of lifelong learning in practice.

School improvement

Having promoted 'improving on previous best' over the past ten years, within the context of a research base of 'school effectiveness' and 'school improvement' – that is to say, ensuring all our schools have targets for improvement for all their pupils, especially those who seem to be in groups which are not improving as rapidly as others (e.g. boys from poor backgrounds and other minority ethnic communities) – our schools are equipped with knowledge of 'what works' in terms of school improvement and a common language with which to visit and compare practice and to learn from research findings. We are moving forward to 'be at the leading edge' because we know that the perpetual renewal of our poorer populations and the need to improve standards of what is possible will need huge energy, commitment, skill and passion to be at the leading edge of practice.

Race, faith and language

Many cities have lost momentum, or a sense of shared direction, because they have not been clearly led and because they have allowed the consequence of their continuing poverty to exacerbate divisions of race, faith and language. It is as though these issues have become 'taboo' subjects, left undiscussed because people have not the courage to discuss them. A learning city must have 'standards of values and inter-faith respect' which it promotes in all its schools, colleges and universities.

Lifelong learning habits

There are cumulative practices which will support lifelong learning as an incentive for all citizens who see health and enough wealth as desirable goals that will lead to sustainability:

1 All courses to contain the first step of further accreditation in their design.

2 A 'primary graduates hall of fame' where primary schools' walls are replete with the achievements and further learning of their former pupils, as examples to present pupils, and whose awards evenings celebrate achievements and accredited attainments of all members – young and old, pupils, staff and parents – of the community.

3 The creation of interlinked learning centres based on libraries in schools, community colleges and business – with open access.

4 Schools devote a set percentage (2 per cent?) of their budgets to further professional development of their staff and whose performance management has an essential ingredient of extending the professional skills of each member of staff.

5 All employers releasing employees for an hour a week, who in turn give an hour of their own time to contribute to some element of the shared agenda of the future where the state funds provision (e.g. in schools, old people's homes, governors, hospitals), i.e. the notion of community service and volunteering being in-built to jobs.

6 Employers set up an e-mail tutoring scheme.

7 Every GP health centre to have an on-site learning centre, whilst surgeries and clinics adopt a 'learning' standard to encourage patients to extend their own learning in the interests of their health and welfare.

8 Universities devote a percentage (2 per cent?) to sponsoring and supporting primary and secondary schools in their areas.

9 Colleges of further education devote a percentage (2 per cent?) for work with secondary and primary schools.

10 Citizens belong to an e-learning foundation committed to collective purchase and exchange of e-learning devices.

11 Supermarkets which devote a percentage (2 per cent?) of their profit to life-long learning foundations.

12 Lifelong learning advocates in every ward: midwives, youth workers, health visitors and librarians.

13 Collegiate academies which cluster a group of schools, a college and a university, working as an interdependent family of learning providers sharing some resources, staff and facilities.

14 A laptop in everyone's lap.

15 Funding incentives which reward diversity and collaboration.

16 Schools voluntarily set themselves targets for the percentage of their 16 year olds who will 'stay on'.

17 'International' specialist schools – places where learners and teachers come from at least three continents.

18 A 'Bring Your Culture to Work Day', challenging education leaders to take up the cause of learning in a rapidly changing multicultural society.

19 Marketing lifelong learning – *It's An Attitude*, a catchphrase that recognises learning is about more than just qualifications and promotes the message that successful lifelong learning policy, practice and delivery requires an attitudinal shift.

These are the priorities of a truly learning city – one committed to remaining vibrant, ever-changing to current knowledge but sure in its values and confident in its unpredictable creativity. In doing so, Birmingham is embracing a new guiding principle: 'In a world of change it's the *learners* who will inherit the earth; whilst the *learned* will remain beautifully equipped to deal with a world which no longer exists.'

7

■ ■ ■

Schools and their Communities in Northern Ireland

Frances and Christopher Bowring-Carr

Principals, teachers, students, and parents working together ... can create within their schools an ecology of reflection, growth and refinement of practice – a community of learners.

(Barth, 1990: 162)

In this chapter the authors will set out some of the constraints on community schools in Northern Ireland, and then focus on two schools to give examples of what is possible once the school has determined to make an attempt at responding to and regenerating the community in which it lives. We start from the premise that in an ideal world the boundaries between schools and the communities around them should be diminished to the point of being invisible. The nineteenth-century concept, which malignly dominated much of the twentieth century as well, was that education was something done to children in a building separate, apart, fenced off from the community, to which parents came in some trepidation and waited at the gate until the children were freed. The twenty-first-century concept is that when parents, the community as a whole and teachers combine with the children then deep learning is possible, and the learning that emerges from such a combination has an influence on the community as a whole. Learning becomes not only something that children have to do but also an activity that regenerates the community and enables its members to live more widely and deeply and, vital to this part of the world, more at ease with itself. What is suggested is that schools can become the monasteries for a secular world. The fullest manifestation of such an idea is the full-service school which:

> ... *puts the best of school reform together with all other services that children, youth, and their families need, most of which can be located in a school building.*

(Dryfoos, 1994: 12)

However, in Northern Ireland the full-service school that Dryfoos describes is not yet in being. There are, however, a number of schools which carry the label 'community'. Their activities, even in the most committed ones, fall somewhat short of the range provided by a full-service school, but they may well be the foundation stones for such schools.

Before turning to the two schools mentioned, it is necessary to look, very briefly, at some of the constraints on establishing a community school in Northern Ireland. Although it is, geographically, a small area, and its population is only 1.6 million, the Northern Ireland education service presents a number of unique features, the collectivity of which gives rise to fragmentation in the provision. First, there are three main categories of school – Controlled (in the main for Protestant children), Maintained (in the main for Catholic children) and Integrated (in which children from both denominations or none are educated). There is also a small, but highly influential group labelled the Voluntary Grammar schools. Second, the majority of the schools are single sex. Third, there is the selection procedure that allocates children to either secondary or grammar schools, which, by its very nature, can divide siblings and friends. Fourth, there is, within the constraints of the results of the 11 plus exam, parental choice, which can mean that children leave the community in which they live to go to a school in a different community. Furthermore, for many of the larger post-primary schools in the cities and larger towns, children are bussed in from quite considerable distances, reducing the feeling of a surrounding community with which a school might feel close kinship.

Added to this fragmentation of provision, there is a plethora of bodies overseeing one aspect or another of education, not all of them with statutory powers, including:

(a) The Department of Education, including the Education and Training Inspectors (ETI).
(b) Five Education and Library Boards (ELBs) (equivalent to LEAs or school districts).
(c) The Council for Catholic Maintained Schools.
(d) The Council for the Curriculum, Examinations and Assessment.
(e) The Northern Ireland Council for Integrated Schools.
(f) The Curriculum Advisory and Support Services (working within the ELBs).

(g) The Regional Training Unit.

(h) Computerised Local Administration of Secondary Schools.

(i) Computerised Local Administration of Primary Schools.

The size of this bureaucracy has a number of effects, one of which is that it diminishes the amount of money from the global education budget that goes directly to schools. Schools in Northern Ireland receive around 75 per cent of the total budget for education, and this comparatively small proportion leaves them, after paying the fixed costs of staff salaries, heating, electricity and so on, with considerably less freedom than their English counterparts to attempt moving outside traditional core activities.

A further constraint on schools is that there has been no clear statement from any of the statutory bodies on the desirability of having community schools, or indeed any agreed definition of what a community school might be. During the 1970s and 1980s, there was considerable interest in Northern Ireland in the concept of community schools, based on the models operating in England. There was, however, no consensus on what a community school should be or do. Those that were deliberately established had few characteristics in common. One school, for example, provided programmes of youth activities and education for adults; another allowed adults to attend regular classes alongside the pupils. Others might house a community library for pupils and adults alike. Overall, the main emphasis was on giving the community access to some of the schools' facilities and there is little evidence of a more regular interactive engagement with the wider community. Despite there being in the 1989 Education Reform Order some attempt to regularise the situation, there is still no official definition of what constitutes a community school.

This fragmentation of both the range of schools and the overseeing bodies has not helped to foster an atmosphere of an educational community. Let us try to define what we mean by 'an educational community'. It is of course easy to idealise the past and look to the old-fashioned local education authority (LEA) of some 25 to 30 years ago as providing an educational community. One of the authors was for some time an HM inspector in England, and able to get to know very well two or three LEAs, one very similar in size to Northern Ireland. Certainly, at the time he was working in this capacity, there was a feeling that officers, councillors and teachers were, if not always on entirely the same wavelength, at least working to the same ends, with a shared past and a shared commitment. An example of this community might be seen at headteachers' conferences in which at worst there was a shared gloom about, for example, lack of resources, and at best a celebration of the LEA's achievements. In Northern Ireland the fragmentation has led inter alia to schools having very different agendas, very different sets of expectations, very different funding. The hypothesis being put forward is that it is easier for a school to be innovative and, most importantly, able to sustain that initiative, if it feels that it is working within a collegium, within a community of educators who are all working to a similar agenda, sustained by a similar philosophy.

One last fact which obviously has had a considerable influence on the Northern Ireland educational system needs to be mentioned, and that is the Troubles of the last 30 years. Clearly this chapter is no place to examine in any detail the causes or outcomes of the incessant violence, but it is necessary to attempt, very tentatively, to hint at what might be an outcome for schools. Throughout the Troubles, schools have been safe bases in which children, teachers and their parents were certain that, whatever mayhem might be going on around them, there was peace and security. However, the very presence of violence outside the school yard and the increasing polarisation of the communities not only made it difficult to discuss the roots of the violence, but also to look at a potential range of community activities in which the school might give a lead:

> *Very few schools, however, provide opportunities for the pupils to consider issues such as prejudice, stereotyping, and sectarianism and the extent to which these are the seed-beds for community conflict.*

(DoE, 2000: 16)

Given the range of constraints that we have attempted to sketch above, schools understandably focused on what they saw as core content. Some schools, however, did look to the communities around them and began links which went further than the normal PTAs and parent evenings.

The first of the two schools that will be looked at in this chapter is a post-primary, all girls' school, St Mary's College, set in the Creggan area of Derry City. It is an area with high unemployment and much battered by the violence of recent years. The number of children in the school on free meals is 64 per cent, against the average for Northern Ireland of 23 per cent and the UK as a whole of 17 per cent. When the current principal took up post, few students sat for GCSEs and the first aim was markedly to increase the success rate in these examinations. The culture of the community, the principal reported, was not geared to tertiary education; indeed was not particularly geared towards the education of girls beyond a certain basic level. An early priority, therefore, was to alter the culture of school so that examination success became the expected norm, and soon it became the norm for the community as well. An additional and essential part of this culture change involved the school's increasing openness to parents and their direct involvement in their children's education.

In the late 1980s, a parent asked if she could join her daughter's mathematics class and the school agreed. A small number of her friends also joined and they all passed the GCSE examination. The following year six parents joined school classes in mathematics and English, and again they succeeded. Soon there were too many asking to come to daytime classes, so parents' classes were switched to the evening. Staff freely volunteered to take these classes. In addition to the examination classes, the school set up a Parents' Writing Group which also proved to be a success. The overall numbers rose to 50 and eventually peaked at 250. In the early 1990s the school received some money to help with the scheme. Around this time, other schools in the area, seeing the enthusiasm of the parents for education, also opened their doors. A good idea which is seen to work seeds itself easily.

In such an area and at that time, a school student's prospect of going to university was limited. There were few expectations of such a move and therefore little encouragement. The school understood that if the community was going to start to regenerate, a growing number of its young people needed to go to further into higher education. The school instituted the Higher Education Liaison Programme (HELP), which is still running. HELP started in a small way in the school, with a small group of students (16) who were thought to be the most likely to get into university. The programme proved such a success that it was opened to all students. An extension, again one embraced by all schools in the area, has been a homework club which has proved most successful. From the start, parents have been deeply involved in the programme. The central aim is to get students and parents to see that tertiary education is a reasonable aim, and the programme has a number of strands.

There is a Saturday school, which is voluntary and to which some 100 students and their parents come. On offer are examination classes, drama, dance and cooking. In the afternoon children and their parents from local primary schools come.

The school has a close link with one of the universities in Northern Ireland and a summer school is held on campus. The summer school is designed to introduce Year 10 students to higher education and better prepare them for it, but parents also go and some have become enthused by the experience and gone on to gain degrees as a result. The school is jointly taught by lecturers from the university, teachers and members of the community. There is a different theme each year and recently ICT, geography and history have been highlighted. At the end of the week-long course a graduation ceremony takes place at which the students wear gowns and process through a packed hall, with grandparents, parents and siblings in prams in attendance. Strawberries and cream are served. It is an occasion which is deeply moving and generates considerable pride in the community.

In a number of other ways, the school has sought to involve both students and parents and, through the parents, the community – making all feel that they have a vital part in it, could contribute to it and gain much from it. For example, the school trained a cohort of parents (10–12) as learning support workers, and this scheme has now expanded. There are now some 20 parents working in the school, continuing their own learning, becoming accredited classroom assistants, and some continuing to university.

The School Council is another way in which pupil voice is given real importance. The council is elected each year, with the election made into an important affair, using polling booths borrowed from the local council. The members of the School Council are involved in establishing a 'Rights and Responsibilities Charter', which is reviewed every two years. The council meets every other week and has real authority, even being involved in the analysis of the senior leaders' (senior management team) management styles. Members of the council attend senior leaders' meetings and contribute. The pupils' council set up the Saturday School and arranged its timetable.

Another way of involving the parents has been the 'Take Your Parent to School' day, and a 'Back to School' day for local employers, designed to show how much school has changed since their own schooldays. The parents' day, for Year 8 parents, attracted only mothers at first, but then fathers complained of being left out and they are now attending. The parents are welcomed to the school, given some idea of what to look for and what to expect and then go with their daughters to class. It is said that daughters give very clear instructions as to the dress code expected of parents on the day. The visit ends with a plenary session with the head of year.

Two final items. First, parents are expected to sign a contract (the Rights and Responsibilities Charter) with the school to make it clear what each expects of the other. The school hall is filled with parents on September evenings at the beginning of the year, as this contract is seen to be at the heart of the relationships which are vital. Second, through the Parent Teachers' Association, parents are now involved in policy making and there is a parent on the Finance Committee.

There was a long history of parents being kept at arm's length by the school. That attitude, combined with the memories which parents had of schooling, meant there was a real gap between school and community. Add unemployment, the Troubles, and very low expectations of what sort of education was possible, especially for girls, and over the years too many young people were excluded from anything but the most basic of schooling. The school has opened itself, literally and metaphorically, to the community, and the community has responded. Glass ceilings that were impermeable before have been removed. Regeneration of a community such as this will take a great deal of patience and time, but the start made is considerable. The school entrance hall, with its welcoming air and parade of the national and international awards won over recent years, is a symbol of the new partnership.

The other school is Tullycarnet Primary School, set in an area of high unemployment in east Belfast. Some of the housing is high-rise flats, marred by the usual problems. The numbers in school have dropped sharply as families have grown older but not moved out of the area. However, as houses do become empty, the reputation of the area means that few, if any, young families consider moving there. Fifty-six per cent of the children receive free school meals. Over the years, the school's realisation of the community's potential, which needed imaginative ways for it to be released, and long-term engagement on the part of the principal in raising monies to help start and maintain a variety of schemes, have resulted in the discovery of a number of ways in which it could become more responsive to the community.

For example, there is a toy and book library which is designed to help teenage parents learn how to play with their children. There is a homework club and an after-school club open to both children and their parents. There is a club to help children prior to the selection process (in more affluent areas, some parents pay for additional tutoring) and the computer suite is open to the community after school hours. The local college of further education helps run this computer club. A room which had become a dumping ground was cleaned out and converted into an art room. Again the community uses it and the school cleaner co-teaches the classes. There is a science club, and through the New Opportunities Fund there are awards for adults passing graded tests.

However, it is the Family Project which is at the heart of this school's involvement with the community. The project is funded jointly by a charity and the school's ELB. An ex-teacher from the school now heads up the project, and there is an outreach worker who visits families that ask for help but are not yet prepared to go to the school to obtain it. There is a crèche which enables women (so far it is mostly women involved) to come to the school during the day. As the numbers of children in the school have fallen, so space has been freed and now the Family Project is in the heart of the school building.

The core of this project is to support the access of the Links Women's Group to the education that they decide they need. For some five years this has been a separate group, and it is the engine of the project. The women in the group set up the courses and do all the organising. They are helped by the community worker, but the day-to-day working and longer term planning of the group are their responsibilities. It is this process of involvement which is central to the philosophy of the project. To people whose own education was extremely limited, whose encounters with schools were not marked by any success, the journey to deep involvement with learning a new skill is carefully stepped. The involvement in coming to the centre and taking up some activity which interests them are the first steps. The actual activity is of minor importance; the involvement is everything. One aspect of the success of the project is visible in the confident animation of the women in the centre, and manifest in the many notices about activities that are or soon will be taking place. There is a buzz and a purposeful quality to the chat and activities. Another outcome, and evidence of success of the project, lies in two of the members starting access courses to university entrance, and another doing a community course. Thirteen did NVQs and as a result six obtained work. The crèche served not only the needs of mothers coming to the centre, but also offered placements to help give the experience the women needed.

The group has also been engaged directly in the community. For example, a subway that is essential for crossing a very busy main road, but marred by vandalism and violence, has been made safe for the community. The group is involved in traffic calming measures and is working to establish a baby clinic. It has set up a 'Baby Bulk Buy', a scheme designed to help young mothers who cannot get to the supermarkets buy essentials for their babies at prices which they can afford. As a side benefit of the scheme, contact is made with these young mothers with the eventual aim of helping them with their parenting and inviting them into the centre. There is also a 'Summer Scheme' to help families enjoy the long summer break.

One of the main schemes in the centre is 'Preparation for Parenting'. This major programme runs for 6 or 12 weeks and it is quite simply a course on how to be a parent. Specifically it includes ideas about how to introduce early language and mathematics to the child and more generally it is about the development of the personal and social confidence necessary for parenthood. The course involves activities at home as well as at the centre. As an extension, the group is now looking to ways of offering post-natal support. The group has written and distributed booklets for parents who are still unwilling to come to the centre and provides activity packs for children during the summer break.

The group recognised that a number of parents, and their children, were ill prepared for entry to school. Therefore, children who are going to join the school in the following September come to the centre with their parents during the summer for three days a week.

Within the school itself, the centre has established a 'Nurture Group' which gives additional help to children who cannot cope with the curriculum. All children are monitored carefully by their regular class teachers up to October. Then 10 to 13 children who are failing to cope come together with one teacher and a classroom assistant in a comfortably furnished room. It is a very casual group, aimed primarily at giving confidence and increased self-esteem in a family atmosphere, but it follows a programme to help them acquire the skills needed to access the mainstream curriculum, supplied by the school. There are settees, a carpet, a relaxed atmosphere and the whole group has break and lunch together. The aim is to enable them to join their peers in the regular classes. As they grow more confident, they spend increasing time in the first year class, but some take until Year 2 before they can go totally into the mainstream. This grouping has the dual purpose of helping the children cope with school, and helping their parents cope with what had hitherto been considerable problems.

Essentially, the project sees itself as being involved with four groups of people. First, it aims to enable children to enhance their personal, social and emotional development, and through that development be able to take an active part in the community, and start school better able to benefit. It aims to enable parents achieve a greater sense of self-esteem, increased confidence in their roles as parents and co-educators of their children, and find ways to improve their own education and career possibilities. Third, the group works with the community, looking to ways of improving facilities and services, encouraging a greater degree of participation in community, and facilitating access to other agencies to improve the quality of life. The fourth group is the school itself, helping to create and embed deeper partnerships between parents and teachers and encouraging the maximum involvement of parents in school life.

Drucker (1993) wrote that we are entering the 'Post-Capitalist society', one in which knowledge is the only meaningful resource. In such a society, schools will change from being labour intensive to being capital intensive. He went on:

> But more drastic even – though rarely discussed as yet – will be the changes in the social position and role of the school. Though long a central institution, it has been of society rather than in society. It concerned itself with the young who were not yet citizens, not yet responsible, not yet in the workforce. In the knowledge society the school becomes the institution of the adults as well, and especially of highly schooled adults.

(Drucker, 1993: 177; original emphasis)

Both the schools that the authors have looked at have begun this transition. There is a slowly growing realisation in Northern Ireland that the scars caused by the violence of the last 30 years, on top of the conflict in the whole of the island of Ireland which has gone on for centuries, will require a different approach if that violence is not to continue indefinitely into the future. These two schools and others in Northern Ireland have realised that:

> The community is the learning environment within which the school or college operates. As every parent knows, the school classroom provides only a small part of what a child, teenager, or college student learns during the course of a week ... A community and its schools are reflections of each other. If one is succeeding, so is the other.

(Senge et al., 2000: 16)

It is extraordinarily difficult for some schools to become more closely involved in the community around them. In some parts of Belfast, for example, where young people and children still in primary school regularly take part in what a principal recently described as 'recreational rioting', it is difficult to see at present how the cycle can be broken. However, there are other more hopeful examples. There is a small primary school in the west of the province that has taken the first steps to become a learning centre for its very scattered rural community. There is a group of schools on both sides of the border that has worked together for some time to heal wounds and improve the education service for both communities. Another group of schools look to each other to begin the process of dismantling the walls:

> The most extensive and sustained of these links involves the seven post-primary schools in a particular area. The project's overriding aim is to 'promote reconciliation between different traditions in NI by fostering tolerance, understanding, and friendship among future leaders'; it has been sustained and grown over the years to involve the students from the schools in a rich variety of initiatives with the aim of developing in each pupil the capacity to co-operate with others in the spirit of courtesy and acceptance.

(DoE, 2000: 23)

There are also many schools that have been imaginative in reaching out to parents and other communities, often as a result of their involvement in cross-community contact schemes, some of which have been funded by the Northern Ireland Department of Education, and others which have been supported by other agencies. In all these examples, it is clear that the schools have accepted the basic imperative of the twenty-first century. That imperative is that if schools and colleges are going to meet the complex and multifarious needs of young people, they cannot take on that task successfully by looking only to their own resources. However hard teachers might work, however long they make the school day, the school alone cannot meet the students' and more widely the community's needs. The school will increasingly look to the community to be involved in the education of young people. The community will look to the school and to local colleges of further education and the university to help meet its lifelong educational needs. Employers will become increasingly involved with both training and education as the half-life of their workforce's knowledge shortens. At any given point in the day it will be difficult to tell who is teacher, who is student, where a classroom is and what it constitutes. The school will lose its monopoly position and learning will become a community enterprise. No other solution will ensure the healthy continuance of our society.

References

Barth, R. (1990) *Improving Schools from Within*. San Francisco: Jossey-Bass.

Department of Education (DoE) (2000) *Report of a Survey of Provision for Education for Mutual Understanding (EMU) in Post-Primary Schools*. Bangor: Department of Education.

Drucker, P. F. (1993) *Post-Capitalist Society*. Oxford: Butterworth-Heinemann.

Dryfoos, J.G. (1994) *Full-Service Schools*. San Francisco: Jossey-Bass.

Senge, P., Cambron-McCabe, N., Lucas, T., Smith, B., Dutton, J. and Kleiner A. (2000) *Schools that Learn*. London: Nicholas Brealey.

8

■ ■ ■

Social Inclusion at The Royal Docks Community School

Pat Bagshaw

Setting the context

The Vision Statement for The Royal Docks Community School

The new school is a resource for the whole community. It provides for all children of the appropriate school age, regardless of ability, need, culture, religion, gender, sexual orientation. It is an equal access school, therefore, but in so being, it recognises that to create equality of access, different needs require differentiated provision. Opportunity and respect sit at the heart of the school.

The school provides learning opportunities for the whole community: for young adults, for the elderly, for women, for men, for mothers/ fathers/parents with small children, for the unemployed, for those with ability but difficulty, for cultural groupings, for interest groups – for anyone who can declare themselves as learners, within the aims of the school.

The school itself is a learning community. It is flexible and adaptable for the future both in its provision and its building. It encourages high standards of work and conduct amongst its students; it encourages achievement in all aspects of learning; it recognises success; it creates an open, friendly atmosphere between learner and teacher, combining mutual respect with mutual enthusiasm to make progress; it recognises that learning is lifelong and that we can all learn from each other through processes both informal and formal.

Profile of the school, including its opening, and attendant difficulties

As an inclusive school, there will be very few schools in the UK which have exactly similar profiles given our complex range of ability and need, and hence our difficulties with 'benchmarking' against 'similar' schools. This school is a new school, opened (late) in September 1999. It is now established, given the circumstances of its opening, i.e. moving late, with approximately 1,230 students (as opposed to one or two year groups) and with, at that time, 120 students with statements of special educational needs.

The general levels of attainment at the point of entry are low against national levels, and although over recent years there have been gradual improvements, levels of literacy remain an issue. Progress against attainment at the point of entry has been very slow, but improvements locally within the linked primary schools with Key Stage 2 results, suggest a trend towards gradual improvements upon which we can build. However, this is not necessarily true for all of our students with statements of special educational needs. The numbers of students with special educational needs in the school – at all levels – are very high, as against the national average. This is particularly true of those with difficulties with low levels of literacy at the point of entry, and we have created ways of addressing that issue.

There are high levels of 'turbulence' as we have quite a high turnover of students, term by term, and across year groups. In addition, currently there are 48 first languages spoken at school. This ranges from a few speakers of a language such as Russian, Swahili or Portuguese to more numerous linguistic groups such as speakers of Bengali or Cantonese. This has increased from 40 first languages when we moved here from Woodside, i.e. within the last three years.

These students include a number of refugee families. Sometimes we know that they are, sometimes not. Many have a history of refugee status. Obviously, we give advice, support and help as needed. Some of the areas where students with refugee status have arrived from over the last two years include Albania, Croatia, Serbia, Turkey, Rwanda-Burundi (usually via another African country), Somalia and Ethiopia. It is worth mentioning that many such families are very fearful of discussing their 'status' as refugees.

The significant challenge for us is the range and diversity of need. We have only one teacher of English as an additional language, as a result of how resources are allocated, but this does not enable us to meet the needs of all those students easily. We have been given some support for work with refugees from September 2001 to Easter 2002.

There remain issues about a persisting local culture of ambivalence towards education, affecting levels of motivation, persistence, participation, attainment and achievement of our children, for example, taking part in examinations, career pathways. We do not subscribe to a 'deficit' model of education and these issues have to be set against the very strong commitment by many of our parents to raising the expectations and aspirations of many of our young people, and to supporting them and the school in achieving the best possible standards for all our students.

This school, like others in this area, has undergone significant 'cultural' changes in the last ten years, as a result of both demographic changes, issues of council housing patterns and changes in the job market. It is worth mentioning that we have a 'skewed' intake into the school, partly as a result of the patterns following upon the 'inclusive education' strategy, partly because of the 'cultural' trends indicated above and also because there is some imbalance in the gender distribution in the school, particularly in Year 8. However, we are an oversubscribed school, attracting students and families because of our facilities and successes.

We have high levels of 'child protection' issues within the school. These issues do affect the motivation and participation of students in their own education, and increase the level of inter-agency work required of senior staff.

The inclusion of a high number of students with special educational needs is an enriching and positive aspect of the school, but requires additional preparation for and awareness from *all* staff. This is also true of students who represent other forms of diversity. It is enrichment to the ethos and culture of the school, but very demanding in terms of being able to meet the needs of such a huge variety.

Unlike many new schools, which open with one or two year groups, we opened with 1,230 students (Years 7–11). This included an unexpected additional group in Year 7, taken in late at the behest of the local education authority. This necessitated rewriting the timetable and shuffling teaching and tutoring staff, thus complicating further an already complicated move.

Our major concern was to ensure that Year 9 and Year 11 students were protected as far as possible from the impact of the transition, given their proximity to public examinations. Despite all the difficulties, we managed to exceed our set 'targets' for the Year 11 students, and continued to improve on our Woodside 'average points score', as we have over the last five years.

Inclusive education

This school has a distinct and different profile from almost any other secondary school in the country. As a result of the local education authority's policy of 'inclusive education', almost all students with statements of special educational needs are placed in mainstream schools within this authority. This school currently has 104 such students on roll, who have been issued with statements of special educational need for a variety of reasons. These are:

- profound and multiple learning difficulties
- visual impairment
- specific learning difficulties
- general learning difficulties (moderate, severe and complex)
- emotional and behavioural difficulties
- speech and language delay/disorder
- autism.

In addition, currently 51 per cent of the school's population is placed on Stages 1–5 of the current Code of Practice.

The new school was built in part to provide for the further development of the local education authority's 'inclusive education' strategy. We now have a developing resource for students with profound and multiple learning difficulties. Currently, we have 13 students in this resourced provision, which will build to approximately 25 in the future. We also are receiving students who have severe learning difficulties. There is no reduction in our standard number to accommodate this provision.

To enable support for all of these many needs, we have a very large and complex staffing structure with detailed timetabling and staffing arrangements to support the operation of these provisions. Further complexities were created for our learning services team recently as a result of the decision made by the local education authority to delegate its centrally held special needs services staff in April 2000. The learning services team is managed by the senior teacher and comprises approximately 32 staff, some full and some part time.

The building is still not complete, but we have continued to establish the school despite these difficulties. Most departments are now properly established in their areas, though staffing shortages have affected this. We have a highly ICT-rich environment in the school, which has interactive whiteboards in every classroom *and* nearly 600 computers available. This provision was made to help accommodate the range of ability and need.

However, the learning services team has expanded in both number and function and this has put pressure on the physical space in the school. We have secured a double mobile installed on one of the tennis courts to assist with this problem.

We maintained the gradual improvement in our attainment levels further at both Key Stages 3 and 4 in 2001, though we had a slight dip in the performance of students attaining 1A*-G at Key Stage 4 in our second year.

Where are we now?

The use of the extensive ICT facilities in the school is developing as the confidence of staff increases. We have provided a number of training opportunities for all staff to develop these skills further. However, changes in staffing make it difficult to maintain this, although we have also managed to appoint some good new staff to replace those who have left – and gone on to promote opportunities in other schools.

Nevertheless, we continue to work to improve the educational offer and opportunities for all of our students and to try to raise attainments and achievements further. The support offered by our informal education team has developed in both confidence and activities undertaken.

We are facing increased difficulties in trying to meet the very wide range of abilities presented by students here. We are trying to deal with this in different ways. In relation to students with special educational needs, we have embarked on discussions with the local education authority about how we are given resources to support this very wide range. In relation to other students, we are moving towards providing different pathways for some students and are planning to divide the Year 10 cohort into two 'broad bands' of ability, building on other measures taken earlier, and the same arrangement is proposed for Year 7 in September 2003. Staffing is our major problem at present. Our perceptions of categories of 'inclusion' at The Royal Docks Community School are as follows:

1   Social and economic which relate to the profile of the school, described above.
2   Cultural, ethnic, linguistic and religious diversity, as described above.
3   Educational needs focusing on special educational needs, as listed above.

Issues and problems

Management of the provision for students with special educational needs

Since moving to The Royal Docks Community School we have had two very different arrangements for the management of this particular provision. The learning services team (staff employed to work with students with special educational needs) was led originally by a senior teacher.

The post holder then moved on and we advertised twice, unsuccessfully, for a replacement. Currently there is temporary post holder leading the team. The senior staff working in the team are appropriately qualified and experienced.

However, the situation became more complicated in the spring term of 2000, when the local education authority decided to delegate more of the budget for pupils with special educational needs. This was primarily in order to comply with the need to reach a greater level of delegation of funding. This meant that we had to take on an increased staffing complement. At the same time, we felt that the financial arrangements made were insufficient to cover the financial commitments needed.

The quality of staff recruited throughout the whole of this time has fluctuated. We have managed to recruit some excellent staff, but we do not always manage to attract people who are necessarily appropriately qualified and experienced. This is particularly true of support staff, for whom the levels of pay are very poor with little career structure and pathway. We do not have enough money to alter this situation. The matter is being considered by the local education authority and should be addressed by the review of 'Inclusive Education' being conducted currently.

An underlying problem for the management and organisation of this large and complex provision is that the funding for 'inclusive education', beyond students funded within specific 'resourced' provisions, is largely done on the basis of the allocation of money by formula. This seemed to work prior to the delegation of resources in 2000. However, the delegation of this funding was done on the basis of actual contact time with students, on issued statements of special educational needs rather than the totality of staffing and other resources required. Since then, our view is that this provision has become consistently more underfunded.

This means that the numbers of teachers and support staff are insufficient to meet the management and organisational needs of what would constitute elsewhere a large special school. Our view is that there exists an additional complication. This is the fact that the model of financing operated may make provision manageable in a primary school, but much more difficult in a secondary school.

The nature of its organisation makes it a much more demanding scenario within which to 'include' and 'integrate' students with special educational needs, particularly for those with complex needs. It is difficult to deploy the current level of staff effectively within the school in order to meet the needs of all students. In secondary schools, different performance and delay and emotional maturity and competence become more marked.

While I recognise the difficulties of managing the financing of teaching and support for fluctuating numbers of students, it is leading us to great difficulties in managing the provision effectively. There is a need for financing to be restructured to provide an appropriate basic staffing structure to meet the needs of such a complicated and wide-ranging organisation.

An essential infrastructure of staffing is needed, depending upon the numbers of students and complexity of provision of their needs, in a given school. Then further provision could be added according to students' needs, if necessary, by formula or by some banding or factoring arrangement. Thought also needs to be given to the administrative and other resources needed for such a provision.

Provision for and management of other forms of 'inclusion'

The range and diversity of students at the school is not only related to the spectrum of abilities, skills, needs and talents. It relates also to other aspects of diversity and issues of 'social inclusion'. These could include social class (the dominant group would be white and working class); religious, linguistic, ethnic and cultural (there are currently 48 first languages spoken in the school and this diversity represents other groupings as given); gender – a fairly balanced intake of boys and girls, but different cultural origins affect the presentation of gender-based issues.

An important observation is that the range of diversity itself tends to promote the recognition of and respect for the ideas which underpin both notions of equality and ideas of social inclusion. Developing policies and practices around these issues is crucial to the growth of the school as a positive and encouraging environment within which students can grow and learn. Notions of 'respect' and 'tolerance' may be focused in some schools on particular aspects such as 'race' or 'gender'.

In this school, all such aspects of attitude relate each with the other. For example, in dealing with student intolerance about a child with special educational needs, it is possible to relate this to a general notion of respect and tolerance. Equally, if you are dealing with issues of racial intolerance, the same thing applies.

All aspects of ethos and attitude can be related to a general standard of 'respect' for the person. This is very important in building an atmosphere which supports the creation of an extremely 'socially inclusive' school. This does not mean that we have solved all problems, or that we do not have any problems or difficulties. However, both our OFSTED report (spring 2001) and a recent visit by two HMIs commented favourably on the very 'inclusive' nature of the school and upon the quality of the relationships between and among students, and staff and students.

Staffing

To run a school like this, it is important to find, secure and retain the necessary range of staffing to support the diversity of need and provision. The staffing currently consists of approximately 86 full-time equivalent teaching staff and approximately 140 staff altogether. Apart from teaching staff, there are administrative staff, curriculum support staff, classroom assistants and some specialist support staff (e.g. reading support workers). The senior management team is made up of a head teacher, three deputy head teachers, three assistant head teachers, one community tutor and a senior resources officer. The finances are large and complicated.

In the current climate, it is very difficult to recruit and, more particularly, to retain good teachers. We do find young staff of very good quality who actively want to contribute to a school like this. However, it is unlikely that we will be able to retain them beyond two to four years, partly because they are very attractive to other employers and partly because we cannot pay them enough to be able to live, work and travel in London, especially if they wish to purchase a property. Equally we want a 'workforce' with a fairly well balanced profile of both age and experience against those young into the profession with ideas, energy and enthusiasm. In the past three years it has become an increasingly difficult matter.

Managing a staff as diverse as this takes a considerable amount of time. Different staff need to be managed in different ways, appropriate to their different roles and responsibilities, different prior attainment and future progression. Some need more direct supervision and accountability than others. There are many more personnel and management issues in a different kind of school.

The management and organisational problems posed in a school with the complexity of this one mean that there needs to be a fairly complex management structure to support the needs of this level of staffing. In addition, different staff have different needs, and sometimes different time scales, within which they wish to pursue further training and development. These need to be identified and supported. Training staff is also a challenge, therefore, given the complexity, the numbers and the range of needs.

Having described the nature and difficulties of the current organisation of staffing for special educational needs, it is important to consider that this is but one element of running a large and complex institution. The organisation of staffing to support special educational needs has to be incorporated into the organisation and staffing of everything else. What I have said about staffing, relates to both 'mainstream' staff and learning services team staff. What I have outlined above applies equally to both.

The challenge is managing a staff of 140, of whom 86 are teachers, some working mainstream, some working with the learning services team, some who are in between the two, and the rest support staff. That in itself poses very complex situations: things like 'equality of opportunity' and 'equal treatment' for all staff; career pathways and opportunities; people working within both 'mainstream' and learning services team; all dealing with often challenging behaviour among students, but being paid very different sums of money for dealing with them.

It has become increasingly true that issues of personnel, training and support, selection of appropriate staff, just having the time, structure and routes to be able to communicate effectively with staff, are all issues that affect a school as diverse and inclusive as this one. To develop notions of 'social inclusion', these have to be explored. For example, it is deemed to be true that it is simply like running any other school. I have to say that it is not. I have run a fairly inclusive school previously, but not with the range of complexities and diversities that this one has. Having sufficient time to plan effectively, giving staff sufficient time to plan effectively for their operation, and for their professional development and for their ability to differentiate and manage in this scenario, are all very important issues.

Administration of paperwork, associated with the Code of Practice, and review and assessment arrangements

We have in the school something like 130 plus students who are 'School Action Plus' in relation to the Code of Practice. This produces an enormous amount of work in monitoring and an enormous amount of paperwork to go with it. The administration of the Code of Practice obviously requires every child to have an individual education plan, annual reviews and then, at the appropriate time, transitional reviews. Proper monitoring has to be done so that targets can be met.

The actual management and time issues are massive and because of the load that has to be distributed among a number of staff, there are issues about monitoring, consistency, and so on. We have one administrative assistant, which really is insufficient for the needs of the school. The figure of about 130 'School Action Plus' students does not actually include the students who have profound and multiple learning difficulties, of whom next year there will be 13. There are a lot of difficulties of a managerial and organisational nature associated with a school that is as inclusive as ours. It doesn't distract from what we think is important, but it does raise issues.

Local education authority – policy and practices

The local education authority embarked on a plan about 12 years ago of developing something called 'Inclusive Education'. In the terms then understood this related to the education of children with special educational needs. Then, following a review of the whole of the educational provision in Newham, quite a large-scale revision of the education system was undertaken at the time. It ended with a huge commitment to education and recognition of the need to raise standards and improve education in Newham. At the same time, they developed the policy of 'inclusion' which meant there was a planned and phased closure of the special schools in the borough and the incorporation into mainstream schools of children who would have formerly attended special schools. That process has gradually developed over the last 12 years and has now ended with the maintenance of one special school.

There was an original plan to remove all, but the policy evolved over a period of time and it was deemed sensible to keep one special school open, to cater for children who really do not best survive, develop and grow in a mainstream school setting. It is recognised at present that there will be some children for whom mainstream education is not an appropriate offer within current arrangements.

The policy has evolved during the last 12 years but there remains a commitment to develop a policy of 'inclusion' which means encouraging the movement of children from special schools into mainstream schools, as interpreted. However, very recently the borough has talked about developing a policy of 'social inclusion' and that does relate to more than just children with special educational needs. There is recognition of the strong connection between 'inclusion' policies as previously understood and inclusion policies which relate to other forms of diversity. There is a developing practice of talking about 'inclusion' in its many forms together. Over 12 years, policy and practices of the local education authority have tilted and a more general 'social inclusion' agenda is now being widely discussed that recognises issues such as religious, ethnic and cultural forms of diversity. It is also about creating more flexible arrangements around and within 'schooling' for all our students.

The policy of 'inclusion' met with great criticism initially. It took a long time for a determined council to overcome the fears and anxieties of many of the parents of children with special educational needs about moving from a special school environment to a mainstream environment. There are still reservations by parents, but largely they have been overcome and diminished by the hard work of the mainstream schools which strive to meet the needs of these very diverse groups of children.

Crucially what the policy of 'inclusion' creates is the opportunity for the school community to address issues of tolerance and prejudice by tackling uniformly all the issues of diversity. I have said elsewhere in the chapter that this is a strength of my school, but I think it is generally a strength within the local education authority. It is possible to make clear connections between the various forms of 'social inclusion' and the various reasons for 'social exclusion' which make sense to people.

To me, the policy of 'inclusion' as developed within the borough, and as developed within the schools in Newham, means that it is really an agenda about equity, justice, human rights, and the quality of provision. It is important that there is real understanding of the reasons why forms of 'social exclusion' occur. This needs to be debated, discussed, understood and developed.

A further aspect of the provision that we have at my school is a commitment to lifelong learning. This is not a separate and add-on notion. The notion of inclusion to me means inclusion of all and that includes lifelong learning. There are issues about special educational needs; there are issues about race, culture, gender, and so on. Equally there are issues about social class and exclusion and indeed of age and exclusion. Therefore a further aspect of work in my school is to promote adult learning in various ways, and this is slowly beginning here. Again, there is nothing very new in this, but these things, in my mind at least and in the commitment of the school, have coherence and are part of the shared vision with which I opened this chapter.

We work to promote the best access for children and their families to education in an area long disadvantaged socially and economically and where a history of educational access has been fraught with difficulties. We provide for adult learning and we have an 'informal education team' which promotes the access and the success of young people in the school. This is led by a community tutor, three learning mentors and a home school liaison worker. We pay for hours from specific youth workers. We have two education welfare officers, employed directly by the school and acting within the remit of the school, in a slightly broader brief than that which would have been envisaged by an education welfare officer in the LEA's direct employment.

This is a strength of the school and supports and underpins the work of others in the school. It adds a dimension of care, pastoral support and family support which I think is also very important in developing the notion of a fully inclusive school.

Conclusion

I have outlined in many ways the advantages of the school's social inclusion agenda throughout this chapter, but there are many difficulties and I have hinted at them. One is most certainly money in terms of inclusion in relation to special educational needs. We still consider ourselves to need more funding and it is a struggle to obtain it. Because of the degree of complexity in running a school that is neither mainstream nor a special school, we have yet to be clear about what is the best model to fund it adequately and not simply to fund the support for children.

As I have said repeatedly, there are very many difficulties in the management of a large and complex institution like The Royal Docks Community School. In my opinion we still haven't got right the framework for running a school like this and we are about to embark on a review of the organisation and management of the school internally.

The biggest problem that I see is effective communication. We need to ensure that all the different people who need to know all the different things get to know them. There is an information overload and at the same time the communication systems that we have in place are not yet adequately meeting the needs of the organisation. It is something we really need to address over the next two years. Then, five years after the school has opened, our structure and organisation will be more secure in terms of meeting the very complex needs of the school and our communication system will be better.

I could perhaps end by saying that the theory of social inclusion and inclusive education is fine. The practice is exceedingly difficult and I have responded to a request to write this chapter positively really because I'm still trying to think my way through how we can make reasonable practice better.

The ethos and nature of this school and the practice of inclusion education here have been acknowledged by OFSTED and the HMIs as being of high quality. I think that it is a product of the hard work of all staff and their commitment to the notion of equality of opportunity and access for all young people in its most diverse sense, and not just in terms of special educational needs.

It is hard work for the staff. 'The Teachers' Pay and Conditions Document' and the emphasis upon 'league tables', 'standards' and target setting sometimes seem very remote activities to my staff. They are teaching classes with perhaps five to seven children in each group that they encounter who are at 'School Action/School Action Plus' in terms of special educational needs; then probably another 10 or 12 children who have got serious difficulties of literacy; and then the added dimensions of children who may be refugees; children from ethnic groupings where their experience of 'equality of access' to opportunities has been restricted; some with English as an additional language, and therefore the issue of many languages. All those things taken together mean that any classroom in our school is very challenging.

'Differentiation' is for the most part an impractical dream in the sense in which it is commonly understood. No teacher can possibly meet the needs of that range of children by adapting for each child, and yet that is what needs to be done. We are 'working towards' an individual education plan for each child. It is the reason why we agreed to plan for a very heavy emphasis upon developing ICT opportunities in the school and to have a very ICT-rich environment, so that we can maximise individual programming and individual access to learning as much as we can. But we are still struggling with all those things. As I have said, theory is fine but practice is extremely difficult.

9

■ ■ ■

Family Learning

Sue Wedgwood

A child's initial learning experiences do not take place in school. The family is a major reference point for emotional security, attitudes, values and learning experiences. When considering the impact of different sources on the development of the child, it is important to acknowledge that from 0–16 15 per cent of a child's working life is spent in school, leaving 85 per cent influenced by family and home environment. The emphasis on parental responsibility dates back to the 1870s, yet in the past, opportunities for parents to exercise any responsibility have been limited, little more than getting them to school on time. However, over the past decade, the scenario has changed; the parent and family influences have increased and more schools are witnessing the benefits of the partnership.

With recent research and a better understanding of teaching and learning, it is not surprising that the family can be a source of inspiration, especially considering the ideology of child-centred learning. However, it would be naive to suggest that all children receive the same support, guidance and nurture at home, and schools face difficulties when trying to provide family learning opportunities for their communities. It is vital that schools and their leaders are well aware of and in tune with the communities which they serve. The context of the school is of paramount importance and should reflect the activities made available to the children, their families and the wider community.

The following case studies of two very different schools, serving very different communities, will highlight the importance of understanding and providing the relevant opportunities for the family to participate in the education of their children.

Case Study One

Through Single Regeneration Budget (SRB) funding, a group of schools embarked on what became known as the 'Family Learning Initiative' (FLI). This initiative was embedded in the philosophy that families did have a vital role to play in their child's education, and that collectively a group of schools could provide these opportunities. Although the schools were geographically very close, their catchment areas were very different. The case study school served a very new private housing estate with approximately 7 per cent of children taking free school meals. The neighbouring schools, however, served large council estates and free school meals were taken by approximately 30 to 35 per cent.

It was very clear from the outset that although the head teachers valued the initiative, it was also going to require a lot of work on top of existing schedules. Other groups of schools had decided to delegate the funding to individual schools, each of which could then provide or purchase resources to address family learning activities. The underpinning belief was that if the initiative was going to work a more innovative approach was needed in order to influence practice in schools, long-term benefits and attitudinal change of all stakeholders – children, parents, teachers and governors.

As a result, a core group representing a wide range of people was established to assess the needs of the community. Representatives were drawn from the local further education college, library service, health, head teachers, youth and community, governors and teachers. An audit of current practice was commissioned so that a full picture of provision could be seen. A major concern was how the initiative was going to be successful and sustainable within an already overloaded marketplace.

Not only was it apparent that the schools were eager to establish family learning initiatives, but also that the wider community was also eager to be part of it. The core group reported to a larger audience and made some radical suggestions in order to launch the initiative effectively and efficiently.

Proposals taken to the steering group

1 To appoint a family learning manager to work across the group of schools. The appointment of an FLI manager was particularly welcomed by head teachers, because it enabled them fully to support the initiative, without having to take total responsibility for its momentum. The appointed manager would play a strategic role across the community, reporting to the core group and meeting with school co-ordinators both individually and collectively.

2 To appoint a family learning co-ordinator in each individual school (plus one management point). Having an FLI co-ordinator was perceived as demonstrating the commitment of the schools and their governors to the success of the project. The extra management allowance addressed the increase in duties undertaken by the FLI, as well as raising the status of the role.

The proposals were accepted by the steering group and the SRB board. Funding issues had arisen due to the thinking time taken before the initiative was finally 'born'. As a group of professionals we were only too aware that there was no quick fix to fundamental issues of parenting and family support. However, we embarked on activities which we hoped would support children and their families, as well as provide sound foundations for the future – when our children became parents.

I feel it important to comment that those of us involved in education had automatically presumed that the appointment of the FLI manager would be a teacher. Our community partners brought us back to earth as we began to realise that the role was much wider than that of a teacher.

Reflecting the needs of individual schools was soon highlighted as an issue within the group project. This was ameliorated as school co-ordinators met with the FLI manager. Schools were able to draw up their individual action plans based on their own needs assessment, as well as having a stake in partnership initiatives.

Examples of partnership initiatives

1 *Library service/bookstart.* All families received a bookstart pack which was delivered by the health visitor. These consisted of books, information about the local library, colourful handouts about 'talk' and the importance of story reading.

2 *Homestart.* This was undertaken by volunteers able to provide support to families with children under the age of 5. Their help ranged from friendship to the family, helping organise budgets within the house, arranging outings and being a vehicle to access other information a family might need.

3 *Links with industry.* A local supermarket joined forces to create 'Shopping to Read' packs and later 'Shopping with Numbers'. Families in the community were able to shop with their children who enjoyed the commercially prepared packs. This made shopping more enjoyable for all concerned and a super learning activity for the whole family.

4 *Basic skills agency.* 'Number Sacks' were created for use across the group of schools. A number sack was a brightly coloured rucksack which contained number activities and games along a theme. Each school had the sacks for a given period of time. Parents were invited to a short presentation and given opportunities to ask questions about the sacks. The activities were enjoyable, non-threatening and very rewarding. These were shortly followed by 'Story Sacks', but this time made by parents.

5 *Health Promotions.* Head teachers and the school-based co-ordinators were given the opportunity to attend a family education forum run by health professionals. This again proved a valuable tool in order to create new partnerships and provide a wider understanding of family learning.

6 *Early Years Worker.* An early years worker was employed to work across the schools to address the needs of the community in relation to early years. This resulted in several initiatives: an admission policy review took place with parental input; crèche workers were provided when schools hosted activities for parents; a directory of information was created for parents with young children. In addition, a mobile crèche was initiated to support the project composed of parents who had trained with the local college.

School-based activities

A questionnaire was sent to parents asking what we were doing well and areas they thought we might improve on. Many staff thought this was either very brave or very stupid. We were delighted with both the response and the quality of information received; it was a good starting point. This also showed parents that their input was valued and a vital component of school development and improvement. (Many of the activities below came about as a direct result of the questionnaire.)

1 *A parent noticeboard.* This was erected at a convenient point within the grounds. Letters home were posted there plus events and activities for the future. Contact names and agencies were also available.

2 *Parent governor surgeries.* These were held once a month where parents had access to parent governors to chat or discuss issues.

3 *Parent governors noticeboard.* This simply had photos and information regarding the parent governors. The questionnaire revealed that 87 per cent of parents did not know who the parent governors were and thought that photographs would be helpful.

4 *Format of open evenings.* Parents had strong views on this issue, especially those who worked full time. Three formats were created to enable a fluid system which encouraged more quality dialogue and time for parents:

- Afternoon activities where parents came to see their child at work and share the experience. Time was also available to talk to staff.

- Appointment system (a.m. and p.m.) for a formal discussion about the progress of the child, agreeing targets and how best parents could support those targets. Where appropriate children accompanied their parents.

- Ongoing appointments throughout the year where half-hour slots were allocated. This took away from staff the pressure of the long open evening process and enabled them to focus and assess individuals within a given time scale, providing quality observations of the child's current performance.

5 *Home–school partnership group.* This was established for consultation on school development and policy. Parents were elected representatives.

6 *Family learning activities.* Staff provided termly projects for their classes and produced handouts for parents to outline the activity and ways they might like to be involved. The activities were varied and not based on paper and pen: e.g. create a miniature garden; display your family tree; make a garment for a toddler; create a scrapbook about someone you admire. Each family had three activities over the year. All contributions were shared and displayed.

7 *Book week.* Parents were invited to take part in quizzes, anagrams and games around books. They were invited to storytime and organised a book-swap for both children and parents.

8 *Family visits.* These were arranged to museums, galleries and events.

9 *Parent and child Design Technology (DT) afternoons.* Challenges were set for the child and their parent to create a given item. Materials were provided and the hall was dedicated to the day. Those children whose parents could not attend were well supported by Year 11 students from the high school, so no one was left out.

10 *Understanding schools (US).* A course was designed for parents who wanted to know more about how and what was taught in school. Comments around making paper aeroplanes and melting jelly had led to many misconceptions from parents who had high expectations of their children. The course was very informal and covered:

- literacy and the national curriculum
- maths and the national curriculum
- science and the national curriculum
- the role of the school nurse
- special educational needs
- the role of the school governor
- how can I help my child?

As a direct result of this course the school nurse set up a monthly surgery, which was well attended. The number of parents who put their names forward for nomination as a governor soared.

11 *Accredited courses for parents by the further education college.* These included a UCAN Parent volunteer course, maths, English and computer courses. A sociology study on the 1960s, 'Absolutely Fabulous', gained media coverage for the parents who donned the appropriate gear for the cameras.

Summing up

All these activities began to impact powerfully on the wider community. Parents from different schools were actively involved in the same event and had a common platform. The whole community gained recognition from much of the activity taking place and the already successful attainment of the pupils improved even more.

Case Study Two

The backdrop to the second case study is very different in terms of the school setting and also my own personal development. As a head teacher I passionately promote the role of the parent and the community in the education of our children and frequently quote the African saying: 'It takes a whole village to educate a child.'

This school was my second headship and was in special measures when I arrived. It is set in a deprived socio-economic area with high unemployment and poor housing; 37 per cent of the children are receiving free school meals. The school building itself was built in the 1890s and is in a sad state of repair. It is a large inner city school with approximately 380 children on roll, 45 per cent of whom are from an ethnic minority background, predominantly Pakistani.

If ever I was fully to understand how important it was to 'know' the school and its community, it was now. The experience gained from my previous school stood me in good stead. However, initiatives can never simply be transferred from one setting to another. School leaders must be sensitive to all the factors affecting school and the stakeholders involved. Once this is established, thought can be given to ways in which the venture can begin.

If our vision is to enhance the valuable partnership between home and school, both parties have to gain recognition and feel valued in their own right. When using the term school here, I mean to include staff too. It was very apparent that the whole school and its community had witnessed a very difficult period post-OFSTED and morale and self-esteem were exceptionally low.

From my perspective, this was the first issue to be addressed. It was necessary to establish a very strong sense of identity. We began with the purchase of a digital camera. When anyone did anything, we took a picture of it. The school became a mirror of positive self-images. This was widened to weekly celebrations of birthdays, courtesy awards and class awards of the week. We took pictures of these too and displayed them to parents, changing them weekly to maintain interest.

Much energy had been directed into addressing the shortfalls of the school, but the people working both inside and outside had little or no control of the process. By raising the self-esteem of all those involved, this could be addressed and included the self-esteem of the parents too. There was an opportunity to involve everyone and actively to acknowledge their input. Many of the parents themselves had barriers to overcome, both in terms of language and their own experience of school, which had very often been a negative one.

It was necessary to open the doors and to communicate actively. This began by simply greeting parents in the morning and at the end of the day joining them at the gate. Home visits were initiated so that every newcomer to school received a home visit. A new glossy prospectus was introduced and parents collaborated on its design. The language used was simple and direct and all documentation translated into Urdu. Simple messages reached home, demonstrating that the school did care what they thought and would listen to their views. A new school uniform was created, once again consulting parents and of course the children. Now awash with bright green sweatshirts and shalwar kameez, the school was a brighter place to be in.

Areas of responsibility were shared amongst the community shortly followed by the School Council and Home School Partnership Team. Parents volunteered for consultative roles such as Personnel, Social and Health Education (PSHE) developments and sex and relationship education (SRE). Celebrations in school reflected the wonderfully diverse population and Eid and Christmas were celebrated together. Speakers were invited to assembly and staff and class visits to the local church and mosque helped widen our approach. If we were to raise the aspirations of the children, then we also needed to raise the aspirations of their parents. The school should become the focal point of the community and be the facilitator of opportunity for everyone.

This was an enormous task which required a shared vision involving staff, children, parents and governors. Prior experience had forged partnerships which I realised would prove to be beneficial, but there were more fundamental issues to deal with working in a socially deprived area. It is easy to tell parents what they should be doing, but a more productive and sensitive approach is to work alongside the family, discussing and consulting at all times.

Health became an area where families were involved; healthy snacks were introduced, with toast and milk an option at playtime providing the nourishment sometimes lacking. Provision of water at all times for the children in class saw behaviour improve tremendously. Parents were consulted on their views and asked if they noticed any changes. Along with the children, parents discussed school meals. As a result halal meat was introduced and the Racial Equality Council (REC) attended the launch. Children who brought sandwiches were not segregated from the other children and placemats and flowers were introduced to make lunchtime a more sociable and pleasant experience. Parents commented on how much the children had appreciated this. The children were encouraged to taste unfamiliar food, especially vegetables, by the school providing plastic spoons. Have a taste first! Handouts and designs by the children on healthy packed lunches were displayed for everyone. As some of the fundamental issues were dealt with, our children and their families were benefiting from an improved attitude to diet. Gaining a Healthy School Award, the first in the LEA, also raised our status.

A menu of opportunities was provided, following a coffee morning drop-in which gave parents a voice on what they would like to see in school. The first-aid course offered by the community college was the beginning of many courses offered to parents. It was very practical, useful and enjoyed by all. Some parents were asking 'What's next?' – always a good sign. Links grew with the college, along with the range of provision it offered.

It is crucial to acknowledge the invaluable role of classroom assistants working in the school and an increased number of volunteers now offering their services. For the more experienced classroom assistants, it was suggested that their valuable work could be recognised via the NVQ route. With a little persuasion and support this original cohort has now completed NVQ2 and NVQ3. The school is a satellite community centre and has 30 students enrolled for the forthcoming year. These students do their placements at school and so our children directly benefit from the initiative. More and more families are becoming involved and are eager to study at the school which is now familiar to them and convenient for child-care purposes.

We are now in a position where parents eagerly look forward to the planning meeting when parent courses are arranged. An interesting viewpoint was expressed by one parent who had recently completed a 'self-esteem' session. 'I feel much better about myself now and I don't always have to study. Let's have some fun courses like aromatherapy, make-up or nail art!' It was this parent who reminded me that learning is fun. It is so easy in these days of targets and accountability to forget that.

In the list of activities that follow I would like to stress again that schools begin at different points. The reader may need to look deeper into the provision of what is termed family learning and how each component links integrally with others.

School-based activities

1 *Eco Council for children and their parents.* The Eco team has been responsible for carrying out a survey in school on conservation, recycling and school ground improvements. As a result we have a community recycling initiative, energy monitors, a community garden built by volunteers, parents, staff and children and new seating in the playground. The council is also represented at the local Green Team and was consulted on a neighbourhood garden. The school has just gained a bronze award for Eco School Status.

2 *Journalist Club.* This is an after-school activity funded by DfES, targeting gifted and talented pupils. The school and parent newsletters begin here.

3 *Together with ICT.* Children and their parents worked for an afternoon in the learning resource suite. When completed, the parents asked for the opportunity to develop this further. Two courses now run, level 1 and level 2.

4 *Family literacy and family numeracy.* Children work in a group, as do the parents, one afternoon a week. On the other afternoon the groups join together. The course has involved trips to the library, museum, supermarket and farm. All parents attended the prizegiving to collect their certificates. (We took their pictures too.)

5 *World of Work Day.* Visitors from a variety of occupations visited school to be interviewed by classes. Parents were invited either to contribute or join in. Visitors ranged from vets to lawyers, journalists to firefighters and a visit from a lecturer who described life at university.

6 *Residential visit at the beginning of Year 6.* This visit was arranged to promote relationships of peers and staff at the beginning of the year. Initially many ethnic minority families were not keen to allow their children to be away from home. We didn't give up: to ensure that all Year 6 went we sought funding from Youth and Community who daily transported those who were not allowed to stay over. This year, the present Year 5 and their parents were given the opportunity to visit one evening in preparation for the trip in September. Our responses show that *all* children are staying this year.

7 *Termly workshops.* Mainly focusing on literacy and numeracy, the workshops are held for the various year groups. They are practically based and provide fun ways for parents to help their children.

8 *Target setting.* Targets are shared and agreed with parents, including information on how they might support the achievement of the target. Translators are booked for this process.

9 *Parent volunteer mentors.* These parents have created a bank of their own resources. They spend time with children who benefit from quality one-to-one time with an adult, playing games and participating in activities together. This provides opportunities that some may not receive at home, or for those children who find relationships difficult to sustain. It is an excellent facility which we will develop further in the future.

10 *Educational Welfare Officer (EWO) surgery.* This is held in school once a week.

11 *Family support worker.* The family support worker is appointed through the Education Action Zone (EAZ) and supports families in a variety of ways. Homestart is also a close partner of school.

12 *Community college.* NVQ2 and NVQ3 for classroom assistants:

- first aid
- computers
- aromatherapy
- drama
- crèche worker course
- aerobics.

13 *Handling children's behaviour course.* This is offered to parents either one to one or as a self-help group.

14 *Family conferences.* These are held termly for those families facing difficulties. All agencies attend to provide quality support to the family and child.

15 *Postcards home.* Every Friday each member of staff sends a postcard which says 'We are all proud of you', writing a thank you for a specific gesture, piece of work, etc. to share with the family.

16 *Telephone home card.* The child is given a card for the office with permission to ring home to tell parents about something they have achieved that day. (We always seem to ring when there is something wrong. Parents were suspicious at first.)

Factors to address

The school-based activities represent some of the initiatives that are currently in place. However this kind of activity is not always as easy as it may seem. There are certain issues which have to be addressed as they arise:

1 *Time factors.*
- It is not always easy to create the time to facilitate community activities alongside school activities.
- Finding the time to contact and physically meet community partners. Diaries were very often difficult to co-ordinate and there were many breakfast and evening meetings.

2 *Space.* Finding space in school to enable courses to take place during the day.

3 *Crèche provision.*

4 *Changing attitudes.* Initially not all staff were committed to the community dimension of school life.

5 *Attracting funding for initiatives.*

6 *Course viability.* The community college would only run courses which attracted upwards of ten people. This created problems when, for example, eight people were interested. The issue raised the fear of creating expectations and then letting people down.

7 *Convincing partners.* It was sometimes difficult to convince FE establishments that the school was an appropriate venue for courses because it was part of the community. Some colleges were not willing to take the risk to see if it was sustainable.

8 *LEA input.* There was an uncoordinated approach by the LEA with respect to some of the initiatives. In some instances the head knew more than the LEA. No one in the LEA had overall responsibility for community education and yet community education inevitably dovetails into many other aspects controlled by the LEA.

Summing up

The success of the school as a community resource is ensured. The school recently secured a Sport England bid and building of a community creative arts hall begins shortly. Obviously we hope to enhance the provision further and draw more partners to our table. We have a vision in which the school will cater for the needs of all the community, young and old, providing routes for even more success.

10
■ ■ ■
New Community Schools in Scotland

Neil McKechnie

The Scottish political context

The role of the Scottish Parliament is to make laws in relation to devolved matters in Scotland. In these devolved areas, it is able, by virtue of the devolution legislation, to amend or repeal existing Acts of the UK Parliament and to pass new legislation of its own in relation to devolved matters.

The Scottish Executive, accountable to the Scottish Parliament, exercises executive responsibility in relation to devolved matters. It is responsible for most of the issues of day-to-day concern to the people of Scotland, including health, education, justice, rural affairs and transport, and manages an annual budget of around £20 billion. The relationship between the Scottish Executive and the Scottish Parliament is similar to the relationship between the UK Government and the UK Parliament.

The Executive was established in 1999, following the first elections to the Scottish Parliament. It is currently a coalition between the Scottish Labour Party and the Scottish Liberal Democrat Party. A First Minister who is nominated by the Parliament and in turn appoints the other Scottish Ministers leads the Executive. Scottish Executive civil servants are accountable to Scottish Ministers, who are themselves accountable to the Scottish Parliament.

The Scottish policy context

Social justice

Social justice is at the heart of the Scottish Executive's work (Scottish Executive, 1999a), integrating services is at the heart of its social justice policy and the New Community School concept is at the heart of its education policies (Scottish Office, 1998). New Community School approaches focus on all the needs of all pupils, engagement with families and the wider community, and integration of formal and informal education with social work, and health promotion. New Community School Projects are expected to become health-promoting schools by providing good quality health education, formal and informal curriculum in health, and by creating safe and healthy school environments (Scottish Executive, 1996b). These initiatives are being taken forward at a time when the national debate on the future of education is underway. Leading and managing change will become critical factors in the implementation and success of the social justice programme.

Education for the future

The National Debate on Education will inform Scottish education for the future (Scottish Executive, 2002a). The nation at large, business and industry, academics and educational researchers contributed to the debate, which embraced issues of values and beliefs, in addition to purposes and requirements of education in the twenty-first century. Developing local strategies for involving communities in processes such as this is one intended outcome of the National Debate. This process can be carried into the individual school. Values-based strategic planning as a dynamic approach, building change into school development planning is an example of this (Scottish Executive, 2002b).

Juvenile justice

Scotland has a unique juvenile justice system for young people under the age of 17 based on Children's Hearings, where trained volunteers decide on what should happen to a particular child following referral from the Reporter to the Children's Panel. The system has been in operation since the late 1960s and has taken juvenile justice, care and welfare out of the courts system. The Scottish Executive has funded various strategies to tackle youth crime. (Scottish Executive, 2002c) particularly in the target group of 16–24 year olds, who account disproportionately for criminal convictions.

National improvement framework

The Scottish Executive has published five National Priorities for education. The Standards in Scotland's Schools etc. Act 2000 legislates for a national improvement framework based on measuring performance against an agreed set of outcomes that relate to the five National Priorities. These measures are very specific in relation to, for example, performance in externally set examinations, and less so in terms of values such as promoting active citizenship. The performance measures are a mixture of quantitative and qualitative measures. Criticism of raw league tables has led to a greater emphasis on benchmarking of similar performing schools with each other, using agreed deprivation measures as a means of grouping schools. Following the publication of 'Smart Successful Scotland' (Scottish Executive, 2001a), there has been a re-emphasis of core skills and an attempt to provide more of an alternative to a traditional academic education for pupils beyond the first two years of secondary schooling. The Scottish Credit Qualifications Framework provides for coherence and progression, and builds upon the Scottish Executive's advice on flexibility in the secondary curriculum. The qualitative performance measures are drawn from a suite of quality indicators for self-evaluation and external inspection of schools ('How Good Is Our School?').

The Act also legislates for the inspection of the education functions of local authorities, with a set of quality indicators available for self-evaluation and external inspection by HM Inspectors of Education. By mid-2002 over half of Scotland's 32 education authorities had been inspected. Various professional and consumer groups have been in discussion with the Scottish Executive with a view to reviewing the process, particularly in relation to benchmarking of performance related to deprivation. As a consequence of the focus on quality issues, there has been a greater recognition of the need for the chief officials of Scottish education authorities to develop leadership skills, including an awareness of the importance of emotional intelligence and the identification of good practice.

Community learning and development

A recent reorganisation of ministerial responsibilities in Scotland has resulted in the Minister for Social Justice being responsible for all areas of public policy in the area of community learning and development, including the professional training of practitioners, community empowerment and community regeneration. Community learning and development are seen as essential to the building of social capital and the strengthening of the capacity of communities and of people to influence planning and service delivery. There is to be dedicated investment in the provision of specialist staff in youth work, community work and community-based adult education and the adoption of this approach by a wider range of public service disciplines.

New Community Schools

The Scottish Executive's approach

The focus of New Community Schools is on the pupils and their families, addressing needs in the round through integrated provision of services – teachers, social workers, community education workers, health professionals and others working together in a single team.

The New Community Schools prospectus (Scottish Office, 1998) outlines the initiative. It lists the essential or defining characteristics underlying the programme:

- A focus on all the needs of all pupils.
- Engagement with families.
- Engagement with the wider community.
- Integrated provision of school education, informal as well as formal education, social work and health education and promotion services.
- Integrated management.
- Arrangements for the delivery of these services according to a set of integrated objectives and measurable outcomes.
- Commitment and leadership.
- Multi-disciplinary training and staff development.

The initiative became a pilot programme in three phases with the third phase announced in 2001.

In phase one, in 1999, schools, nurseries and family centres joined the New Community Schools programme. Projects were based on proposals submitted by local authorities, in partnership with the Health Service and others. Phase two was announced a year later. The Scottish Executive is now supporting the rollout of the new community school approach across education authorities. Accordingly, all 32 local authorities were requested by the Scottish Executive to submit a development plan for approval. West Dunbartonshire was well placed to expand its rollout programme, given that this approach had been adopted at an earlier stage in the phasing of development grants from the Scottish Executive.

New Community Schools address the fact that there are many factors which affect achievement at school, and that it is necessary to look at achievement in the widest sense; on their own schools cannot address all the barriers to children's learning. A team approach is key – integrated provision of services and integrated response to needs and aspirations. In New Community Schools, teachers, social workers, community education workers, health professionals and others will play their part as members of a single team working together to provide the services which individual children need. Personal Learning Plans, developed and discussed with parents, are seen as crucial in meeting the full needs of the children and their families. While implementation has been slow, there are expectations that they will be subject to further development and evaluation.

The vision is being realised incrementally through key strategies such as community planning; community learning; integration of education, family support and health education/promotion; partnerships with statutory and voluntary sectors; and strengthening the links with business enterprise/social economy.

Leadership and the development agenda

Synergy in cultures and style is a major aspect of the development agenda – requiring vision and effective leadership at all levels in the agencies concerned with the social justice programme. This necessitates recognition of the range and diversity of environments within which change is required. A move from traditional, bureaucratic approaches of command and control with agencies working in isolation from each other in order to deliver their own aims, to promoting greater use of neighbourhood management to deliver services is required (Quong et al., 1998). Measuring progress and tracking change over time will be critical to ensure that change results in improvement. To this end, the Scottish Executive is preparing indicators which will assist, for example, in relation to employment in deprived areas, educational attainment, health improvement and child poverty.

Evaluation

Since April 1999, when the first 37 New Community School pilot projects were launched, a national evaluation team has been tracking the programme. The team has reported on the early indicators of progress. Local diversity and flexibility have been encouraged and examples of good practice and achievements will inform the development programme and lead to better integrated children's services and real and lasting change. The researchers have identified that cross-agency liaison and practice have been substantially enhanced in the first year of the programme. The indications are that multi-agency working and service delivery depend on appropriate management, funding and governance structures, as well as high levels of commitment from key individuals in local authorities, the New Community School programme and school management. West Dunbartonshire has concentrated on these areas, enabling it develop as a New Community Authority.

West Dunbartonshire: A New Community Authority

West Dunbartonshire is situated to the west of Glasgow between Loch Lomond and the river Clyde. It comprises 70 square miles and 96,000 people. There are three main towns, Alexandria, Dumbarton and Clydebank. The area is well known for its engineering heritage, whether through the manufacturing of Singer sewing machines, or as the birthplace of some of the world's greatest ships. It has pockets of severe deprivation, the second worst in Scotland. A high proportion of people live in rental accommodation, mostly via housing associations, with low housing ownership. Citizens of West Dunbartonshire are unhealthier and have a shorter life span than most of the rest of Scotland. However, there are some successes in inward investment and it is a safe place to live.

There are attractive areas on the waterfronts of both the Clyde estuary and Loch Lomond. The council vision of providing the best services and enabling the potential of all citizens to achieve is matched with positive examples of communities building the capacity to empower their own lives. Scotland's first national park at Loch Lomond, opened summer 2002, providing a focus for leisure and tourism.

Vision and ownership

West Dunbartonshire Council, as a New Community Authority, seeks to tackle social exclusion, promote active citizenship, enable lifelong learning, raise standards of attainment and promote healthier lifestyles – an agenda which can only be achieved through partnerships with families, communities, other agencies and better integrated services.

Improving the co-ordination and integration of services to address needs and make effective use of resources is the goal. This is increasingly happening through partnership planning, for example, Health Improvement Plans, Social Inclusion Partnership Plans and Community Planning.

Integrated planning

The West Dunbartonshire approach for developing and delivering its New Community School initiative has three strands: the first is establishing and maintaining interagency mechanisms at strategic, operational and practice levels; the second is interagency training and development; and the third is supporting school cluster development planning.

Planning at strategic level comprises a steering committee, membership of which includes the Leader of the Council and Convenor of the Education Committee, directors and senior officers of Education and Cultural Services and Social Work and Housing Services, the two NHS boards, the Social Inclusion Partnership, Enterprise Company, Police, Further Education College and the Careers Service. Serviced by an integration manager, its purposes are fivefold: to plan, monitor and evaluate the initiative; to match resources and ensure added value; to provide leadership; to take strategic action; and to ensure and promote the effectiveness of the initiative.

At operational level, three sub-committees were set up, chaired by the integration manager and each with a specific focus: lifelong learning, pupil and family support and health. Membership comprised senior managers of the relevant partner agencies represented on the steering committee. The roles and functions of the sub-committees have been regularly reviewed and, where appropriate, incorporated in other interagency structures as the widening social justice agenda has evolved.

An implementation group, reporting to the steering committee and chaired by the head of educational development, with representation from Social Work, Psychological Services, Quality Development, school Cluster Co-ordinators, and Lifelong Learning, was established in 2000. Serviced by the integration manager, this group meets regularly to ensure a co-ordinated and coherent approach to service developments at school level.

Training and development

How change is managed will determine the success of the social justice programme. However, it is important to differentiate between leadership and management as the leaders and the managers are in the communities and agencies where change is to be affected.

Skilling staff in ways of working which actively promote community learning and development is becoming increasingly important. First, in bureaucracies the reliance is largely on positional power within a hierarchical structure. However, if members of the community are to be actively involved in the planning process and delivery of services, the new partnerships require leadership and management styles which are somewhat different.

The authority and its partners have been working with the University of Strathclyde on an accredited training module for staff who have responsibility for transmitting the New Community Authority vision and for planning and delivering services through effective interagency working. The module 'Developing Better Integration' will enable key leaders and managers to contribute, through the training opportunity, to the development of a collective vision for the authority, the management of change and interprofessional working, and give evidence of leadership skills in building a system for the future with client-centred outcomes.

School cluster development planning

Still in its infancy, interagency school cluster planning is believed to have a vital part to play by increasing ownership, building on good practice, and setting and achieving realistic targets which have a local expression. The real challenges are in building the team and developing the individual, as well as delivering the task. While schools will continue to be managed by head teachers, in the case of cluster planning the leadership role may, in fact, be assumed by any of the partners.

Management structures

In the course of developing an integrated management approach to support the New Community School initiative, politicians, officers and partner agencies in West Dunbartonshire agreed a New Community Authority vision and a structure to support interagency planning at strategic, operational and practice levels. This approach aligns with Adair's (1983) model of action-centred leadership. Irrespective of the local situation, adapting Adair's model, the centre point of the overlapping circles is the social justice vision of the Scottish Executive as opposed to a single leader.

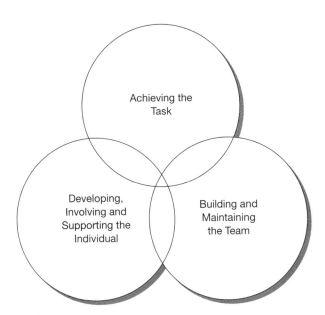

Figure 10.1: The West Dunbartonshire Council (WDC) approach and leadership model

The WDC approach to rolling out and sustaining the new community school approach relates to Adair's (1983) action-centred leadership model. This identifies three key elements: the task, the individual and the team.

The approach adopted by WDC to achieve the task of rolling out the new community schools model has focused on developing the individual; for example, by identifying members of staff as key change agents and through building effective teams to secure the vision, plan the strategy or deliver the services. The emphasis is on achieving the task through the individual and the team. The balance between the three areas has fluctuated over phases of the new community schools programme. The release and development of people's potential has been one of the key drivers of change. Consequently, there has been some tension between traditional command and control management practices common in many organisations, including schools and education authorities, and leadership practices. The latter approach focuses on people, inspires trust, deals in relationships and teamwork, gains commitment and requires coaching and facilitation skills.

Case Studies

The case studies that follow illustrate how the vision had been translated into action, dismantling the barriers to learning through working in partnership with individuals and groups and promoting citizenship. They also show elements of individual development (Jacqui's Story), team development (White Mice) and task delivery (Bellsmyre digital community), with social justice being the focal point of the action. Everyone has the potential to be a 'spotter', a 'referrer' or an 'expert'. In the New Community Authority, these roles are often inextricably linked.

Jacqui's story

Jacqui was a school cleaner in the first New Community School project. A mother of two pupils at the school, her own experience of school was of failure. A 'non-achiever', her recollection was of feeling stupid, being at the bottom of every class and never asking for assistance. Having failed to achieve at school, she had no reason to believe that she had the ability to achieve as an adult. Cleaning duties in the home economics department were to change this view. One of the teachers recognised Jacqui's skills in communicating with disaffected pupils and provided the necessary support, encouragement and advice which saw Jacqui meeting up with the school-based community education worker, and her return to school as an adult learner, and then to a post as a special needs auxiliary. Not content with her own adventure into learning, Jacqui was next concerned to provide support, encouragement and advice to friends and socially isolated adults in her community to enable them to re-engage with learning through the New Community School programmes.

White Mice

The White Mice project is an example of community capacity building, where local expertise and experiences are harnessed to develop curricular programmes, which address issues of citizenship. Asbestosis is one of the legacies of the shipbuilding industry on Clydeside. 'White mice' was the nickname of the powder-covered asbestos workers in the shipyards. A local action group, Clydebank Asbestos Group, is engaged locally and nationally on a range of issues, including family support, community health, legal issues, welfare benefits, environment and sustainable development. A partnership with Clydebank Asbestos Group, education staff, the arts adviser, the health services and a youth theatre company, White Mice brings together a travelling gallery exhibition with materials and science experiments for primary and secondary pupils, a cross-curricular information and teaching pack, a broadcast quality film on historical and current environmental issues, and drama workshops for pupils, families and the wider community.

Bellsmyre digital community project

Digital inclusion is a central theme of the Government's Social Justice agenda. Access to ICT is a prerequisite for the delivery of other key strategies of the Scottish Executive, particularly lifelong learning and adult literacy and numeracy. The Digital Scotland Report includes a vision which recognises that improving access to ICT to disadvantaged groups will make training and education more accessible and will provide access to new employment opportunities, the focus of the digital inclusion strategy (Scottish Executive, 2000). ICT presents opportunities to promote social inclusion and capacity building. A community within West Dunbartonshire, Bellsmyre succeeded in winning a challenge competition to become a digital community.

Personal computers, internet access and associated peripherals are to be installed free in every household in the community, some 2,000 homes. Learning hubs will be established in primary schools in order that ICT learning and training can take place.

Access to learning and other content will be via a community portal. The network will allow specially developed school-based learning systems to be accessed at home, reinforcing classroom work and offering parents the opportunity to become more involved in their children's learning. Much of the content will be of a local nature, and community groups are already engaged in the process of identifying the content they want to see available.

ICT training will be provided for each connected home, and initially volunteers from the community who have been identified as 'digital champions' will be able to support neighbours as a result of receiving more advanced ICT training. This will leave a legacy in the community of competent ICT users.

The project lends itself to online or e-learning and links are being developed with a number of learning providers to support this type of delivery. A virtual learning environment has been developed, supported by the local further education college. Content from this has been developed with input from a range of partners including community educators, under a European Community funded programme. The aim of the digital community project is to become self-managed and a community trust is being considered. This project not only begins to address the Government's Digital Inclusion Strategy, but also builds capacity through the medium of ICT. Learning is enhanced across the family, not only with the e-learning accessed by adults, but the promotion of stronger links with school-based learning into the home ensures a family-wide approach is adopted.

Conclusion

The Scottish Executive's approach to New Community Schools is rooted in the Social Justice agenda. The delivery of the programme in West Dunbartonshire has developed through a particular model of action-centred leadership, where the focus differs according to the outcomes of strategic planning, by attempting to reflect local circumstances through integrating services at school cluster level. The ability of organisations, communities and individuals to meet their own needs while still contributing to the delivery of the vision of West Dunbartonshire as a New Community Authority is promoted.

References

Adair, J. (1983) *Action-Centred Leadership*. London Industrial Society Press.

Quong, T., Walker, A., Stott, K. (1998) *Values-based Strategic Planning: A Dynamic Approach for Schools*. New York: Prentice Hall.

Scottish Executive (1999a) *Social Justice: A Scotland Where Everyone Matters*. Edinburgh: Scottish Executive.

Scottish Executive (1999b) *Towards a Healthier Scotland: A Route to Health Promotion*. Edinburgh: Scottish Executive.

Scottish Executive (2000) *Report of Digital Scotland Task Force*. Edinburgh: Scottish Executive.

Scottish Executive (2001a) *A Smart Successful Scotland: Ambitions for the Enterprise Networks*. Edinburgh: Scottish Executive.

Scottish Executive (2002a) *Better Communities in Scotland: Closing the Gap*. Edinburgh: Scottish Executive.

Scottish Executive (2002b) *The National Debate on Education*. Edinburgh: Scottish Executive.

Scottish Executive (2002c) *Scotland's Action Programme to Reduce Youth Crime.* Edinburgh: Scottish Executive.

Scottish Office (1998) *New Community Schools: The Prospectus.* London: Scottish Office.

National Evaluation of New Community Schools Pilot Programme in Scotland: Phase 1. Institute of Education, University of London. Interchange 76 Scottish Executive (2002)

11

■ ■ ■

Open Schools in Sweden

Marianne Lundholm

Marianne Lundholm works in, promotes networks across and researches developing open community schools in Sweden. Here she draws on extracts from conversations with three school principals and describes, for purposes of reminder and reflection, the significant work of John Dewey (1935) on (in the vocabulary of the USA) school administration.

Background to school and society in Sweden

When elementary schools were introduced in Sweden, during the middle of the nineteenth century, it was an agricultural country. Then the school and its teachers held central positions in the countryside. 'The school in the middle of the village' was where teachers established themselves, along with the clergyman, the parish clerk and the organist, as important authorities in the village. They were used by villagers for different writing tasks. The school premises were often used as a community hall, and the pupils were taught to help to clean them and to keep the fire burning.

With industrialisation and urbanisation the school became more isolated from the surrounding community. As in many other European countries, a selective school system was developed with elementary school for the majority and an intermediate school leaving examination (*realskola*) and secondary grammar school with higher school examination (*läroverk*) for those who were considered especially talented and expected to get higher positions in society. In all schooling, obedience and training for collective work was stressed. In the curriculum of 1919 for the elementary school there was a special subject, local geography and history (*hembygdskunskap*), in the lower grades. Some weeks of continuation school (*fortsättningsskola*) completed compulsory education after six or seven years' elementary school. In the continuation school civics (*medborgarkunskap*) was introduced.

Fresh ideas about schooling and its aims were developed after 1945. The intention was to make the school an instrument for democratisation – an antidote to the recent history of authoritarian governments in Europe and the emphasis on obedience in schools.

Comprehensive schools of nine years were established, promoting pupils' independent work individually or in groups. An important aim for the development of these schools during the 1950's to the national curriculum of 1962 was to encourage pupils to learn about the surrounding community, its associations, working life and nature. The new subject of social studies was introduced and, during the last year of schooling, a vocational guidance programme with some weeks' work experience in local enterprises and organisations. The pupils also investigated the local community through interviews and study visits, often in groups.

A new curriculum was introduced in 1980 that stimulated thematic studies, projects with interdisciplinary themes, often involving investigations in the local community. However, many representatives of the traditional school subjects, especially in the universities, were critical of this way of studying and anticipated that it would threaten the subject knowledge of the pupils. A so called knowledge movement was started that favoured more direct teacher-led, subject-oriented studies. This movement was for some time rather successful and influenced, among other things, the new teacher training reforms towards the end of the last century.

Through this period of management and curriculum decentralisation many schools have strengthened contact with the surrounding community. A national school committee in 1997 introduced the concepts of 'The Open School' and 'The School as a Cultural Centre'. It stressed that contact with the local community has two different dimensions. One is learning from the resources of, and co-operation with, the community and near environment. The other is to enable the school and its premises be a resource for adults in the local community. Much has been learned from teachers networking through the International Community Education Association (ICEA). Contacts with schools in Denmark and England have been especially important.

A network called 'The Open School' has been working to support schools through exchanging experience of different activities. It has worked in close connection with another network, 'Health Promoting Schools', attached to the Swedish Institute for Public Health (Folkhälsoinstitutet). The network works in co-operation with the institute and the Swedish Integration Board in supporting a three-year project to promote the idea of the open school in the suburbs of big cities with many immigrants – 'The School in the Middle of the Suburb' (*Skolan mitt i förorten*). Though project funding is at an end, the work is now promoted and undertaken through a national association for 'The Open School'.

Elisabeth Sörhuus, Hjulstaskolan

Elisabeth Sörhuus has been the Principal of Hjulstaskolan for 15 years. The school is 31 years old and is situated north-west of Stockholm in the sub-region Spånga-Tensta. It serves pre-school to 9th grade. Many immigrant families live in the catchment area of the school. When she first came to the school 65 per cent of the children had a mother tongue other than Swedish; today it is 98 per cent.

One month before this interview a researcher visited the school on a project run by the Swedish National Board of Education with government funding, called 'Alternative Success'. Elisabeth Sörhuus refers to this project in her conversation.

Q: *In what ways have you begun to engage with the community in your role as a School Leader?*

ES: Prior to my appointment I knew the head of the school. We had worked together on student democracy issues.

The community has changed during these years and I usually say that we have the pupils we have. We do not want the area to be so segregated, but it is wishful thinking that it could be different. Almost no Swedish families live here and many families are, from time to time, moving around. A year ago, 30 per cent of the pupils moved within the year.

I have realised that my job is not only to lead the school, but to be part of the development of the community in a constructive way, which I also try to persuade my staff to believe. I was helped to do this when the researcher visited our school and said that our school is 'marked by exclusion'. This school has a special duty that other schools do not have.

In our daily talks with parents we can hear how difficult it is to get into the spirit of community, how impossible it is even for educated people to get a job and how easy (but personally hard) it is to be put aside and excluded. Therefore, we cannot say that our mission is to teach only the basics or we must also work on having the families incorporated into Swedish society and thereby give the children better opportunities. I believe in the equal value of all and, in the school, we have to give the pupils the best conditions by strengthening their self-esteem and self-confidence.

Q: *How has this served to improve the quality of work in the school for students and teachers?*

ES: The recognition that our pupils have a natural social ability and openness that will favour them in the future. We open up and start the processes that will strengthen their self-confidence.

We run many projects where we recognise the pupils' backgrounds, language and culture. We train cultural guides in ten different languages. They tell the history of our area. We take people for a cultural walk in the community. Instead of their language being a burden, they learn that their language is an asset.

I think that this kind of work directly influences the pupils' attitudes to school and to learning in a positive way.

Q: *How does your work improve achievement and lifelong learning?*

ES: Looking at our development during the last years our marks are better and more pupils are passing their examinations. It is a little risky to look at statistics; children come here who have never been to school before, some directly from a war zone. They cannot catch up on these years. We also consider that our goals are comfort, well-being and safety. We sometimes feel sure that the school is as important to them as their families.

The school is also open afternoon and evenings three days a week. We invite younger children in the first place and encourage their parents to come with them to feel that the school is theirs. Teachers stay to sit and talk with the pupils and the other adults who come.

We are also planning how to utilise the parents' backgrounds, experience and knowledge. We also run classes for parents. They thought it was wrong to come to school and just talk; they wanted to do something. Now we have computer classes and one in woodwork led by a female teacher. This has encouraged mothers to come. Food and diet is another class. When starting these we met parents who had never been here before. So we are beginning to achieve the aim that they feel that the school can mean something to them.

Q: *How have you engaged with leaders in the community?*

ES: The parents are our most important partners. But I can also see that I have to work outside school to reach the objectives I describe and my vision for this school. So I try to open the school more, though it is sometimes a question of resources. I try to get associations in, to make the school a natural meeting place. To reach those goals I have to rely on the community.

Additionally, I am a member and chairperson of an association, Tenstagruppen, which is an association for different interests in the community. It works for those who live and work here and deals with issues that are significant for our community. Everybody who is interested can become a member, like people from the local authorities, landlords, tenants' associations, representatives from other associations and the church. There is room for sharing information and it gives me an invaluable network of contacts to reach out to, to be able to do things outside school.

Q: *What skills, knowledge and qualities of leadership do you think you need as School Principal?*

ES: You must have a vision, as well as energy and power to implement it. Be sure not to get drowned in paper; there is something more important. The motive for me is to make a contribution for a better world. I think it is necessary to realise, when you take on this kind of commitment, that it is the community you are really employed for. Your colleagues must have the same belief. You cannot work alone but must be a team of leaders. There must also be personnel in the school who accept your values and people who are driven and able to turn vision into reality.

Q: *How are you supported in leading your community school work by local and/or national policies?*

ES: If you are not engaged in the community when you come here, you have to change. You get involved and supported by parents and pupils.

Jonny Axelsson, Ekenässjöns Skola

Jonny Axelsson is the head of a compulsory school, Ekenässjöns Skola, with 220 children, grades 1–6. It is situated on the outskirts of a small town in southeast Sweden. The area includes both industry and farming. The district is characterised by its businesses, Free Church traditions and active associations of different kinds.

Jonny Axelsson took over a very traditional school. This was a challenge for him. 'Something had to be done', by which he means – to open the school. The word open is very important to him. There is now a strong movement for 'the healthy, open school' in which he is engaged.

Q: *In what ways did you begin to engage with the community in your role as a School Leader?*

JA: We started by trying to get the district library into the school. The aim was to arrange a natural meeting place. We use the phrase 'A centre of learning' – a school and a meeting place for learning.

The other important thing was to start working according to the new curriculum. That meant doing and learning different things in different ways, to individualise learning. That caused complaints from parents. We realised that we had to go out and explain our way of thinking.

Q: *How did you use others to lead these initiatives. How did you delegate?*

JA: When it comes to delegation the teachers respond in different ways. Some want to work with study visits, some with retired people in our school. The main thing is teacher's attitudes, to be open to new ideas, to dare to take a step into the unknown and try to see if it works. Then it is important that I, as a leader, do not criticise when things go wrong but, instead, see it as an opportunity. The more you open up, the more the ideas come.

Q: How has this improved the quality of work in the school?

JA: Regarding the practical situation, our stock of books is better, we can use better premises, e.g. the chapel on the other side of the street with good seats and microphones. When you raise the awareness of the parents about the importance of education, then you also raise the quality of schooling for children and that is more important than good seats. That is my main issue in much of school development – to bring together school, children and parents in a meeting about the importance of our community's future.

Regarding lifelong learning, we run computer courses for adults. There are painting courses, study circles run by a study association, courses and study circles in English run for a business company.

We have some comprehensive curriculum goals. One is pleasure and purposefulness in work. This is easier to attain by working outside the school, in real life where students can see why they need particular knowledge. Curiosity, desire to learn is another goal. Self-confidence is yet another. By recognising and respecting individual cultures, the individual is valued and confidence grows. Research in Sweden has shown that the achievement in basics has improved when people learn in this way.

Q: How have you engaged with leaders in the community?

JA: I am a member of a network of mainly business people who are not only leaders but also employees. There is a priest from the nearest chapel and, sometimes, the head of the parents' association joins us, sometimes a teacher from our school. We meet for lunch and talk about the future, about the circumstances for the companies nowadays. We discuss the role of the school in the society. Tomorrow I am invited to a breakfast meeting at one of the big companies to talk about my work. I will talk about teaching and learning today.

There is also co-operation between the group of school leaders in the municipality and a local bank. Eight principals meet with the leaders from the bank to discuss common issues.

Q: What skills, knowledge and qualities of leadership do you think you need as a School Principal to engage with the community in order to improve the quality of education service provided by your school?

JA: You should be humble, fearless, daring, safe and curious. None of these traits can be studied at university; they come from your inner personality. I have met some inspiring people who have given me energy, many thoughts and ideas. I read from specialist and other literature.

Q: *How do you see your role as a leader of the personnel in the school?*

JA: I want to inspire them with hope for the future, set a good example, see possibilities, dare to make mistakes, to have courage; because the teachers do what I do. If I dare to make mistakes, they also do.

Tom Hagman, St Botvid Secondary School

Tom Hagman is the Principal of St Botvid Secondary School, covering ages 16–19 years, with 600 students and 60 teachers. The school is situated in the centre of a suburb southwest of Stockholm. It was moved to there only two years ago. It had a difficult period during l996–7 when the school was adversely portrayed extensively in the media. The result was a bad reputation that still has to be handled. Tom Hagman was appointed leader of the school in l999.

The school is organised into three centres, with teachers working predominantly in one centre, all with common goals. The school is administered by the Department for Education and Work in the municipality. The majority of the elected board members are social democrats and left wing.

The school follows several different programmes covering natural sciences, English, business administration and tourism. An aesthetic programme offers 'Music and the New Circus' in co-operation with a circus company educating artists and performing. The school also has a special programme with 40 students with learning difficulties.

Many of the youngsters have parents with different ethnic origins, which means that the students are multilingual and Swedish is their second language. The demand on the personnel in the school is to focus on the fact that, in the future in Sweden and in other countries, there will be a great call for people who can 'read' cultural differences and with knowledge of language. Today, these merits are often not recognised and valued when applying for jobs.

Q: *In what ways and how did you begin to engage in the community in your role as a School Leader and how did this serve to improve the quality of your work?*

TH: For me it is natural to establish links between the school and its community. I believe that the school is an important part of the community, today the most important part. Thus it is the responsibility of the school to link to the community. The school encourages the community to feel proud of its school and, with joy, satisfaction, confidence and peace send their children to school. Thus the school or the School Leader cannot be anonymous. When the Principal is walking in the community, people should know that this is the Principal of the school. Then you have laid the first foundation stone.

Q: In the community of your former school, what kind of 'initiatives' did you undertake?

TH: It was towards the parents as human beings. I recently heard from a colleague there that she sometimes meets parents in the school yard. This had become an intersection for all paths from the houses to the centre since we cut down the turnstiles. Then it became a natural meeting place and it became a park arranged for families to sit in summer evenings, to barbecue and talk together in a social context.

It is quite clear that this influenced the dialogue and made it easier to secure more openness. The parents developed a feeling that the school was meant for their children, not the contrary. It also had an effect on the formal co-operation. Each class had a class board of representatives for parents that met once a month to discuss the school and the children in the class. Their points of view were passed on to the work teams and the local advisory board with parents and staff. This all contributed to better quality education.

Q: In this school, how have you engaged in the community and how has that improved your work?

TH: We are starting a parents' association in each class and this should be a process parallel with issues of democracy relevant to the young students. Since the upper secondary school for many years has traditionally made no contact with parents, this is a major reorganisation.

We co-operate with the biggest Syrian Orthodox Church in the Nordic countries, being built next to our school. Young people, some of whom are students at the university, come here one evening a week to help our students with their homework. This is open to all students of the school, irrespective of religion. These university students are really role models for further learning. I see this as a first step to organise future co-operation with different associations.

We have also recently started a project with Swedish Television. Three journalists now co-operate with the editors of our school paper.

We are planning a computer education programme for the staff at IKEA situated close to us in the community. We have had computer classes for retired people where the students are teachers/instructors. We plan to arrange these again soon.

Q: How do you engage and co-operate with other leaders in the community?

TH: Each curriculum programme in the school has an advisory board consisting of business people who take on apprentices (from amongst our students), other representatives and one of the school leaders. Through these boards we have a continuous co-operation with the business leaders near us. Our business programme is partly located at local companies. Tourism in our social science programme involves students working for six weeks in other countries, like the USA, France, Spain and Turkey.

Recently we held a training course for a consulting company that works with networks for leaders. We arranged a programme for one day including me lecturing on leadership. The former head of our students' council, now studying at the university, contributed a session. Our students were involved in discussion groups with the company on the theme of young people's view of the future.

Q: What qualities of leadership do you think you need to improve the quality of education served and provided by your school?

TH: To co-operate you must be very humble, very sensitive and listen. Try never to get into a situation of defence, but create openness for criticism. The staff must feel that I am the best possible guarantor for their working environment and conditions, thereby guaranteeing the best possible education for the students. I want people to talk to me and not about me, to tell me their problems and I will try to answer their questions. The teachers are the professionals, but should feel free to come to me and ask for help. My strategy today is that I support fully those who are open for development and change. I do not press others.

If you can let your belief in people's own power permeate the whole organisation, the collective power will definitely lead to success.

Q: In the curriculum, the responsibility to co-operate with the community is very seldom directed at the principal but at the teachers. How do you feel about this?

TH: When I take a job as Principal I also take responsibility for the community where the school is to take an active part for the development of the community. For me, it is quite natural, it is the same as if I were a head in a small country village with fifty families. To be the head of a school also means to be in charge of developing and sharing the responsibility of not letting the community die. The work today needs a sharing and exchange between all parties to make it possible. The days when the school worked on its own in isolation are over.

A reflective framework

The author draws heavily in her work on the ideas of John Dewey. Here, she uses a discussion on the 'problems of public school administration' (in USA) and 'of the ways of meeting them' (Dewey, 1935) as an outline framework for reflection on her conversations with school leaders.

The problems are complex and may be presented through three phases composed of conflicting factors. The first phase involves superintendents, principals and supervisors being engaged in both the direction and the practice of educational enterprise:

> *... the intellectual phase of responsibility and function of the administrator. He or she not only participates in the development of minds and character, but participates in a way that imposes special intellectual responsibilities.*

(Dewey, 1935: p.9)

Second, administrators are particularly charged with personnel matters. The principal needs to co-operate with members of the school board, to deal with politicians and to meet parents of varied views and ideals. A superintendent is an intermediary between the teaching staff and the public. Dewey identifies many routine tasks. In particular, he notes that these can so dominate that the other prime phases are lost. Administration at this point becomes isolated.

Dewey suggests that an administrator can deal with these things effectively only if s/he is able to unify them into a comprehensive idea and plan. It is especially important that the directly educational phase of the work is unified with the social relations both inside and outside the school. Different aspects of the administrator's work tend to combine and conspire to nullify their positive effects. For Dewey, the only way for the administrator to avoid this is to focus on clear ideas and principles of place and function for the school in the wider context of society, from local to national. Only from such clarity can the integration needed be attained.

The first step to this integration developed by Dewey is clarity of focus and direction in leadership. What is the social function of the school? Is it to perpetuate existing conditions or to take part in their transformation?

Also important is the degree to which the administrator achieves the integration of the educational with the human and social relationships aspects of the work. Here, the school develops as a co-operative community with shared intellectual and moral responsibilities across the community.

Finally Dewey promotes adult education to be a necessary part of the job in the sense that the public is brought to understand the needs and possibilities of the creative education of the young:

> *He will realise that public education is essentially education of the public directly, through teachers and students in the school, indirectly through communicating to others her/his own ideals and standards, inspiring others with enthusiasm of her/himself and ... staff for the function of intelligence and character in the transformation of society.*

(Dewey, 1935: p.10)

Reference

Dewey, J. (1935) 'Toward administrative statesmanship', *The Social Frontier*, 1, 9–10.

12

■ ■ ■

Schools and Community Education: An Integrated Concept

Yardena Harpaz

Community schools in Israel

The elementary community schools organisation in Israel was established in 1977 to help regular state schools become community schools. The belief underpinning its establishment was simple: the relationship between all the educational processes that affect children, for example, their families, schools and other informal agencies, cannot be ignored. Currently, the organisation is an integral part of the Israel Association of Community Centres which is a governmental association belonging to the Ministry of Education.

The idea

The basic conceptual framework behind community education regards the school as being open to its environment in the sense of being a meeting point for people, resources and organisations. This creates a process which contributes to the comprehensive quality of the academic, educational, social, cultural and community achievement of pupils. The community school operates in co-operation with local authorities, institutions and other establishments in the community, e.g. community centres. Partners in the community school are pupils, parents, teachers and other citizens. The community school meets the community's needs via its programmes.

The planning and decision-making processes take place within the context of a variety of frameworks within classrooms or management structures, for example, community committees and councils. There is no one model through which the idea is carried out. The overall organisation of a community school encourages schools to create their own purpose and mode of operation specific to their own requirements, via training and consultation.

The idea of integrating community education into the conceptual framework of schools has now been disseminated and accepted within the educational system. In 2001, 500 community elementary schools were active all over the country: public secular, public religious and in the Arab, Druze, and Bedouin sector. Currently there is a long waiting list of schools interested in joining.

The characteristics of a community school

The community school exists as an educational, social and physical resource for the community. School programmes are influenced and planned according to the specific requirements and needs of the various groups included in the school community. A systematic process of planning, implementing and evaluating programmes exists in the community schools. All significant elements of the school's community participate in this process. The community school programme consists of a combination of compulsory and extracurricular programmes in, for example, social programmes and studies, arts, culture, sports, etc. These are aimed at various target populations. The community school's resources encompass all the human, professional, financial and physical facilities that exist within the various target populations and organisations.

The organisational structure of the community school facilitates local partnerships and co-operation in the decision-making process and these influence school policy and programmes. There are a variety of different forms of local partnerships beginning with those in the classroom – every classroom has a classroom leadership group consisting of parents, students and teachers – and also exemplified in community councils, committees, task-specific teams, etc.

Methods of operation

Community education is based on a holistic and comprehensive philosophy. For the purpose of realising this philosophy, the community school uses the following methods:

1 Creating interaction with the other organisations in the community which influence children. These ties are based on the specific characteristics and needs of a particular community and, uniquely, facilitate the contribution of all parents to the educational process.

2 Developing knowledge, learning skills, behaviour habits and value systems, while providing pupils with opportunities to act as active and involved citizens, contributing and influencing the communities they belong to.

3 Bringing together the combined resources of the schools and their environments: actualising the human, professional, organisational, physical and fiscal potential existing amongst students, parents and teachers within the community.

4 Systematic co-operative work through belief in organisational structures which consist of a combination of parents, teachers and pupils, working together in classroom leadership groups, community committees, ad hoc task groups, advisory councils, steering committees, etc.

The secret of partnership: the whole is larger than the sum of its parts

Training of community schools is done by consultants and advisors from the elementary community schools organisation working in teams in six regional units across the country. The training is provided personally to the principal and others. Joint workshops are provided for parents, teachers, social workers and other relevant professionals with the purpose of enabling parents, teachers and principals to become leaders of the community education process in schools.

Intensive consultation and advisory support is provided by the elementary community schools organisation for up to four years, according to the specific development needs of each school. The community schools organisation also enables each school to access its training and information resource centre. The role of this centre is to collect, develop and renew information about the programmes and methods of work that are happening within the domain of community education in schools.

Within the framework of ongoing improvement and renewal processes in a community school, the following issues are emphasised:

1 Developing client-directed organisational culture – inculcating attitudes of 'service' in the school, so that, for example, teachers are perceived as clients of the principal, parents and pupils as clients of the teachers.

2 Creating an authentic community-oriented curriculum.

3 Developing autonomous, self-managed community schools.

4   Developing joint programmes between community centres and community schools.

5   Advancing dialogue between community schools in various sectors, for example, religious, secular, Jews and Arabs.

6   Monitoring and reviewing issues of community development within the school.

Community schools

The programmes provided vary from school to school and emerge from the needs and aspirations of the local community. They include joint activities for pupils and their parents, activities designed to foster the development of community-oriented student councils, cultural and artistic activities, sports, leisure time and recreational schemes, programmes on ecology and environment, good citizenship and co-existence. The school conducts extra-curricular activities consisting of extended programmes beyond the regular hours and sessions of the formal education system.

The school functions as an integrated comprehensive system designed to influence and be influenced by pupils, their families and the school surroundings. A public advisory council is formed, drawing membership from parents, neighbourhood residents and representatives from the local municipality, other neighbourhood organisations and school staff. The function of this council (which also includes topic-specific sub-committees) is to identify needs, transform ideas into operational objectives and help community school staff create a budgeted programme in accordance with the policy determined by the council.

Amongst the prerequisites for the operation of a community school is the consent and readiness on the part of the principal to assume full responsibility for the expanded activity of the school. In addition, teacher involvement is absolutely necessary. Teachers must assume an active role in encouraging parent participation in, for example, developing programmes and curricula with a community orientation, committee membership, etc. It is important that teachers identify with the responsibilities and commitments which stem from changing the institution into a community school. The involvement of the teachers is the essential factor in ensuring the integration of the formal system with that of the informal one.

The mission statement of a community school

To challenge and assist the school's leadership to make real the process of partnership between school, family, and community. This partnership has as its aim the achievement of a comprehensive academic, cultural and social climate in the school and in the community.

Basic assumptions regarding the co-operative processes

1 Co-operation is expressed in the process by which various education agencies share authority and responsibility.

2 Parents are responsible for their children's education and therefore have the right and obligation to be partners in the educational process taking place in schools.

3 The involvement of parents and the local community in the educational process enables the creation of a climate to increase motivation and, consequently, improved academic achievement.

The school in its environment

The school's environment is made up of a range of internal and external stakeholders:

1 Task environment:
- clients
- suppliers
- competitors' organisations
- complementary organisations
- local and national agencies.

2 External environment:
- social factors and trends
- cultural factors and trends
- economic factors and trends
- political factors and trends
- technological factors and trends
- religious factors and trends.

Community curriculum planning

Figure 12.1 shows the key relationships in developing a curriculum for the whole community. The key principles underpinning such planning are:

- maximising choice;
- studying the whole community, not just school;
- developing subjects relevant to the community.

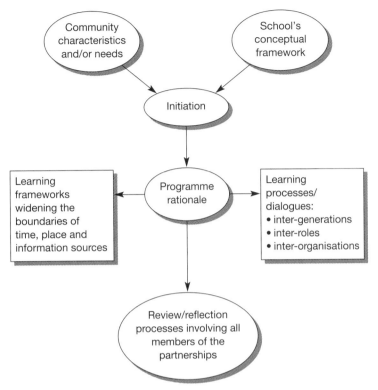

Figure 12.1: Community curriculum planning

Studying under one roof

A variety of people can be found 'studying under one roof' for a variety of reasons. Those found working in same environment may be immigrants new to the country, young couples, young single people, students in full- and part-time education, parents continuing or beginning to study later in life, senior citizens and teachers.

Building relationships between the community centres and community schools

This necessitates the identification of the two organisations and an awareness of the unique aspect of each. Plans need to made in a co-ordinated and co-operative way. Teams need to be built to create partnerships.

Caring communities

'Caring communities' is a system of integrated services in the school, which has as its focus family and community. The community school serves as the centre around which all agencies participating in this project meet, join in and are trained together to work for achieving the aims of the same community, which they all serve. It takes a whole village to rear a child. However, creating a partnership among all those concerned, including the clients themselves, takes time. Examples of the aims of such a programme include the following:

1　To assure the welfare and security of the children and their parents, by expanding the range of responses for those in need, including mutual assistance from members of the community.

2　To strengthen and enrich the community's support network for parents and children, by increasing the community's cohesiveness and capacity to intervene on behalf of the children and their families.

3　To offer enrichment and nurturing and to reduce gaps in the capacity of children and parents to take advantage of rehabilitation and continuing education.

Operational objectives

The operational objectives are: to increase the number of families supporting or participating in school activities, including assisting those in need; to define the sources of information and measurement tools; to evaluate information from questionnaires for parents and reports of those who are conducting the programmes.

The central ideas of the operational objectives are to define the needs and responses of the residents and to activate staff leaders who are credible in the community. The school is the central source for revealing risk and dangerous situations and the recruitment and utilisation of community resources in order to provide support and assistance for individuals in crisis situations and those with difficulties functioning.

The programme's potential partners

The formal systems which provide the programmes' potential partners include the community government authority, local and government education systems and welfare systems, as well as physical and mental health systems, the local and government legal system and the Israeli police department.

As well as the range of formal systems, there is also a variety of informal systems, for example, residents (youth and families), business and crafts organisations and individuals, along with public associations and voluntary organisations. There are the traditional and religious frameworks as well as locally elected public figures.

There are clusters of preventative services which can also be involved, including in-school and after-school tutoring, drug-free recreation opportunities, programmes for 'latchkey' children and pre-employment and job placement services.

13

■ ■ ■

South Africa: Educational Leadership and the Community

C.J. Gerda Bender and Jan Heystek

The South African education context

The South African Minister of Education has identified the school–community relationship as one of the priorities for education, namely that schools should be the centres of community life (Department of Education, 1999: 9). At present in South Africa the priority of the school–community relationship is becoming a reality by implementing Tirisano, the school effectiveness programme, in all provinces. This means that parents and community members are officially involved in the whole school evaluation and school improvement programmes. Through these programmes we are slowly building a culture of parental and community involvement (Department of Education, 2002a). The Minister of Education stated in his report on *Call to Action: Mobilising Citizens to Build a South African Education and Training System for the 21st Century*:

> *The school will truly become a centre of community and cultural life if its facilities are being put to use for youth and adult learning, community meetings, music and drama, sports and recreation. An idle school is a vulnerable place, inviting vandalism. A busy school is a place the community will protect, because it is theirs. There is a role in a community school for religious bodies, businesses, cultural groups, sports clubs and civic associations, both to serve their own requirements and to contribute to the school's learning programme both in and out of school hours.*

(Department of Education, 1999: p.9)

The communities within which schools are located strongly influence their development and vice versa. This is a basic ecosystemic understanding. The local community reflects values, norms and conditions common to the broader community and to the social system as a whole. These in turn are reflected in the school. The reciprocal or reverse process also holds true (Donald et al., 1999).

The school–community relationship always needs to be considered in the broader social context. Problems that a school faces need to be analysed and addressed within an understanding of broader social issues, particularly those involving power relationships. In South Africa, it is critical to understand how the dynamics of race, social class, gender and other areas of exploitation and oppression in society as a whole influence what happens in every school. Unless these issues are understood in their broader context, they are unlikely to be addressed in any one school in an effective way.

Schools are part of the community – and the economic and political system – in addition to being part of the larger departmental education management and governance system. The location of the school in the larger system has implications for the effectiveness of governance and management because it is at this level that education policies are actually implemented. For the schools to achieve goals that are pedagogically sound, and which governance and management should aid, communities, school districts, departments of education and the government must have a suitable governance and management culture and capacity. One is overestimating what schools can do if one overlooks the role played by the other sub-systems in successful school governance and management. Problems of crime, vandalism, gangsterism, community apathy, inadequate finances in the department of education, teacher militancy, violence, ethnic division, decline in economic resources, unemployment and others, not only affect the immediate community in which they occur, but also have a bearing on effective school governance and management (Ngcongo and Chetty, 2000: 80). It is against such a background that Ngcongo (1997) argues for the establishment of strong and sustainable partnerships between schools, education departments, local communities and business in the transformation, governance and management of schools.

The aims of schooling have been and continue to be reshaped. All these endeavours are initiated by the state with opportunities for public input. School education is not to be offered for the school's sake but for the child, family, community and the whole social system. It is offered for the holistic development of the child (intellectual, cultural, moral, emotional, socio-economic, physical development). In South Africa, the parent community as well as the learner population in schools are changing rapidly. The school caters for learners from diverse societies in terms of culture, race, moral–religious values and beliefs (Rambiyana and Kok, 2002: 10). The authors hold the ecosystemic perspective as reference for education, stating that education is a function of home learning, school learning and community learning.

The aim of this chapter is to present a broad perspective and understanding of education in South Africa followed by a discussion on the school–community partnerships.

The education system in South Africa

The South African education system is in a state of transition. Laws, rules, regulations and policies regarding education have been drafted on an unprecedented scale. Since 1994 a number of education acts have been passed by parliament: South African Qualifications Authority (SAQA) Act 58 of 1995; Labour Relations Act 66 of 1995; National Education Policy Act 27 of 1996; South African Schools Act 84 of 1996; Education Laws Amendment Act of November 1997; Higher Education Act 101 of 1997; Further Education and Training (FET) Act 98 of 1998; Employment of Educators (EEA) Act 76 of 1998; and Employment Equity Act 55 of 1998. The Act most relevant for this chapter is the South African Schools Act (SASA) 84 of 1996 and a brief description will follow under education policy (see p.147).

South Africa's education system accommodates more than 12.5 million learners. There is a sizeable and growing private school and college sector (Department of Education, 2002b).Formal education can be categorised into sectors and levels. The sectors, which are closely linked to particular levels, are public ordinary school education, independent school education, special school education, technical college education, teacher training and technikon and university training. A public school may be an ordinary public school or a public school for learners with special education needs. The levels are pre-primary, primary, secondary and higher education. General and further education and training are concerned with all aspects of school education, Adult Basic Education and Training (ABET), community education, Early Childhood Development, technical college education and distance education.

The South African education system is divided into three levels: the national, provincial and local (or school) levels (see Table 13.1, p.144), for a schematic representation of the education management and governance system.

Table 13.1: The governance, structure and functioning of Education Support Services (ESS) in South Africa
Source: Adapted from Mashile (2000: 92); Lazarus and Donald (1995: 48). Envisaged by the NCESS/NCSNET (1997).

NATIONAL LEVEL		
Head of Department of Education	**Forums** Disabled People's Organisations (DPOs) Non-Governmental Organisations (NGOs)	* Ensure accommodation of diversity. * Removal of barriers in education and training.
Co-ordinating Structure: Each of the six sections of the Department of Education represented.	**National ESS council**, comprising senior representatives from each ESS area and from relevant national organisations.	
PROVINCIAL LEVEL		
Member of Executive Council (Education)	**Forums** Provincial Education Departments (PEDs), DPOs, NGOs	* Capacity building for district offices.
Co-ordinating Structure: Each of the six sections of the Department of Education are represented.	**Provincial ESS council**, comprising senior representatives from each ESS area and from other relevant provincial organisations.	
DISTRICT LEVEL (Community Centre)		
Several district offices per province	* Support CLBTs. * Develop preventative/developmental programmes. * Individual assessment of learners (only when asked by CLBT).	
Support Personnel: Psychologists, doctors, nurses, social workers, etc.	**District/Community ESS council**, comprising representatives from each ESS area and relevant organisations.	
SCHOOL LEVEL (Centre of Learning)		
School Governing Boards (SGBs)	* Identify, assess and support learners (LBED).	
Centre of Learning Based Team (CLBT): Mainly educators, although others can also be represented.	**ESS sub-committee**, comprising representatives from the school's ESS team, principal, teachers, parents, relevant community organisations and learners.	

National level

At the national level the Ministry of Education has been established. The Ministry comprises the Minister of Education, the Deputy Minister of Education, advisors and administrative staff. In terms of the Constitution, a minister is accountable personally to the president and the cabinet for the administration of his/her portfolio. The Department of Education is part of the organisational structure of the Public Service and is headed by a director-general assisted by deputies. The mission of the department is to ensure that all South Africans receive lifelong education and training of high quality. The functions of the department include:

- provision of educational policy support to the department;
- planning, co-ordination, development and management of the higher education system;
- development, evaluation and maintenance of a national policy, programmes and systems for general and further education and training;
- management of human resources in the education sector and the rendering of corporate services.

The department is divided into four main branches each headed by a deputy director-general:

- Systems and Planning: provides policy support services to the department.
- Higher Education: plans, co-ordinates, develops and manages the higher education system.
- General and Further Education and Training: develops, researches, evaluates and maintains national policy and systems for general and further education and training.
- Education Human Resources and Corporate Services: manages human resources in the education sector and renders corporate services.

In addition, there are two other branches headed by directors, the Parliamentary Office and the Education Department Support Unit (EDSU). The purpose of the Parliamentary Office is to render services to the director-general and the Department of Education. The EDSU's purpose is to render support services for the transformation and organisational development of the provinces (Mda and Mothata, 2000: 3).

Provincial level

Each of the nine South African provinces has a Member of Executive Council (MEC) responsible for education in the province. The Provincial Education Departments (PEDs) are responsible for the general administration and management of education institutions (other than universities and technikons) in their provinces and the setting and administering of provincial examinations, in accordance with national policy and other relevant statutory provisions. These include the general provision of education (e.g. provision of resources and employment of educators). The PEDs can promulgate their own acts in education which must be within the framework of national education policy (Mda and Mothata, 2000: 4).

Local level (school level)

At this level, the governance of schools is the responsibility of School Governing Bodies (SGBs). These structures are made up of elected representatives from parents, educators, non-educators and learners. Learners can only be represented in schools offering Grade 8 and higher. The functions of these governing bodies include:

- determining the language and the admission policy of the school;
- drafting and adopting a constitution for the school;
- drawing up a code of conduct for learners;
- preparing budgets;
- developing a mission statement for the school;
- making recommendations to the provincial head of department on the appointment of educators and non-educators (Mda and Mothata, 2000: 4; (Department of Education, 2002b).

The school governing body, led by parents, exercises a trust on behalf of the parents of the community and functions as the indispensable link between the school and the community. This is a new concept for most communities in South Africa. Therefore a great effort is put forward to ensure that governing bodies, especially in poor communities, are given the support they need to become strong and viable. The Ministry of Education has an interest in ensuring that all public school governing bodies become members of governing body associations, which can represent them in dealing with the education authorities and provide valuable technical support to their members (Department of Education, 1999: 8).

The school principal, who represents the provincial department of education and is head of the school management team, has the crucial role of professional and administrative leadership and is responsible for the standard of learning and teaching in the school. The principal needs to forge a working partnership with the governing body, so that they can jointly serve the vision and mission of the school in the community. Both parties require guidance in exercising their respective roles. It is therefore important that the school leadership team, headed by the principal and the governing body in each public school, is given the opportunity to create a sense of common purpose and mutual support (Department of Education, 1999: 9).

Education policy

The South African Schools Act (SASA) 84 of 1996 was passed by the Department of National Education and its aims are:

- to provide a uniform system for the organisation, governance and funding of schools;
- to establish minimum and uniform norms and standards for the provision of education at schools;
- to ensure the provision of quality education across the school system;
- to amend or repeal certain laws relating to school.

The content of the Act includes stipulations regarding (a) admission to public schools; (b) ages for compulsory attendance; (c) discipline; (d) language policy in public schools; (e) freedom of conscience and religion in public schools. Guidelines are provided for the establishment and maintenance of public schools; the status of public schools; the composition, powers and duties of school governing bodies; the closure of public schools; funding of public schools; payment of school fees. Guidelines are also provided for the establishment and registration of, and subsidies for, independent schools.

Schools as centres of the community

A functioning school is a true community in its own right, and an indispensable centre for the wider community's social and cultural needs and interests. But for this to happen, we need peace and stability in schools and in the environment of schools. Schools must therefore be rendered safe for learners, teachers, staff and the community.

(Department of Education, 1999 p.10)

It would be incompatible with the notion of 'community', as well as a denial of basic rights, if public schools ignored their responsibility to children with special needs, and their parents. Public schools should be, by definition, inclusive, humane and tolerant communities. Schools must be assisted to create an enabling environment for parents whose children have physical disabilities or other special needs, so that early identification can result in appropriate advice and placement. To the greatest extent compatible with the interests of such children, the ordinary public school in the community should welcome them and provide for them.

(Department of Education, 1999 p.10)

At the heart of the school as an organisation are leadership and management. These two factors hold together and develop all other aspects. Leadership and management are not only the concern of principals or heads of department; all teachers are leaders and managers, within their classrooms, in the school and in the community at large. Learners likewise need to be given opportunities to develop leadership and management skills and strategies as basic life skills. An effective school is one in which leadership and management capacity are developed in all members of the school community through ongoing personal and professional development and structural support.

School–community partnerships

School

Schools are organisations and organisations are systems. In every organisation there are particular aspects or elements which make up that organisation, and each of these needs to be functioning well if the school is to be effective in achieving its goals. Any poorly functioning element will have a ripple effect through the whole system. Likewise, any well-functioning element will facilitate the positive development of the school as a whole (De Jong, 1996). The goals and purpose of a school, influenced by national and regional policies, affect the particular way in which the school as an organisation structures itself and functions (Jordaan and Faasen, 1993). Schools are open–closed social systems. This means that they attend to their unique business and are not insulated from what happens around and therefore are in continuous interaction with other systems outside them, including the local and broader community, and the social system as a whole. Schools are complex social organisations, with many people and functions. Various elements of the school as an organisation can, however, be identified: namely the culture and identity of the school, strategy, structure and procedures, technical support, human resources, leadership and management, the social context (whole social system). These different elements are inter-dependent and continuously interact with one another (Donald et al., 1999).

Community

Many problems experienced by learners and teachers, and by parents and families, are related to a conflict between the values of the school and the values of the students as reflected in their particular cultural, family and peer group backgrounds. In South Africa, the language issue and values associated with it have created much tension in the past. These issues are still far from resolved in the present. Value conflicts are also common in relation to religion, whether and how sexual education is handled in school, and around the content and relevance of the syllabus. Generally, parents who have the choice send their children to schools that most closely reflect their own values, be it religious, social class or language. This is not always possible, however.

Issues of race and the associated value conflicts in South Africa are of particular concern. Although the legacy of apartheid is specific to South Africa, the issue of racial integration has been a concern in many other countries. This raises some important issues which have to be faced in the classroom, the school as a whole, the families and communities concerned and of course at the level of policy making. It brings with it many problems and challenges, particularly because issues of social class are often embedded in racial dynamics. The move towards racial integration in South African schools, even if slow, is crucial to bridging conflicts of value in the society as a whole. It creates its own particular challenges, however. For example, a working-class, black learner who attends a traditionally middle-class, predominantly white school often has great difficulty with fitting in socially and academically. There are many reasons for this, but a conflict of values is likely to be one of the main reasons. Further difficulty may arise if the learner, in trying to live up to the values and expectations of the school, then becomes estranged from his own family. Such issues need to be addressed sensitively and perceptively in schools. They constitute one of the major challenges if school–community relationships are to break down the barriers that have been established in the past. Although it is easier if there is a match between community and school values, this does not mean that working-class children should only go to working-class schools (Siann and Ugwuegbu, 1980 in Donald et al., 1999). Rather, it suggests that schools, and the education system as a whole, have a tremendous task of addressing diversity across social class, race, language and other categories, so that schools do in fact respect the values reflected in different communities (Donald et al., 1999).

Community involvement in schools

Parent involvement

Along with the democratic process in South Africa, there has rightfully been an emphasis on parents and communities having more involvement in and control over the development of their schools (Department of Education, 1996). The South African Schools Act of 1996 officially establishes the priority of the Minister of Education regarding the relationship between parents, the community and schools. According to this act, parents with children in a specific school must be elected as legal members of the particular school's official school governing body (SGB). However, parent involvement needs to go beyond election onto the school's governing body and participation in parent–teacher meetings. There are many other constructive contributions to the life of the school, which might include:

- involvement in lifeskills education programmes and acting as teacher aides to help address special needs in the classroom or school;
- involvement in the teaching of particular skills, topics, or areas of information (among any body of parents is a wide range of knowledge, skills and expertise which might be shared with learners);
- involvement in fund raising for the school;
- involvement in sport, cultural and other extramural activities;
- involvement in maintaining the equipment and facilities of the school.

Across the world, there is evidence that constructive involvement of parents in the life of the school holds great benefits for the school, the learners, the parents and their mutual relationships (Bauch, 1994: 53–7; Khan, 1996: 61; Rambiyana and Kok, 2002; Wolfendale, 1992: 55).

Success at school depends on the triangle of interaction of three components: the teacher, the parent and the child (learner). A working partnership between parents and teachers enhances the probabilities or chances of successfully helping the child and getting involved in school activities. Parents could, for example, be involved in such a partnership on three levels, namely: helping and showing an interest in the homework of their children; assisting the school with specific tasks; and serving on the official governing body. Academic activities must be the focus point at all these levels of the partnerships.

Other non-parental members of the community may also be members of the school governing body, and usually such persons will be co-opted because of their expertise. The principal is an ex officio member of the governing body. It is this official representation that is important for the school manager in order to manage effectively in favour of the school and community. One of the best ways to improve education is to strengthen parents' involvement.

Parents as supporters

Involvement at the first level includes parents as monitors and supervisors of learners' homework and progress. Parents also assist their children with homework and assess their progress in the school (Bauch, 1994: 53–7; Khan, 1996: 61; Wolfendale, 1992: 55).

Every parent can be actively involved at this level. The level of literacy of parents may be a problem, but even if parents cannot read or write they can assist their children. Their interest and motivation will have a positive effect on the standard of the work of their children. This is the level where parental involvement really can improve the standard of education. According to Khan (1996: 59) and Gene and Stoneman (1995: 569), parental involvement in school activities has a positive effect on the academic achievements of learners. If parents experience the positive results of their involvement, it may motivate them to be more involved in other school activities. In this way the school and parents may benefit from improved involvement.

Educational leaders must assist parents so that parents will know how to assist their children. Effective communication and regular meetings between parents and teachers will assist in improving parental involvement at this level.

Parents as assistants and participants

At this level parents are on the continuum from parents who voluntarily assist teachers on field trips, to parents who serve as aides to teachers in the classroom. Parents may also be officially employed as teachers in schools (Bauch,1994: 53–7; Khan, 1996: 61; Wolfendale, 1992: 55).

At this level of involvement, parents will probably need more skills and knowledge than at the previous level. The numbers of skills and levels of knowledge of parents will depend on the type of school, whether it is a primary or secondary school and with what parents will be involved. Parents with specific skills and knowledge, not necessarily academic knowledge, may join children on field trips. This will enable teachers to spend more time in the school to complete administrative tasks or to prepare for future lessons.

To assist teachers in the classroom will involve some training (empowerment) for teachers and parents. This type of assistance may be more effective in primary schools than in secondary schools. It may range from listening to learners reading and assisting with group activities to the supervision of a class if the teacher is absent. It will be important to select the correct parents and work strictly according to rules and regulations because there is legislation that may have an influence on the involvement of parents in classroom activities. Factors that may inhibit effective involvement at this level include:

- teachers being afraid that parents may challenge their authority and knowledge base in the class;
- parents not having sufficient knowledge to be of effective assistance in the classroom.

This type of assistance may be especially important in classrooms with a large number of learners where teachers want to use group work as an instruction method. This will ensure that learners receive more individual attention and in turn will improve the standard and quality of education.

Parents as managers

The third level of involvement is when parents are part of official governing structures in schools and are initiating and implementing change in schools (Bauch,1994: 53–7; Khan, 1996: 61; Wolfendale, 1992: 55).

This level will most probably demand the highest level of competencies, skills and knowledge from parents if they want to be effectively involved at the management level of schools. Parents who are illiterate or not well educated may either not have a huge influence on the management of the school or the principal and teachers may dominate them. This domination or feelings of inferiority towards the teachers and the principal may result in very limited or no participation by parents. Parents who lack skills and knowledge should be empowered. By empowering parents and treating them as equals, such parents can make a positive contribution to the management of schools, even if they are not highly skilled.

Schools must ensure that the necessary structures are in place to accommodate parents who want to be involved in school activities. Schools, especially principals, must initiate activities that will motivate parents to participate. Often parents do not know why and how they should be involved in school activities. Schools must empower parents with the knowledge and opportunities to become involved in school activities. Although the departments of education are in the process of training members of the governing bodies, it must be a continuous process because new members are constantly being elected to governing bodies (every three years).

One of the authors, Heystek (1999) carried out research on the reasons why parents do not participate actively in school activities attended by their children. The respondents mentioned the following reasons – in order of priority from the most important to the least important:

- Parents' negative attitude towards the school. Parents feel that the teachers are qualified and salaried for their task. Parents apparently do not even know that they should and can be involved in school activities, or how they can be involved.
- Parents' feelings of inferiority towards the teachers. The study showed that the parents did not consider themselves capable of assisting the teachers, while the teachers indicated that most parents lacked the skills and knowledge to be effective assistants in the academic field.
- Knowledge, skills and competencies of parents and teachers.
- Demographic reasons. Although these reasons are not high on the list of important factors, they are more important in rural areas where parents do not have transport.
- Teachers' negative actions and attitudes. The fact that some activities such as committees in the school governing body did not even exist at most schools could well mean that schools do not make provision for structures or opportunities of parental participation. Parents' low level of participation, even where there were structures or opportunities available for participation, could indicate that the schools did not adequately encourage their parents to get involved, or perhaps even, that teachers did not want the parents to be actively involved in school activities (Heystek, 1999: 109–13).

Broader community involvement

How can the broader community be involved in the school? Parents are certainly important, but there are others who might be involved, including:

- religious, civic and other leaders in the community;
- relevant non-government and community-based organisations (NGOs and CBOs), particularly those that deal with issues directly relating to the life of the school;
- people in the helping professions;
- indigenous or traditional healers, particularly within the notion of inclusive Education Support Services (ESS);
- the formal and informal business sector, as well as the professional sector, particularly in terms of facilitating a closer linkage between education and work.

Community representation also needs to be reflected in the governance structures of the school. Representation from and involvement of all of the above sectors are also particularly important within the context of Education Support Services (De Jong et al., 1995). The scope of ESS, according to the Ministry of Education (1996) encompasses at least all education-related health and social work, vocational and general guidance and counselling, as well as other psychological programmes and services, and services to all learners, including learners with special education needs (ELSEN) in and outside mainstream schools. Table 13.1 (see p.144) provides a broad picture of the proposed interacting levels of governance, structure and functioning of Education Support Services (ESS) in South Africa. The role of councils at the national and provincial level is more directed at overall policy development and co-ordination, curricular planning and resource allocation. The role at district/community centre and school level is more specific to the management and co-ordination of practice. The importance of including parents and representatives of relevant community organisations cannot be over-emphasised. The area of education support services provides one vital possibility for developing closer school–community relationships since the issues which are of central concern to Education Support Services are also areas in which parents and community members can make particular relevant contributions (Lazarus and Donald, 1995: 48).

Apart from all these benefits, it is also important for youth to learn about life in their particular communities, and the best people to present a realistic view of 'the world out there' are those who live and work out there. We are so used to thinking of education as something that must take place in a particular building called a school. Learners could be provided with numerous invaluable educational experiences outside the school building. One of the ways in which a teacher can use the community as a setting for learning is through work placements, apprenticeships or service learning. Learners are established in work placements for short or longer periods of time in formal or informal work environments. In this way they can observe and experience different career and work options, as well as learn specific work-related skills.

The school's contribution to the community

There are many ways in which the school can help to build its community. Schools are expensive facilities which have historically only been used at certain times of the day. One obvious way to become a useful resource in the community is to find ways to use the school and its facilities for local community education and development. This requires administrative co-ordination, but the possibilities are endless.

Adult and community education classes in the evenings, at weekends and during school holidays are immediate possibilities. Use of halls and sports fields for local community events is another possible way of sharing resources.

Schools can provide cultural activities that would further the development of the local community. The school could be a centre for art, music and other cultural activities. Learners and teachers may play a role in such activities, but they need not feel they have to take on the full responsibility and time involvement. There are always others who will be prepared to do this.

Educational programmes for parents and general community members are a particularly valuable resource that schools can offer. Teachers have a great deal to contribute in this regard. The education support arm of the school could play an especially important role in programmes relating to problems such as drug abuse, life skills, parenting and sexuality.

The relationship between the school and its community can be developed through various indirect ways as well. The more the school managers, teachers and learners are involved in the development of their community and the more community people are drawn into the life of the school, the more chance there is of building a strong and constructive relationship (Donald et al., 1999).

Strategies and principles for best practices

School leaders and community members share a common purpose and vision: ensuring a positive future for children, their families and their communities. Educators and community members can work together when they approach each other with respect, take time to build trust and define ways that their assets can be used to reach shared goals. Education managers aspiring to be educational leaders must be skilled builders of community. Teamwork and collaborative efforts are necessary in creating a community-oriented school where all members are guided by common vision and purpose.

From a South African perspective and experience on whole school and school–community development, the following principles with particular relevance apply:

1 *Developing a sense of ownership of the school and its goals.* This is crucial in learners, parents and other members of the community. It is the only way a joint sense of commitment to dealing with both the origins and results of contextual disadvantage can be developed. To achieve a sense of ownership, a lot of determined action will be necessary both within the school and between school and community. Relevance and flexibility must be introduced into the curriculum so that it meets the needs of all learners.

The basic rules to building the ownership are to find out about each other's interests and needs; reach out to potential partners on their own turf with specific offers of assistance; spell out the purpose and terms of joint efforts, including who will do what, by when; work out the problems as they arise and change the approach when necessary. Build out from success by sharing positive results and encouraging expanded efforts.

2 *Developing a positive school culture.* In particular, making school a positive experience for children who have suffered social and economic disadvantages is a difficult but very important task for school managers and teachers to undertake (Donald et al., 1999).

3 *Effective organisation, management and leadership.* These are central to the development of educational institutions that are able to accommodate a diverse range of learning needs. In this regard the abilities of education managers to manage and provide appropriate support services to address learning difficulties and exclusion should be greatly enhanced. Education managers should participate in ongoing professional development programmes that will assist them to develop management and leadership skills which are essential to accommodating diversity and addressing learning difficulties and exclusion.

Further, guidelines for best practices should focus on prevention. Preventing the complex, wide-ranging, and interacting contextual causes of development and educational risk is an immense task. It is one that has to be tackled at all levels of society, from the broadest aims of reconstruction and development, to specific and local health and educational interventions. The following principles may be useful in shaping a school manager's specific engagements with prevention:

1 *Work with others (networking).* Seek the advice, help and support of colleagues, ESS personnel, community workers and NGOs. This will draw you into a network of others who can give you both strength and direction in what you do. In this way a leader can build a team, a shared commitment and professional effectiveness. Such a network also helps to avoid wrong or inappropriate action.

2 *Involve the learners in preventive action in the local community (service learning).* Older learners can become engaged in life skills education programmes with pre-schoolers, for instance. Developing a sense of community responsibility and caring is very much part of the value of *ubuntu*, which is an age-old African term for humaneness – for caring, sharing and being in harmony with all of creation. As an ideal, it promotes co-operation between individuals, cultures and nations, which may be of such importance in South Africa as a developing society.

3 *Examine your own values and assumptions about what you believe is 'good' and 'bad' and be open to the values of others.* The emphasis here is that the greatest flexibility is required if preventive action is to be negotiated, owned and effectively carried through in a truly collaborative way.

4 *Work actively through the notion of resilience and protective factors.* Building on the assets that people already have, or might be helped to develop, is particularly effective as a strategy for helping people to cope with stress. (For example, work on the value of social support networks and how to develop them.)

5 *Always be aware of the factors that cause the stress in the first place.* Preventive action, particularly collective action, which addresses these factors at school, in the community and particularly at state level, needs to be taken at the same time and with equal vigour.

6 *Build positive school–community partnerships.* School experiences and the role of the manager can be important protective factors in the resilience of contextually disadvantaged children. This depends entirely on the school experience being positive and affirming. Critical dimensions of prevention, therefore, are working on the whole school context itself (Donald et al., 1999).

In an endeavour to build strong community–school partnerships, the authors recommend three interrelated approaches:

1 *The school should be a community centre.* It should serve both as a resource for lifelong learning and as a vehicle for the delivery of a wide range of services (including education support services). School resources such as buildings, technology and well-educated staff can provide a range of educational and retraining opportunities for the community, for example, adult and community education programmes.

2 *Sociological inquiry into the community.* For example, learners study the community by assessing needs and mapping assets, monitoring environmental patterns and documented social developmental community projects through interviews and essays (doing research).

3 *School-based enterprise (SBE).* This places a major emphasis on developing entrepreneurial skills whereby learners not only identify potential service needs in their rural communities, but also establish a business to address those needs.

These three interrelated approaches provide a way to think about how schools and communities can work together for mutual benefit. The values of these community-based learning experiences are the long-term benefits of leadership development, a renewed sense of citizenship and a revitalised sense of community.

References

Bauch, J.P. (1994) 'Categories of parent involvement', *School Community Journal*, 4 (1), 53–60.

De Jong, T. (1996) 'The educational psychologist and school organisation development in the reconstruction of education in South Africa: issues and challenges', *South African Journal of Psychology*, 26, 114–19.

De Jong, T., Ganie, L., Lazarus, S. and Prinsloo, W. (1995) 'Proposed general guidelines for a lifeskills curriculum framework', in A. Gordon (ed.), *Curriculum Frameworks for the General Phase of Education*. Johannesburg: Centre for Education Policy.

Department of Education (1996) *South African Schools Act*. Pretoria: Government Printers.

Department of Education (1999) *Statement of the Minister of Education, Prof. K Asmal: Call to Action: mobilising citizens to build a South African education and training system for the 21st century*. Pretoria: Government Printers.

Department of Eductaion (2002a) *Implementing Tirisano: The School Effectiveness Program. National Conference on Whole School Evaluation*. Pretoria: Department of Education.

Department of Education (2002b) http://www.education.pwv.gov.za. (Visited 12 July 2002.)

Donald, D., Lazarus, S. and Lolwana, P. (1999) *Educational Psychology in Social Context: Challenges of Development, Social Issues and Special Need in Southern Africa*. Cape Town: Oxford University Press.

Gallagher, D.R., Bagin, D. and Kindred, L.W. (1997) *The School and Community Relations*. Boston: Allyn and Bacon.

Gene, H.B. and Stoneman, Z. (1995) 'Linking family processes and academic competence among rural African American youth', *Journal of Marriage and the Family*, 57 (3), 567–79.

Heystek, J. (1999) 'Parents as partners in schools: so important, but why so unreliable?' *Koers*, 64 (1), 97–113.

Jordaan, A. and Faasen, N. (1993) *Whole School Curriculum*. Cape Town: Cape Education Department.

Khan, M.B. (1996) 'Parental involvement in education: possibilities and limitations', *School Community Journal*, 6 (1), 57–68.

Lazarus, S. and Donald, D. (1995) 'The development of education support services in South Africa: basic principles and a proposed model', *South African Journal of Education*, 15 (1), 45–52.

Mashila, O. (2000) 'Education support services', in T.V. Mda and M.S. Mothata, *Critical Issues in South African Education after 1994*. Kenwyn, SA: JUTA.

Mda, T.V. and Mothata, M.S. (2000) *Critical Issues in South African Education after 1994*. Kenwyn, SA: JUTA.

Ngcongo, R.G.P. (1997) 'The role of principals as educational leaders'. Unpublished MEd dissertation. University of Zululand, South Africa.

Ngcongo, R.G.P. and Chetty, K. (2000) 'Issues in school management and governance', in T.V. Mda and M.S. Mothata *Critical Issues in South African Education after 1994*. Kenwyn, SA: JUTA.

NCESS/NCSNET (1997) *Quality Education for All. Overcoming Barriers to Learning and Development*. Report of the National Commission on Special Needs in Education and Training (NCSNET), National Committee on Education Support Services (NCESS). Pretoria: Department of Education.

Rambiyana, N.G. and Kok, J.C. (2002) 'Parents' expectations of public schooling in the Northern Province of South Africa', *South African Journal of Education*, 22 (1), 10–14.

Wolfendale S. (1992) *Empowering Parents and Teachers. Working for Children*, London: Cassell.

14

■ ■ ■

Outgrowing our School Uniform: Reconceptualising the Health and Education Interface

Michelle Anderson

To a child being on the wrong end of the trend is not a sign that it's time to dig in and defend the old position; it's a signal to cut and run. Progress depends on these small acts of treason.

(Lewis, 2002: 12)

Introduction

This chapter explores leadership within the community from the particular perspectives of education and health. Specifically, the chapter provides an overview of the relationship between education and health as it relates to the life outcomes for children and young people. It goes on to identify some recurrent themes to be addressed by both systems, examples of promising practice and some of the barriers to and enablers of reform at the health and education interface. The chapter concludes with a checklist of some palatable and perhaps not so palatable suggestions for a way forward.

The examples and information in this chapter arrive out of a recent Winston Churchill Fellowship to the United Kingdom and Canada and a knowledge of various programmes in Victoria, Australia.

A rationale for a stronger health and education interface

Health and well-being are inseparable to learning and developing for the future (Anderson and Foster, 2001). For most children and young people, continuity of learning is something they take for granted and indeed have a right to expect. However, for an increasing number of children and young people, their access to a continuous learning experience is interrupted. This happens for reasons related to, for example, social and economic disadvantage, family life crises, chronic illness, mental health, experiences at school and relationships with peers. These pressing problems are likely to be compounded if the education and health systems do not effectively build bridges of professional engagement and partnership or, as Caldwell (2000: 2) puts it, we do not become 'effective in spanning the boundaries in the delivery of services in support of "all students in every setting"'.

The interface of health and education has become more entwined and blurred. At its best it reflects a 'no boundaries' approach with a mutually developed understanding and commitment to the joint roles that health and education play in supporting children, young people and their families within their local community. At its worst barriers crop up, with beliefs and ideologies historically related to one or other of the systems leading to competition, rather than shared agendas of support for families (Anderson, 2001).

To suggest that leading change at the health and education interface is going to be easy would be misleading. However, as Regional Director of over 140 primary, secondary and specialist school settings in Victoria, Australia, Steve Marshall says we can continue to jump up and down and go higher and higher, or we can decide to leap forward. One has the appearance of change; the other is about real transformation. The fundamental reason we need to leap forward, as opposed to just do more of the same but better, is that for every success story there are numerous others where circumstances and conditions have had negative impacts on outcomes for the child or young person. In other words, despite in more recent times growing health and education budgets, the problems faced by children and young people are on the increase. These include mental health disorders, chronic illness and literacy disparity based on socioeconomic status (AIHW, 2002). Health and education need jointly to address this problem.

Taking up this challenge a number of programmes and services have been established in Australia, UK and Canada to lead change at the health and education interface; for example, at the Women's and Children's Health,

Royal Children's Hospital Melbourne, University of Melbourne, UltraLab, Essex and Ontario Institute for Studies in Education, Toronto. Some of the characteristics of these new programmes and services include valuing 'consumer' input and participation, maximising the use of information communication technologies, designing more effective communication and programme frameworks across health and education and producing new forms of professional development that meet the changing needs of the professions. These changes are dramatically influencing education for children/young people within, for example, the hospital setting. However, as much as these changes suggest a new future for hospitalised and other children and young people unable to access more traditional pathways of learning, a series of problems remains. These problems are both conceptual and practical.

The conceptual issues range over how to best conceptualise the health and education interface, how to define health, how to transform education for the increasingly large numbers of children and young people disengaged from and disenchanted with traditional school settings, how we conceptualise inclusion, and how to define participants. Also, there is an increased focus on how to conceptualise the new issues emerging as we begin to use the new technologies and understand their capacity. The practical problems relate to: traditional patterns of service and professional attitudes amongst the two sectors; fragmentation within sectors; funding; sustainability of government support of new initiatives; partnerships between health and education, schools and other settings; better ways of involving children, young people and their families; and the use and implementation of technologies and the training of staff.

These conceptual issues and practical problems need to be viewed within a comprehensive evaluation framework. Both education and health are cornerstones within the community for shaping and influencing the outcomes of children and young people. Each draws significant policy, financial, media and research attention. With this attention comes also an increased accountability and impetus to improve service capability and provision and yet a narrow understanding of evaluation persists. We use a range of evaluation methods, such as planning and consulting, but it is the accountability of programmes and services that remains the dominant measure of success. Unfortunately that measure, more often than not, is narrowed to a set of quantifiable data that misses the complexities of real life at the interface of health and education. Accountability is an important component to evaluation but it is just that, a component. A greater range of evaluation methods could be better understood and utilised by education and health and to do this we need to develop our capacity to evaluate jointly programmes and services from their outset.

Waiting for change and the weight of change – it's time to change!

As education and health professionals we have all felt the weight of change. In this context we are probably some of the most adaptable professionals in the workforce. New curriculum, new policies, new referral procedures, new performance measures are just some of the changes that have swept through the systems over the last five years. Changes have often been imposed within a framework that has insufficiently recognised the equal need for implementation support.

While we feel the weight of change, so too do we tend to wait for it. With each new change of government, change of minister or change of organisational structure we wait and brace ourselves for more change. However, as noted in a recent UK publication (NCCSDO, 2001), 'What changes all the time but stays the same?' The answer: the National Health Service. The answer could also read: health and education. No wonder we have felt, at times, burnt out and sceptical about the reasons for and benefits of proposed changes. We get all fired up and excited about a development but, as Fullan (1993) suggests, only reach a superficial level of exploration or implementation before, for example, the funding ceases. The result: change, but fundamentally things remain the same.

To avoid the repetition of sameness masquerading as change, the focus must be on the needs of children/young people. Rather than waiting for change or feeling the weight of change, we as education and health professionals have a significant leadership role to play in the government's setting of and response to key directions. We are in a prime position to comment on the translation of policy into practice and on the further research needs of the field. Up until now this important role has been marginalised and misrepresented to the community. Often concerns about conditions and pay, although very legitimate needs to be addressed, have overshadowed the significant research, policy and practice contributions that professionals are contributing. A reciprocal relationship between government and professions that breaks through that cycle of sameness is required. Encouragingly this is beginning to happen. To illustrate my point, when visiting Canada, a fabulous discussion between school principals and other educational leaders undertaking doctoral studies was taking place (something they were doing in their own time with little support other than their respective organisations' blessing). The discussion was about the type of leadership required in schools today and in the future. Inevitably frustrations about the government's accountability measures and procedures came up in discussion, as did the complexity of schools and their relationship with other services within the community. For a while the discussion seemed to reach a stalemate until one principal shared her strategy to ensure the needs of children are met: 'creative insubordination'. She went on to say that this was not about being disrespectful about the government's requirements but involved not interpreting them so literally. In this instance the principal had moved beyond the technical 'know-how' of leadership to a level of confidence in her ability to anticipate creative ways to meet desired and prescribed outcomes (Beckett, 2000). Leading at the interface of health and education will require professionals to move beyond the technical.

Leading at the health and education interface

A vacuum exists between professionals' 'interest and intent' to have stronger links between health and education and their actual 'capacity and action' to make it happen. Excellent literature is available about community development and the relationship between the determinants of health and education (Bond et al., 2001; Edgar, 2001; Fullan, 2000; Putnam, 2000; Shelton, 2001). Each describes successful schools as having deep roots in community. However, very little literature can be sourced about what the 'interface' of education and health looks like or how it can better jointly operate to improve the life outcomes for children and young people. As key pillars within the community, to understand the health and education interface is also to lead change.

An 'interface' occurs when two things interact and link in such a way that a circuit of power is created to produce a seemingly effortless energy source. We can all remember how, when learning to drive, it seemed incredibly difficult, but when it 'clicked' it seemed perfectly effortless – so much so that when asked to teach or explain the process to another we had trouble trying to make our thoughts and actions explicit. It seems in promoting a stronger interface between health and education we are somewhere between being the novice learner driver and the more experienced driver trying to make explicit our thoughts and actions.

Until recently the systemic links between health and education across policy, practice and research have been somewhat tenuous. More often than not individual relationships and single 'issues' rather than whole of government agendas have driven these links. This level of response was the norm within schools. Interventions tended to look for curriculum solutions, focus on single issues (for example, drugs), be short-term 'add-on' programmes increasing the workload of willing staff, or only identify students 'at risk' (Bond et al., 2001; Glovers et al., 1998).

Emerging themes and examples of promising practice

Worldwide there is evidence of paradigm changes at policy, practice and research levels that will shape and transform our future health and education agenda. In this section I discuss five interrelated and interdependent themes to be addressed if we are to improve the life outcomes of children and young people. Examples of promising practice from the UK, Canada and Australia that address one or more of the themes are also discussed.

Retention and engagement in learning of children and young people

In a recent speech, Estelle Morris, UK Secretary of State for Education and Skills, noted that in the UK 42 per cent of all permanent exclusions from school occur in the first three years of secondary schooling. Of these permanent exclusions, 84 per cent are boys. This situation is not unique to the UK and presents a fundamental challenge for many societies.

Alternative pathways for learning are needed. Characteristically to the fore in the more successful initiatives are the needs of the child or young person, high expectations for the child or young person to own the learning process and outcomes, and collaborative approaches across education, health and the community.

One example is an innovative initiative at Ryerson Polytechnic University, Toronto: Providing Education by Bringing Learning Environments to Students (PEBBLES). Ryerson has successfully developed and trialled video conferencing and robotics technologies to support children in hospital to participate directly in their classroom. The system has two components: one located in hospital and one in the child's school classroom. Principles such as equity and access underpin this student-focused design and use of PEBBLES. The school-based PEBBLES is a colourful yellow egg-shaped unit. The child, in hospital, uses a game-pad to operate the mobile unit's camera which has the capacity to look up and down, right and left, zoom in and out, and a mechanical hand on the side of the unit can be raised, just as the child would do if physically present, to ask a question. Professional development is provided to the teachers and peers to prepare and familiarise them with PEBBLES. Support is also provided to the child within the hospital so they can self-direct their sessions with the class. A negotiated learning plan between the hospital, family, child and teacher is established. Analysis of case study data of PEBBLES in action has shown social, emotional, physical and learning benefits for the child (Fels and Weiss, 2001).

Another example is the work of Ultralab in Essex, UK. The team at Ultrab have investigated, with some highly successful outcomes, an alternative pathway of learning through the online research project 'Notschool.net'. This project, commenced in September 1998, has encouraged 100 young people, phased in over a period of months, to engage in a new learning environment. The young people (termed 'researchers' because they had an active part to play in the project) have at least one thing in common: a traditional school learning environment does not work for them. The reasons for this are diverse, including phobia, disruptive behaviour, illness and pregnancy.

Notschool.net involves a team of people from across education, health (as relevant to the needs of the 'researcher'), Ultralab and the community. The programme provides face-to-face learning opportunities but a distinguishing factor is its provision of IT equipment and 24/7 internet access at the 'researcher's' home. This creates, as the team found, an opportunity for siblings and parents to use the technology and develop their own knowledge and skills.

The 'researchers' enter information into a secure website community and are then encouraged to share their ideas with other 'researchers', mentors (i.e. people with specialist knowledge) and buddies (i.e. successful undergraduate or postgraduate students who act as online friends). The programme builds on the interests and strengths of the 'researcher' with an identified expectation of evidence of activity from the 'researcher' each week, for example, developing an art portfolio. Criteria for interaction between participants were developed, as was an intervention response.

External evaluation of the 'NotSchool.net' initial pilot (Duckworth, 2001) and the subsequent final research phase report (Ultralab, 2001) has found that a number of factors influence the engagement and retention of young people in learning. These factors include: the identification of 'researcher' strengths and interests; development of support networks at home, community and online; appropriate installation and training in the use of the equipment; high expectations of regular contribution from all participants in the programme; and the use of terminology that is deemed non-threatening, inclusive and respectful to the contributions of all participants. Time to establish links between health, community and education services and with the 'researcher' was important. Typically it took three months to engage the researchers. Once engaged, learning was rapid, with requests for access to accreditation routes.

Inclusion policies and practices

Retention and engagement of children and young people in learning is dependent on the conceptual and practical approach to inclusion. Defining, understanding and implementing a framework of inclusion that encompasses the needs of children, adolescents and their families is complex. Health tends to emphasise the developmental needs of the child or young person, whereas education tends to emphasise inclusive attitudes and practices with regard to teaching and learning, and to academic achievement.

To add further complexity to the views and approaches put forward about inclusion is the larger social context of exclusion. 'There are approximately eleven million children in England [and] four million of them are living in families with less than half the average household income' (DoH, 2000: 1). Edgar (2001) notes that in Australia 770,000 children live solely with one parent while Dwyer and Wyn's (2001) research reveals a chaotic, complex and non-linear life pathway for young people that firmly establishes patterns of work and study whilst still at school. These statistics and research are a salient reminder that an agenda for an inclusive community cannot be viewed in isolation of changes in family and work life in society in general.

Inclusion is high on the agenda for governments in the UK, Australia and Canada. There has been a shift in viewing inclusion as only for those at the fringe or 'at risk' to meaning inclusion for all children. However, tension still surrounds the intention and reality of achieving 'success for all'. Many working at the frontline of health and education express a level of scepticism about government commitments in this area.

Professionals in both health and education, whilst wanting to be enthused by the 'inclusion' agenda, are cautious in praising this direction, worried it may turn out to be efficiency driven rather than child outcome driven. This becomes particularly evident when speaking to teachers about inclusion and student academic achievement, and about inclusion and resource allocation. Both impact on intent and actual capacity to develop inclusive environments for children and young people.

Within this reality, however, there are a number of interesting joint initiatives at a policy, service and professional development level that are tackling head-on the tensions that surround policies of inclusion.

For example, in the UK the Department of Health provides an annual grant to each local authority. The local authority must use this money to demonstrate how they are addressing the issue of 'social exclusion' through policy and practice. Until recently local authorities responded to a questionnaire sent back to the Department of Health. Significant learning opportunities for the health and education system and the local authorities were missed because of inadequate information sharing. Enter the National Children's Bureau (NCB), London. NCB, amongst many of its other significant policy and research initiatives, now has the responsibility to collect, analyse and advise government on the findings of these local authority initiatives. The NCB is in a position to use the data to act as a critical friend, distribute information about examples of good practice and advise government of particular actions or predictive outcomes.

Another example can be found at the Royal Children's Hospital (RCH) in Melbourne. Traditionally, hospital schools have operated as a parallel practice to the child or young person's school of origin. For 30 years, the Royal Children's Hospital School in Melbourne played an important part in providing continuity of education. Children and young people from Prep to Year 12 who were required to stay in hospital for long periods were provided with an educational service at the hospital. Teachers from the then Victorian Department of Education worked in ward areas, predominantly at the bedside and in classrooms located within the hospital. The school's role evolved but the time came in 1998 to acknowledge changes in the delivery of health services over the past two decades. These changes have seen hospital admission trends towards reduced inpatient stays and increased outpatient or multiple admissions, technological advances offering increased options for mitigating distance and isolation, and the implementation of conceptual frameworks that are weighted towards prevention and early intervention (Closs, 2000).

The RCH changed its approach to the education of children when a joint venture of the hospital and the Department of Education and Training (DE&T) saw the launch in 1999 of a Royal Children's Hospital Education Institute (RCHEI). Governed by a board of directors comprising senior health, education and community members, the institute's message is simple: a child or young person's connection is with their own peers and school community. To support this message the first phase of the institute's work has seen a refocusing on strengthening the capacity of professionals, equipping them to better support children and young people; the encouragement of collaborative relationships with the children or young people themselves and their families; and research into creative solutions to bridge gaps caused by distance, health circumstances and peer or professional understandings.

Another area of relevance has been the reframing of practice through professional development. Key government documents in student welfare within the Victorian context have been influential in shaping views about the role of schools and school personnel and their relationship to health services (Department of Education, 1998a, 1998b). This has had a significant impact on professionals' understandings of inclusive practices, but less impact on professionals' capacity to actually reorientate service provision towards a prevention and early intervention focus. To address this issue the Catholic Education Commission of Victoria (CECV) in 1999, as part of a Youth Services Strategy on Mental Health, commenced a strategic sponsorship of teachers in leadership positions with the University of Melbourne's Faculty of Education. This alliance with the university supported experienced teachers to undertake and complete the Postgraduate Diploma in Educational Studies (Student Welfare). At the beginning of 2002 over 400 teachers had participated in the course with a further 100 teachers expected to complete the course by the end of the same year. The programme seeks to equip teachers with technical skills in counselling and interpersonal and group processes but with equivalent emphasis on student welfare and the socio-political context, school–community partnerships and organisational change (Freeman and Strong, 2002).

Partnership process and outcomes

Transformation of communities requires a transformation in our understanding of what constitutes a community partnership. We have probably been involved in projects, programmes or initiatives with a group collectively called a partnership. However, problems can arise if the terms of partnerships are not clear. When we unpack what is happening in our approaches at the interface we find often that health undervalues education and education treats health as an event to be managed. This observation might provoke a defensive response from those working in health and education, because at the core is our desire to do what's best for a child. But that is not at all what is being questioned. What is being questioned is the context in which we work as health and education professionals. Usually we are brought together across the health and education interface out of a reaction, necessity, situation or circumstance to do with a child or family. But the sort of partnership needed to bring about deep change is one that is about a sustained commitment. If the relationship remains at the superficial or event management level, both systems miss out on important opportunities to enhance their working relationships, and more significantly, improve the outcomes and experiences for children and families who have little choice but to negotiate their way between the systems. An explanation for the missed opportunity lies in the recognition that both systems are established on a platform of hierarchy and history that works against implementing current theories of inclusion and partnership. Thankfully, this is changing. In the UK, next to the significant investment in developing community partnerships, is the significant investment being made in the role of leadership. One such example is the joint work of the University of Manchester, the National College of School Leadership and head teachers from nine schools.

This 18-month research project is focusing on 'Linking Behaviour, Learning and Leadership' to increase the capacity of schools to respond to the needs of all learners. The method of collaborative research being implemented has evolved out of other work at the university (i.e. National Research Networks, a project of the Economic and Social Research Council's Teaching and Learning Research Programme) and from the identified questions of participating schools (Ainscow, 2002; Ainscow et al., 2001).

The researchers provide theoretical frameworks and processes to assist schools in identifying, implementing and evaluating different needs and strategies. The schools propose questions they would like to see answered in their particular contexts. Over a period of two days, three school representatives from the eight other schools involved visit and gather evidence to support that school's inquiry. Then all the schools and researchers get together and support each other to work through the evidence collected as it relates to the questions being proposed.

Six think-tank sessions take place each year, with all researchers and school leaders meeting to discuss draft materials around particular questions being addressed by a school. Various case studies addressing such topics as partnerships and data collection and uses are being developed, and it has been proposed they be used through the National Professional Qualifications in Headship (NPQH) programmes and the website of the National College of School Leadership. A framework of themes and issues from all the case studies and think-tank sessions that other leaders can access is also being developed. The success to date of this collaborative research approach has been linked to such things as: being head teacher led; the practical and personal relevance of the work being done; the sustained opportunities for collaboration; the willingness of participants to be 'vulnerable'; and a national interest and distribution base for new ideas and insights.

The success of this type of collaboration also draws attention to how we as professionals learn best. Professionals' engagement in learning is a crucial element in influencing outcomes for children and young people.

Professionals' engagement in learning

An observation is that while health expects its professionals to move on, education typically does not. I have encountered three reasons for the attitude in education that professionals should stay put: that the system can ill afford movement because of the critical shortage of qualified, experienced and available teaching staff; that encouraging movement leads teachers not to return to the classroom; and that, for many people, becoming a teacher is a vocation and lifestyle choice.

When considering what actions to take to strengthen the interface of health and education it could be proposed that more opportunities be given for sustained inter-professional collaboration and staff development. My experience and observation is that we pay lip-service to the notion of 'sustained' and that conceptual and practical reasons (e.g. ideas of what constitutes a professional development framework at the interface and the practicalities of support through time and funding) exist as to why this is the case. As Barber (1997: 224) noted: 'the first step towards making teaching attractive should therefore be an attempt to convey the reality more accurately'. This reality for teachers is complex and, just as it is for their students, extends beyond the classroom into the realms of health and the broader community.

What I find fascinating is that the very basic need of time is not being sufficiently addressed. Building partnerships of inter-professional collaboration and learning is an intellectual investment that takes time. We know this and yet we persist with the practice of snatching time because we feel ill-prepared for the realities of teaching, of a deep belief and commitment to making a difference and sometimes simply because we are told we have to.

The UK Department for Education and Skills (DfES) notes that over the next ten years it intends to increase staff flexibility. How this translates into action will be interesting to observe as other countries, like Australia, are pursuing similar agendas. This vision provides opportunities to invest in professional learning that expands the horizons of teaching and crosses the boundaries of health and education. It also provides a platform of change in education different to previous change platforms which have centred on organisational structure or changing teachers' individual practice.

Broadening the network and circle of influence of 'frontline' professionals in education and health is an important characteristic of this new platform of change. Leading by example is the development of a new Masters course by the University of Melbourne, Centre for Adolescent Health and the Youth Research Centre. The 'Masters of Youth Health and Education Management', to commence in 2003, brings centre stage the issues and needs of youth in the context of education, health and community. The uniqueness and currency of this course to the emerging needs of professionals lies not only in its content but in its conceptual and organisational design. From the outset a team of health and education professionals from each of the organisations have worked together developing shared understandings of youth across health and education. The course represents over 18 months of work by the team and aims to draw on the organisations' significant experience and expertise in the youth field to:

- promote learning about effective cross-sectoral practice in communities and networks;

- develop, strengthen, implement and evaluate community initiatives to support young people;

- extend the evidence-base about what works to enhance community capacity to support young people (Wyn et al., 2002b).

The reality is that health and education whilst blurred in their practices still operate in very different domains. We have seen significant advances in the use of information communication technology (ICT) for children in relation to such things as the global classroom. With respect to health we have seen significant advances in the use of technology in such things as tele-medicine. However, we have not seen the same level of sustained interest in engaging professionals across health and education in online communities of learning. In this respect ICT is an under-utilised resource. In fact the use of ICT in professional engagement in learning provides interesting models for leading change at the interface between health and education.

At the Ontario Institute for Studies in Education (OISE), University of Toronto, 'Knowledge Forum' has been developed as an online tool that supports deep learning and reflection to solve communal problems. A collaborative research programme between OISE and Toronto Rehabilitation Centre is being undertaken to foster professional development and continuous learning and reflection across a range of disciplines and positions within this health setting (Russell, 2002b).

'Knowledge Forum' provides an online learning platform within which communities can be established. It has within its design many of the features that enable the use of ICT, such things as a clear online identity, conducive operational design features and user accessibility.

The project involves an identified community of people, in this case professionals from Toronto Rehabilitation Centre, proposing questions or problems relevant to, for example, policy or practice. These appear as 'idea' bubbles on the computer screen to which others then contribute suggestions or reflections or share common stories. A number of learning communities can be created within the one group of people participating. As with all new tools, participants do need to be trained and supported in their use.

Knowledge is the key focus, but knowledge transformed into action is a key outcome. The characteristics and benefits of this programme can be identified as follows:

1　*Communal access to everyone's work.* For example, the programme automatically authors people's work so participants can search to see who has read or added to their views.

2　*Expectation of expertise.* Everyone is expected to operate at a level of expertise. This is not about 'skill' expertise but rather the expectation that all knowledge is valued. Those who perceive they have more to contribute to a particular area are expected to use their expertise to 'scaffold' the capacity building knowledge of others.

3　*Outcomes.* The learning platform provides a learning environment that generates knowledge and solutions to practice problems for the professional.

4　*Historical record.* The reflective practice of 'Knowledge Forum' captures historically what would never be revealed in a face-to-face meeting.

5　*Capacity to import material.* Pictures, graphics and charts can be imported as a background screen or prompt for online discussion.

6　*Changes practice.* The tool creates the opportunity for participants to move from merely exchanging information to creating new knowledge that is grounded in practice.

7　*Flexibility.* The tool allows for flexible approaches to collaboration. Participants can be involved in real-time discussion or not. Professionals can work on the same issue but according to their own schedules.

Accountability measures

It is ironic that the final theme for discussion, accountability, is often the first raised by health and education professionals. As the boundaries at the interface blur, differences in outcome measures of systems are highlighted. For example, traditionally health reports focus on mortality and morbidity, while education reports focus on academic achievement. These differences work against the development of collaborative partnerships because, from the outset, measures of achievement are not shared.

As illustrated in this chapter, leadership in the development of concepts and practices that engage children and young people and the professionals who support them are anything but traditional. Why then do we persist with traditional measures of success, measures that, as Wyn (2002) observes, are narrow in their definition, linear, formula driven and at odds with the life contexts of children and young people and professionals?

Systemic leadership and support ultimately are only possible if policy directions align with evidence from practice and research across health and education. A promising development is found in Toronto, Canada. Here an interministerial group across health, education and corrections has been established to question existing legislation and review inconsistencies and directions related to common problems. A cross-appointment of an officer has been made to co-ordinate the group. Developments like this, initiated at the most senior levels, offer significant potential to reduce duplication, expense and, more importantly, improve the provision of services and outcomes for children and families.

However, cross-appointments will remain merely a meeting point – meant to have a systemic impact but with little influence – unless truly supported by both systems. What does this mean? Again it comes back to our understandings of partnership (sustained with mutual resource commitment); capacity to change the context (so that professionals' engagement in learning is expected, supported and regularly reviewed); an interrelated valuing of research, practice and policy (e.g. evidence of the different perspectives participating in planning, implementation and review); and commitment to children and young people (i.e. focused on improving their life outcomes).

Enablers and barriers to leading change

For each of the examples above, professionals encounter a number of enablers of and barriers to leading change at the health and education interface. We can all readily identify barriers to change at the interface because they seem to 'jump out at you'. More often than not, they provide the 'story of the day' – of frustration or annoyance – that professionals and families alike have to tell a sympathetic ear. These barriers include inconsistencies between policy directions and front-line experiences; problems that arise if the conceptual understanding and practice of partnerships is not clear; tensions between the need for staff development, which is future oriented, and the here and now service requirements of children and young people and their families; and the lack of willingness to share information, for example, the attitude: 'You don't share information, you "own it" and get credit for it.'

An equal challenge is our ability to articulate and put into action enablers at the health and education interface. A range of enablers linked with the personal qualities of individuals, the appropriate development of personnel, the context in which professionals operate and the type of content they deliver combine to promote positive interactions between systems. The individual commitment of staff; professional development that prepares and supports individuals and organisations to develop partnerships; cross-appointments that promote and value the opportunity to bring together diverse networks of individuals and organisations which might otherwise remain at arm's length; access to resources as an important lever for networking and partnerships; and the provision of information that is practical, relevant and accessible by the target audience all come to mind.

As a platform, the quality of the relationship, at an intra- or inter-professional, or organisational level, is the key to successfully transforming traditionally held professional concepts and practices. This requires professionals to 'loosen up' – to be prepared to show their vulnerability when it comes to building and sustaining partnerships. We need to be honest about our successes and our failures.

There is a difference between 'presenting' an idea or proposal and actual 'engagement' with other parties. A relationship can get stuck at a superficial level where only the 'best practice' or 'best features' of an organisation are on display. This type of presentation sets up a false reality. Real engagement allows the less positive aspects of practice and outcomes to be part of the reality discussed and learnt from. This movement towards a 'warts and all' approach relies significantly on a foundation of trust and mutual respect being established from the outset of the relationship. This can be formally or informally established, for example, by agreeing to the purpose of sharing the information and use of information by all parties. If deep change or reform is the desired outcome then this will not occur if the 'partnership' comes across or is perceived as a threat.

Developing a checklist for action

Developing relationships at the interface is based on trust, commitment, mutual respect, mutual growth and benefit, and it is goal oriented. The examples of new initiatives discussed in this chapter are moving towards a formalisation of this type of relationship at a more systemic level than in the past. Whilst not yet accomplished, a number of concepts and actions common to these initiatives can be identified, combined and presented:

1   *'Go in' before 'Going out'*. Establish a reliable baseline rather than jump to a proposed solution or outcome. Analyse need first. This appears to be more successful and meaningful when the people involved or impacted by the action have access to developing their skills in evaluation. This builds confidence and encourages a continuous engagement between development, implementation and review.

2   *Schools are 'the' core social centre* (OECD, 2001). Assist schools to provide a frame of reference for the community. This is not about the school 'carrying the load' but rather acting as a platform, a meeting place and gathering point. With this comes reciprocal responsibility and accountability.

3   *Be transparent*. Share information toward building awareness and understanding. Encourage transparency by sharing baseline information with the local community (health and education professionals, parents, community and business services), for example, establishing an online community environment and/or newsletter/publication.

4 *Balance power differentials.* Take every opportunity to include, involve and value children's and adolescents' contributions to their own learning and development. Mutual respect is the baseline for relationships.

5 *Review access and usability of information.* 'Decode' the idiosyncrasies of the various professions within health and education so that common language and shared meanings can develop. Access and usability also require clearer goals and statements about the type and appropriate use of the information to be shared within the community.

6 *Compare weekly or monthly data.* Track and transfer information between settings more effectively to ensure the goal of continuity of learning, for example, better use of ICT and education passports.

7 *Establish networks of support.* Articulate clearly and implement peer guidance and support. This involves moving from a 'showcase' model to a 'warts and all' approach, learning from success, difference and difficulty.

8 *Transform staffing arrangements.* Encourage and promote cross-appointments by both systems to strengthen the interface between health and education. Allocate time to embed joint health and education collaborative initiatives with children/young people in day-to-day school life. This demonstrates the community understands the relationship between the systems to improving life and learning outcomes for children/young people.

9 *Develop partnerships of professional learning.* Promote sustained and expected collaboration across health and education at all levels of engagement, i.e. policy, research and practice. Encourage staff opportunities for movement within fields and be creative about the use of time by, for example, implementing genuine online learning environments that take into account the need to recognise identity, community and time.

Conclusion

This chapter has taken a cross-section of community to magnify the interface of health and education in the belief that to understand this interface is also to lead change. It has presented a rationale for examining the health and education interface and why we need to move beyond the masquerade of change to actions that will lead to deep systemic reform. Five interrelated and interdependent themes are suggested as key emerging areas to be jointly addressed by health and education: retention and engagement in learning of children and young people; inclusion policies and practices; partnership process and outcomes; professionals' engagement in learning; and accountability. Offered throughout are promising examples from Australia, UK and Canada. These initiatives in research, policy and practice are challenging many of the conceptual and practical problems faced by professionals in their endeavours to improve the life and learning outcomes for children and young people. Palatable and not so palatable suggestions of ways forward challenge us to rethink our understandings of partnerships, the roles of education and health professionals and how government supports our lifelong learning. In each of the examples within the chapter the pictures created of the health and education interface were as varied and complex, as they were similar and straight-forward. What becomes clear however is that we have a choice: we can dig in and defend our old position, or we can cut and run. Which do you choose?

Acknowledgements

I would like to acknowledge the support of Dr Sara Glover, Director Education and Training, Centre for Adolescent Health, Melbourne and Professor Johanna Wyn, Department of Education, Policy and Management, The University of Melbourne and Director, Australian Youth Research Centre, in the development of this chapter.

References

Ainscow, M. (2002) 'Linking behaviour, learning and leadership: a collaborative research project'. Notes from Head Teacher ThinkTank, University of Manchester, Head Teachers and National College of School Leadership, 17 April.

Ainscow, M., Booth, T. and Dyson, A. (2001) 'Understanding and developing inclusive practices in schools'. A Collaborative Action Research Network Paper presented at the American Educational Research Association, April, Seattle, USA.

Anderson, M. (2001) 'What does the health and education interface look like?' *Royal Children's Hospital Education Institute, Year in Review*. Report from the Executive Manager, Education Resource Centre, Royal Children's Hospital, Melbourne, Victoria, Australia.

Anderson, M. and Foster, S. (2001) *Health and Education: Promoting the Dialogue*. Health and Education Consortium Profile Paper. Royal Children's Hospital Education Institute, Melbourne, Victoria, Australia.

Australian Institute of Health and Welfare (AIHW) (2002) *Australia's Health 2002*, Melbourne AIHW.

Barber, M. (1997) *The Learning Game: Arguments for an Education Revolution*. London: Indigo.

Beckett, D. (2000) 'Making workplace learning explicit: an epistemology of practice for the whole person', *Westminster Studies in Education*, 23, 41–53.

Bond, L., Glover, S., Godfrey, C., Butler, H., Patton, G. (2001) 'Building capacity for system-level change in schools: lessons from the Gatehouse Project', *Health Education and Behaviour*, 28 (3), 368–83.

Caldwell, B. (2000) 'Notes for boundary spanners: passing the public good test in the quest for world-class schools'. Keynote address, Australian Principals' Centre (APC), Incorporated Association of Registered Teachers of Victoria (IARTV) and the Royal Children's Hospital Education Institute (RCHEI), Leaders as Networkers: Connecting Education, Health and Community, Conference, 28 April, Melbourne.

Closs, A. (ed.) (2000) *The Education of Children with Medical Conditions*. London: David Fulton.

Department of Education (1998a) *Framework for Student Support Services in Victorian Government Schools*. Melbourne: Department of Education.

Department of Education (1998b) *Individual School Drug Education Strategy Guidelines*. Melbourne: Department of Education.

Department of Health (DoH) (2000) *Framework for the Assessment of Children in Need and their Families*. London: The Stationery Office.

Duckworth, J. (2001) *Evaluation of Notschool.net Research Project Initial Pilot*. Chelmsford: Cutters Wharf Consultants.

Dwyer, P. and Wyn. J. (2001) *Youth Education and Risk: Facing the Future*. London: Routledge/Falmer.

Edgar, D. (2001) *The Patchwork Nation: Re-thinking Government, Re-building Community*. Pymble, NSW: HarperCollins.

Fels, D. and Weiss, T. (2001) 'Video-mediated communication in the classroom to support sick children: a case study', *International Journal of Industrial Ergonomics*, 28, 251–63.

Freeman, E. and Strong, D. (2002) 'PD in student welfare: a CECV strategy to support teachers', *Learning Matters*, 7 (1), 10–11.

Fullan, M. (1993) *Change Forces: Probing the Depths of Educational Reform*. London: The Falmer Press.

Fullan, M. (2000) *Change Forces: The Sequel*. London: The Falmer Press.

Glover, S., Burns, J., Butler, H. and Patton G. (1998) 'Social environments and the emotional wellbeing of young people', *Australian Institute of Family Studies, Family Matters*, 49, 11–16.

Lewis, M. (2002) *The Future Just Happened*. London: Hodder and Stoughton.

National Coordinating Centre for NHS Service Delivery and Organisational Research and Development (NCCSDO) (2001) *Managing Change in the NHS: Making Informed Decisions on Change. Key points for Health Care Managers and Professionals*. London: NCCSDO.

OECD (2001) *Schooling for Tomorrow. What Schools for the Future?* Paris: OECD.

Potricus, R. (2000) *Bowling Alone*, New York, Simon & Schuster

Putnam, R. (1995) 'Bowling alone: America's declining social capital', *Journal of Democracy*, 6, 65–78.

Russell, A. (2002a) 'The role of epistemic agency and knowledge building discourse to foster interprofessional practice in a Canadian hospital'. Paper presented at the American Educational Research Association Annual Conference, New Orleans. (http://ikit.org/fulltext/2002AERAAnn.pdf)

Russell, A. (2002b) 'Using progressive inquiry to support interprofessional health care teams to collaborate and build knowledge: a Canadian perspective'. Invited keynote speaker at the 21st Century Learning Environments Conference, State of the Art Conference, Karolinska Medical Institute, Stockholm, Sweden. http://www.stateoftheart.nu

Shelton, J. (2001) 'Consequential learning: outcomes from connecting learning to place'. Keynote address, Education Foundation Summit, Thinking Community: Futures in Education, 18 October, Melbourne.

Ultralab (2001) *Not-School.Net Research Phase, Final Report*. Chelmsford: Ultralab.

Wyn, J. (2002) 'Young people and social change: shaping new, participatory research agendas'. Keynote address, Centre for Adolescent Health Symposium, 18 July, Royal Children's Hospital, Melbourne.

Wyn, J., Glovers, S., Davies, L., Freeman, L., Strong, D., Cahill, H., Gleeson, J. and Robinson, N. (2002b) 'Master of Youth Health and Education Management'. Course outline, University of Melbourne, Centre for Adolescent Health and The Youth Research Centre, Melbourne, Victoria, Australia, June, 1–4.

15

■ ■ ■

Educational Leadership and the Community: Principle and Practice in Australia

Nick Thornton

Australian schools, more particularly schools in the second most populated state, Victoria, play a significant leadership role in the communities in which they are situated. This role is not so evident in the major cities in Australia of which there are few, by comparison with Britain, but in more isolated settings the school is often the hub of local activity.

Australian experience shows that building school–community relationships takes time. It is the responsibility of educational institutions actively to search out opportunities to engage those who would not normally or naturally have contact with educational settings. Leadership does, of course, play a key role in the promotion of such ventures and often the great successes depend on the capacity of the initiator of the partnership to cede influence to others.

> *Effective leadership for school–community partnerships is a collective process during which school and community go about developing and realising shared visions.*

> (Kilpatrick et al., 2002 p.25)

Commonly, we expect that school leaders will not only be able to walk across the water but also turn it into wine! Sometimes these expectations are unrealistic but in communities where the school is the centre point of the social fabric, the principal or head teacher plays a very significant community leadership role. All of the good theory we respect about parallel or distributive leadership may not be how the local community perceives the role. The expectations of local communities are sometimes context free. In the old days bank managers, believe it or not, played a similar role.

The Kirkpatrick et al. (2002) study conducted by the Centre for Research and Learning in Regional Australia (CRCLA) points out that the leadership process was facilitated by certain individuals in each of the communities studied, most notably school principals. Often referred to as boundary crossers, principals provide a bridge between school and community. Principals legitimise potential school–community partnerships and play an important role in ensuring there are ongoing opportunities for interaction for all community members, as well as facilitating the development of structures and processes that foster group visioning. In essence, their transformational leadership practices empower others as effective players in the leadership process.

In the past decade in Victoria schools have become increasingly self-managing, so much so that 95 per cent of the state education budget is under the direct control of the governing body and the principal or head teacher plays an increasingly important role in finding creative ways to link the school and the community. The development of the principal's role from what could be described as a superior teacher/supervisor to one that became clearly focused on educational leadership and community development has its genesis in the 1970s. Successive state governments in this period recognised the need to transform a nineteenth-century educational bureaucracy to an organisational structure that ceded more decision-making responsibility to individual schools. While the changes brought about by the Kennett government's introduction of the Schools of the Future in 1992 had an enormous impact on the scope of the principal's role, Victorian schools had already enjoyed a large degree of local autonomy through the increased powers granted to School Councils in 1974. In that year School Councils were given a range of powers including:

- the capacity to enter contractual arrangements for school maintenance and improvement and the joint use of facilities by the community;
- the employment of ancillary staff;
- the administration of grants made to the council.

These powers were unique in the Australian school system and may go some way to account for the early identification by Victorian principals of their pivotal position in schools and their emerging role as leaders in a contested local environment. With the granting of powers to School Councils in 1982 locally to select principals, the status of principals vis-à-vis other teachers was made even more stark and may have been crucial factor in the development of separate professional associations for principals.

During the 1990s the Victorian Department of Education, under the leadership of Geoff Spring, a new Education Minister, Don Hayward, and the consultancy of Professor Brian Caldwell of Melbourne University, was exploring ways to refocus the administration of education, from a central bureaucracy to schools themselves. This had obvious implications for school principals, in terms of workloads and new kinds of professional responsibilities, particularly in the area of personnel management.

The Schools of the Future policy of the Liberal (conservative) government in Victoria implied enormous changes in the role and responsibilities of school principals. It sharpened the attention of educational bureaucrats and principals alike to the need for better programmes for the preparation of teachers for school leadership roles, as well as the ongoing professional development of principals. It also suggested that old bureaucratic models were ill-suited to the delivery of an educational product that must be responsive to a rapidly changing local and international environment and gave a green light for principals to explore new ways of doing things within their schools and with the community.

The case studies that follow are not schools in rural settings, but the principals display many if not all of the leadership characteristics or competencies found in the CRCLA study.

In Victoria, in 1998, the state Department of Education and Training commissioned the Hay Group to develop a set of leadership 'capabilities' which were designed to capture the new responsibilities of leaders in the devolved setting of the 'School of the Future' (Power et al., 1999). In one way or another the Hay Group have developed school leadership capabilities or competencies in Britain, New Zealand and Singapore as well as Victoria and there are quite startling similarities despite differences in nomenclature. For the purposes of this discussion the key capabilities are seen as the following:

- a passion for teaching and learning
- big picture thinking
- influencing others
- achievement focus
- maximising school capability
- leading the school community.

It is not difficult to make the link between the evidence gathered in the CLCRA study and these capabilities, which define excellence in school leadership. In their final report to the Department of Education and Training in Victoria, the Hay Group assert: 'There are different combinations of requirements for success in school leadership roles. This is not a one size fits all model ... in fact there are different paths to excellence' (Power et al., 1999: 13).

With this general framework of leadership characteristics in mind, let's see what happens when we apply them to some exemplary practices in developments in two Victorian schools. The case studies are Deer Park Secondary College in the western suburbs of Melbourne and the Brookside School at Caroline Springs, a satellite housing development on the outskirts of the same city.

Case Study One: The Deer Park Educational Precinct

Bert van Halen has been principal of Deer Park Secondary College for about 15 years. Bert is a very experienced school leader who has a continuing interest in the development of his colleagues and can legitimately claim that he has prepared a number of people for principalship.

In addition to significantly revising the learning and teaching strategies in the school, Bert has developed a long-term plan for involving the community in the school and for the provision of a wide range of interrelated services. This work is leading edge and provides a template for other education precincts to use as a model. All of the key leadership capabilities are evident in the proposal.

The opportunity to develop a precinct proposal in the Deer Park area arises largely from three new housing developments commenced in the late 1990s and still continuing. It is expected that when the three developments are completed there will be an additional 7,000 families in the area, which will necessitate a complete rethinking of the educational and community facilities required.

With this in mind Bert van Halen and his team developed a plan to meet these needs. This plan not only addresses future needs but is cognisant of the fact that current educational arrangements do not adequately deal with student needs in respect to future employment prospects and do not meet the norms for literacy and numeracy at primary levels. Juvenile justice statistics, which indicate considerable breakdown in social structures, are also of concern now and for the future and must be addressed at the earliest possible opportunity. Keating (2002) proposes that educational precincts have much to offer in planning and providing for the future. He defines precincts as spatial or virtual linkages between education and training providers across different sectors and possibly other organisations for the purposes of:

(a) enhancing the quality and diversity of provision of programmes and services;

(b) building vertical and horizontal pathways in education, training and employment;

(c) improving the quality and distribution of educational outcomes;

(d) building a greater capacity for collective responsibility for the interests of students.

These purposes presuppose that aspects of the planning and management of the delivery of programmes and services are located in the precinct, rather than the individual providers and central authorities.

The big picture for this proposed precinct includes the vertical and horizontal integration of education, health community services, juvenile justice, aged care, family and child care, arts and sport and recreation services. This will mean the reconfiguration of present services better to locate them relevant to community need and the creation of a series of new services by drawing in a range of community and business enterprises. New capital expenditure will also be required and facilities constructed will be purpose built in order to reflect both the purpose and culture created and driven within the precinct. In developing a final budget for the precinct there will be elements of both disposal and acquisition and this of itself will be a task of patience and determination.

Central to the precinct concept is a reconfiguration of education provision and this has been characterised by breaking education provision into three distinct phases: pre-school and early years; middle years; later years.

Pre-school and early years schooling

This phase includes the co-location of pre-schools and schools so as to take advantage of economies of scale and to allow for shared programme development. Presently these services are managed separately, giving rise to inefficiencies and an inordinate amount of transition arrangements.

The new arrangements provide opportunities for pre-school and school staff to work together and create powerful formal and informal professional development opportunities. The new concept proposes that these joined services are described as family centres and would include family, parenting, child rearing and health services on a number of sites within the precinct.

A broad range of health, local government and education professionals would be working together to ensure that there is a seamless process in place best to prepare young children for the learning opportunities ahead of them. Where specialist needs exist, for example, support for children with disabilities, this new arrangement will be able to provide strategic and meaningful early intervention on behalf of the child.

Middle years of schooling

This phase includes Years 5 to 9 and represents perhaps the biggest challenge. Both Australian and overseas research show that this is the time when many students become disengaged from learning and patterns of failure become more evident. The precinct concept allows educators to rethink provision through the development of new formal structures, purpose-designed curriculum and more appropriate pedagogies. In many ways this is the most important contribution to education provision because getting it right in the middle years provides for substantial success in the later years of schooling. In the middle years provision it is proposed that the School of Education at the local university be involved in research and programme development conjointly with the schools. The focus is on adolescent development, resilience, connectedness and peer support. Continuing research building on a significant middle years project conducted in Victoria over some years has much to offer those responsible for the redesigned programmes that go with middle school reform.

Later years of schooling

In the later years of schooling the Victorian government has established a clear target. It is expected that by 2010, 90 per cent of young people will complete Year 12 or its equivalent. It is also highly desirable that near universal participation in post-secondary education and training be the norm. The later years include Years 10 to 12 and the aim is to develop a managed individual pathway for every student as they move to post-school education and training.

All the stages of schooling in this model assume that children and young people will also be involved in a range of community activities such as the arts, recreation and sport. There is an expectation that they will contribute to the support of the elderly via participation in community service programmes and that many will also play a role in the necessary governance structures to support community facilities.

In order to implement this proposal amongst the 15 existing government primary and secondary schools within the precinct, new sites will need to be established and existing sites modified or in some instances closed. This will take significant courage and a capacity to set aside personal interest for the benefit of future schooling options. These negotiations will be emotional and politically delicate and their successful outcome will again be evidence of the high-level capabilities we expect of outstanding school leaders.

The other key aspect of the proposed precinct is that it will establish a Precinct Pedagogy Institute (PPI), which will play a central role in leading the learning. The PPI will also play a role in monitoring and maintaining quality of provision and with appropriate partners will conduct research and provide professional development for precinct personnel.

In developing this concept and the working proposal, Bert van Halen has with his leadership team demonstrated all of the key leadership capabilities indicated above. So have many members of the precinct development team. It is expected that if the precinct proposal is accepted by the stakeholders there will be in place an reinvigorated community with a strong commitment to, as Tony Blair puts it, 'provide joined up solutions to joined up problems'.

Case Study Two: The Brookside School

Gabrielle Leigh is the principal of the Brookside School, which was developed at the end of the 1990s as a new school in a new community at Caroline Springs on the western outskirts of Melbourne. The school was custom built as part of a single campus that includes independent and Catholic primary schools as well as the government school. The three schools share some facilities and have all been networked from the day the doors were opened.

As part of the development of the school there has been a significant focus on a thinking curriculum. Staff thinking styles were assessed as part of this process and found to provide a comprehensive spread over the four quadrants which are used as a framework. This framework guides the way in which the leadership team and the teaching staff go about their daily work.

Gabrielle stresses that taking on something as radical as a thinking curriculum requires a degree of 'strategic abandonment' (Caldwell, 2002), but in implementing the strategy it is important not to 'throw the baby out with the bathwater'. Previous good practice needs to be able to survive and flourish in the new paradigm. While the school had no additional funding in its exploration of these new directions, consistent with the spirit of Brookside, the costs were shared amongst the three partner schools.

Flexibility is vital in the Brookside development. For example, tennis might be provided for one term, replacing performance arts, or there might be one term where science becomes a curriculum focus. That kind of decision, ensuring an overall balance in curriculum provision, within the context of limited resources, has implications for the employment of teachers. What the students need determines the curriculum: the curriculum determines the choice of teachers.

The Caroline Springs three-school campus was consciously established as a centre for the new community – both educational and social. The developers built the schools first before the construction of the houses began, and pre-planned the installation of networking throughout the community.

Since the early days of 1997, the Caroline Springs campus has been based on commitment to a number of principles including lifelong learning, optimal use of learning, information and communication technologies, a philosophy of sharing and new forms of ownership and structures.

In practice, these principles are applied by way of an intranet, which connects all students with home and more widely into a range of locations in the community. There is also considerable sharing of buildings, play areas, curriculum and sporting facilities. For example, inter-school sport teams are made up of students from the three schools rather than three teams from the three separate schools. Joint meetings for the three schools' staffs are held once a month and vertical planning teams meet together on a regular basis so planning and implementation are shared.

Clearly, the new school culture is built on mutual trust and common purpose. Going deeper, the foundations include passion, emotion, hope, alliances, tapping of expertise within and beyond the school, responsive leadership and celebration. All of this is not to say that there have been no obstacles to overcome. Central issues such as governance structures, the building of a different style of leadership team and of course, changing personnel have an impact on the capacity of the school to deliver consistent excellent outcomes for children. The model has much to recommend it and progress so far exemplifies the importance of having a leadership team in place that has the high-level skills and attributes (capabilities) necessary to deliver good outcomes.

Both of the case studies convey a clear message. The capacity to enhance outcomes for children turns on the collective wisdom of the school and its community. It is foolish to believe that schools can exist outside their community and smart schools tap into the resources which the community has to offer. Good leadership ensures that this will happen.

References

Caldwell, B.J. (2002) 'What do experiences tell us about the future of schooling? Contexts, trends, challenges and opportunities'. Paper prepared for the APC Summer Institute, Reconfiguring Schools for the 21st Century. Published in summary form in *Australian Principles Centre Monograph*, No. 9. Melbourne APC.

Keating, J. (2002) *Educational Precincts in Victoria – A Discussion Paper*, Melbourne APC.

Kilpatrick, S., Johns, S., Mulford, B., Falk, I. and Prescott, J. (2002) *More than an Education: Leadership for Rural School–Community Partnerships*. Report on Project UT-31A. Canberra: Rural Industries Research and Development Corporation. Reported in *Campus Review-Education Review*, 12 (23), 41–2.

Power, Paul G. et al. (1999) *Excellence in School Leadership – Creating a First Class Learning Environment*. Melbourne: Hay Management Consultants.

16

■ ■ ■

Extended Schools: The Dream of the Future?

Julian Piper

> *My vision of Britain is of a nation where no one is left out or left behind, and where power, wealth and opportunity are in the hands of the many, not the few. Investing in that vision is an investment in the future of our whole country, and is in everyone's interests.*

(Tony Blair, Cabinet Office, 2000: p.1)

> *I recognise that we need to work together with other Departments and agencies if we are to provide the help and support that schools need. We therefore need to develop approaches that require closer working partnerships between Departments and agencies ... Schools Plus activities can make a real difference to the lives of pupils and others in the community. I look forward to working closely with everyone involved in taking the agenda forward.*

(Estelle Morris, DfEE, 2000: p.1)

Local and national governments have attempted to solve the problem of social exclusion or deprivation in a rather piecemeal (some might say 'haphazard') way. Policies have often lacked co-ordination and the dispensing of large amounts of cash has often been ill-considered and based on headlines (such as riots) rather than any kind of overall local strategy. The evidence from areas that have seen considerable investment through, for example, Inner Area Projects, City Challenge and other large-scale initiatives does not generally support the view that major sustainable improvements have been made to the lives of the poorest neighbourhoods. It is suggested that among the key reasons for this are the short-term nature of many of the programmes, the continued erosion of social capital, a lack of understanding of the background to the decline of neighbourhoods and a serious failure of local and national agencies to work together and build partnerships that would sustain the initiatives and continue into the future.

The wide gap between poor neighbourhoods and the rest results from a complex combination of factors. Some of the factors are social and economic changes that have affected many countries. When these combine, they create a complex and fast moving vicious cycle. But, over several decades, the policies and actions of central and local government have not been good enough at tackling these issues; and sometimes they have been part of the problem.

(Cabinet Office, 2002: p.8)

The Labour government, when returned to power, began a major review of a whole series of aspects of life, which related to the issue of social exclusion. Eighteen Policy Action Teams (PATs) were set up to look at key areas where there could be an impact, in an effort to ensure that any future investment would result in clear benefits and demonstrable improvement in people's lives. These ranged from basics such as jobs (PAT1), skills (PAT2) and business (PAT3) to more innovative areas such as community self-help (PAT9), arts and sports (PAT10), joining it up locally (PAT17) and better information (PAT18). The overall conclusions of all these reports were clear. They suggested four key imperatives: (a) reviving the economy; (b) reviving the community; (c) improvement in services; (d) leadership and joint working (Cabinet Office, 2000).

A further look at these priorities shows how strongly education features within them. Reviving economies includes a strong emphasis on improving skills, especially in IT, in order to enable people to become economically active. Reviving communities is linked to promoting arts and sports and to building community capacity through empowering local people. An increase in Schools Plus activities, improved family support through referral points (e.g. schools) and on-the-spot delivery of services (e.g. through schools) are seen to be important in improving services. The role of schools in community leadership links to greater local, regional and national priorities in order to ensure that there is better co-ordination of activities and a local strategy is developed. It is clear that strong partnerships at all levels are required to deliver this neighbourhood renewal agenda and schools could be well placed to be at the heart of the local activity that will deliver it.

At the same time, schools face a problem. The drive to improve standards is ever pressing and inescapable. The obstacles to higher attainment in some communities seem greater than ever. However, when Maslow's (1970) hierarchy of needs is taken into account, the desire of pupils to learn is not at the top of the list. According to Maslow, there are general types of needs (physiological, safety, love and esteem) that must be satisfied before a person can act unselfishly. He called these needs 'deficiency needs'. As long as we are motivated to satisfy these cravings, we are moving towards growth, towards self-actualisation. Satisfying needs is healthy. Blocking gratification makes us sick or evil. In other words, we are all 'needs junkies' with cravings that must be satisfied and should be satisfied or else we become sick. Schools are becoming more familiar with the signs of needs of their pupils and examples of good practice in provision of breakfast clubs and supper clubs (in order to satisfy hunger) are now commonplace. Similarly, a renewed focus on the security of pupils through anti-bullying policies, behaviour policies and an increase in CCTV in some schools helps to ensure that the pupils are not primarily concerned about their safety. Some schools are providing training in emotional literacy for teaching and support staff and the provision of activities designed to build self-esteem has long been seen as essential for many schools.

Schools are often, therefore, trying to compete in a contest where they are almost sure to lose unless they address many other issues first, or at least simultaneously. Force field analysis also suggests that simply putting more energy into opposing cultural and poverty-driven difficulties will be counter-productive. The opposition simply increases in proportion so that little progress is made. Such analysis states that a more successful approach is for schools systematically to work away at the opposing pressures, ideally with the support of other local agencies, and eventually turn them to work in their favour.

What are the causes of these oppositional features? One of the critical ones is the deprivation of the communities surrounding many schools. If schools were to work with other agencies (including other departments of the local authority) to reduce the effects of poverty and deprivation, it might be easier to encourage individuals to learn. Leicester City Council, shortly after gaining unitary status, held a series of 'witness' events in different wards. The format of these landmark events was that the directorate listened for several hours to testimonies from key professionals working in the ward about their perceptions of the issues in that area. It was significant, not only because the individual directors of services heard from other professionals outside their field, but also because the professionals heard a more complete view of their area by listening to each other. During this consultation, it emerged that one deprived ward, although relatively modern, had the highest incidence of noise abatement notices served, the highest incidence of environmental health problems and the highest proportion of looked after children in the city. In other words, many families suffer from sleep loss, poor health and are dysfunctional or in the vicinity of dysfunctional families. All these issues have a dramatic effect on children's receptiveness to learning and such myriad problems can only begin to be solved by a collaborative approach such as that proposed in the new legislation and through neighbourhood renewal strategies.

A second issue is the lack of value placed on education in many communities for a whole variety of reasons, too many to illustrate here. If schools were able to work in partnership with other community groups to effect a cultural shift, the work of schools might be held in higher esteem and everyone involved in the community might seek to support the values held by the school. Other difficulties are posed by the sheer volume of initiatives that are placed on schools. This is especially difficult when these are not viewed in relation to an overall local and neighbourhood strategy.

Seen in this context, it becomes clear that the work of schools is inextricably entwined in the neighbourhood renewal/social exclusion agenda. Social inclusion cannot be achieved without schools, and schools cannot continue to drive up standards without social inclusion. We must then ask why it is not happening universally, what are the obstacles and how can they be overcome.

The Policy Action Team 11 (Schools Plus) report made significant recommendations which will, as they continue to be implemented, have a major impact on this close relationship between schools and their communities (DfEE, 2000). This is especially so in disadvantaged communities, but not necessarily so. Why should the benefits of extending the role of schools simply be limited to those living in poverty? The recommendations included the following:

1 Provision of at least three hours' study support for every student.

2 Extended opening hours at schools (including extending the school day for students).

3 A network of One Stop Family Support Centres.

4 Improving the quality and breadth of school business links (building on good practice such as Playing for Success, mentors and work experience agents).

5 Greater involvement of the community in the school and the school in the community (including promoting supplementary and mother tongue schools, Schools Plus Teams and Community Learning Champions).

6 Recognising success (work with OFSTED to identify effective community activity, enhancements to Initial Teacher Training and other awards).

7 Extending and improving schools' links with parents (new ways of engaging parents, family learning and family support).

Several of these recommendations have now been piloted in a number of different LEAs and schools and they have been further refined. At present the term 'extended school' is used to describe those that are working towards the implementation of these recommendations, particularly where a multi-agency approach is being developed in order to provide not only the extended activities and opening hours, but also a range of additional services on the school site. This term is only a 'working title' of such initiatives and may be replaced by a 'new branding' if one can be found. The indication that this would be developed in the Education Act 2002 was published in the *Schools Achieving Success* White Paper:

> *Many schools already recognise the benefits for them and their communities of providing additional services to their pupils, pupils' families and the wider community. Most schools already provide some before or after-school study support; some provide space for sports or arts activities, community groups or Internet access; others work closely with other public bodies to provide integrated services such as health services, childcare or adult education. We shall legislate to make sure that there are no barriers to schools developing these innovative approaches.*

We will establish pilots to test out such 'extended schools' and generate examples of good practice. And where schools have already demonstrated the advantages of this approach we will help them develop further to become Centres of Excellence, and celebrate their achievements.

(DfES, 2001: p.3)

This commitment is repeated in the Summary of the Education Bill 2002 which states:

This has the potential not only to benefit the wider community, but also to drive up standards in the school, by engaging the community in the mission of the school.

(DfES, 2002a: p.10)

How do 'extended schools' differ from the existing models of community schools and colleges and from previous concepts? It seems to me that the major difference lies in the philosophy behind it. We have already seen how many earlier efforts at regeneration failed to provide sustainable benefits to the people who were the object of the initiatives. This was often because the improvements were simply cosmetic (such as improving environmental features) and failed to engage the people who were the object of the activity. In a similar way, many community schools provide a range of activities to which the community is invited or allow their facilities to be used by the public. The justification often promulgated is that the school is at the heart of its community and that the capital resource of the school is such that it should be used by everyone, not just its core population. However, merely opening the facilities of the school to the community does not necessarily engage local people in the values and core purpose of the school.

The entity represented by the term 'extended school' is certainly a close relative of the 'integrated community school' that was modelled particularly by Leicestershire and Cambridgeshire and promoted by such as Henry Morris, Stuart Mason and Andrew Fairbairn, as indicated in the introductory chapters to this book. Indeed, in terms of philosophy, there may be little difference between the modern notion of an extended school and the integrated community school as some of these pioneers envisaged it. However, in actual practice the integration achieved, where successful, was often because the school succeeded in providing a range of services or resources by itself for its local community. This often involved expanded senior management teams to include staff with a specific responsibility for community activities. It was designed to achieve collaborative working, which would ensure that the needs of the school and community did not come into conflict with each other, but rather maximised the benefits of co-existence. It was also to ensure that the resources available were used to benefit the whole community rather than any distinct interest group.

In reality, the partners were not equal and, to a large extent, they are still not equal. The model sometimes failed to achieve its objective because of difficult relationships between head teachers and community managers (most notably over confusing line management between the school and the LEA). Often, and especially since the advent of local management of schools and the increased drive to improve standards policed by the DfES, league tables and OFSTED, difficulties have been caused by a domination of the needs of school pupils so that community needs have been pushed into second place. Shortage of cash and increased compartmentalisation of funding have also played their parts. In spite of these pressures, it is a tribute to the leadership of many head teachers and community staff that examples of good practice of the use of complementary skills and resources to maximise benefits for schools and their communities still abound. Those who have continued to wave the integration flag and have demonstrated its benefits are now seeing their ideas come of age.

There is currently a variety of different models of community involvement in schools which have grown up over the years. What follows is an attempt to characterise a number of these models and define them according to the extent to which the community has a stake in the development. It is not exhaustive, but illustrative of a process. The true picture is, in reality, a continuum and some aspects of each of the three following models may be present in any one situation. For schools wishing to embark on the road to greater community involvement, it may be that this continuum also represents a developmental process from which they can see some steps that are feasible in their own current situation. Integration or 'extension' does not happen over night. The route by which a school travels towards the extended school model will be important and may involve elements of the other models described below.

The 'joint use' model was favoured by many local councils in the 1970s and 1980s as a means of providing leisure facilities for the local area. Sometimes school sports facilities were shared during the day but, after school a manager and staff from the council would take over the running of the amenity and offer pay-as-you-play opportunities as well as some coaching sessions. Heads would sometimes convene campus liaison committees, or their equivalent, to sort out any potential conflicts of interest. There were thus two tenants of the premises who operated in their own defined time zones and, if all went well, neither side was really aware of the other's existence. There were clear benefits to both sides of this relationship. Schools often inherited substantially improved sporting facilities and the shared cost of maintenance provided financial benefits to both partners. It was not only councils that partnered schools in this way. Babington Community College in Leicester became the home for the Leicestershire Badminton Association as a result of an injection of £90,000 into the original building programme in 1981 which enabled the addition of a sports hall dedicated to badminton but shared with the school throughout the day.

The 'co-ordinated' model has been developed alongside the joint use model. Often schools provide other facilities for the community. Perhaps the school library becomes a local facility for the whole community. Surplus classrooms are rented out to local parent and toddler groups and in the evenings and sometimes at weekends adult education providers or faith groups use other spaces. Schools thus develop a vision of how their facilities might best be used and, by developing the co-ordinated model, enable other groups to make use of them, often, but not always, with some income generated as a result. Premises staff or site managers are as key as head teachers in the successful management of this co-ordinated approach since they can be agents for peace in situations where different users have different requirements of the same space. Sometimes the local user groups have management committees but these remain largely independent of each other and of the school, focusing on their own activity and purpose.

In the 'integrated' model, staff, pupils, governors and parents are aware of the inclusive nature of the school and its involvement with community groups, businesses, agencies and families. Whilst there are frequently staff who have a primary function to work with specific areas of activity (i.e. it is not necessary for community staff to teach or for all teaching staff to have community responsibilities), managers of different aspects will be seeking to maximise the benefits of collaborative working. Teachers are keen to encourage contributions from other adults to the curriculum. Community staff endeavour to harness the skills of the community to support the school. For example, school pupils may act as tutors for adults in basic computing classes or as guides and receptionists when visitors are expected. Youth workers and teachers collaborate to provide maximum benefits for young people through a variety of different approaches. Secondary pupils may lead activities in local primary schools, nurseries or even old people's homes that are linked to their own national curriculum targets. Older members of the community can be recruited to assist with reminiscence activities to enhance relationships between different generations.

This is but a brief example of possible activities, but the list is almost endless and many examples are showcased on the Community Schools Network website at www.cedc-csn.org.uk. In this model, governors have a key role in the overseeing of the site and the links between the activities for each of the client groups. This may be through a specific committee or through a community association. In the best examples, community members and groups are encouraged to contribute ideas and skills at all levels and feel a part of the institution, sharing its aims and its values.

So what is different now as we consider the 'extended school' and what is distinctive about its philosophy? This model might be best considered as a further development beyond the integrated model described above. In order to understand what it might look like, we need to return to the changes in rhetoric and practice in regeneration. Here the new focus is on empowerment of the community in a variety of different ways through 'joined up' thinking and working. The aim is to ensure that local agencies are working in creative partnership to support local people in determining the priorities and solutions to local problems. Many of these activities involve families and many involve an element of learning or acquisition of skills. Schools now find themselves surrounded by myriad potential partners with targets and outcomes that link closely to their core purpose. This addresses one of the other key priorities of both neighbourhood renewal and schools: the issue of early intervention. The partners are often able to support the school in dealing with some of the lower, but more pressing needs of families (see Maslow, 1970) that interrupt the progress of learning which is so central to schools achieving their targets. They are also able to intervene earlier where there are problems. There's another important difference too. As highlighted in the *Schools Plus* report (PAT11), OFSTED has been encouraged to consider the ways in which schools work actively in partnership with their communities and the benefits accruing to pupils as a result. This will surely be a very powerful incentive for head teachers to consider more actively the way in which they and their school can engage with parents and others in order to drive up standards still further.

What do we mean by an 'extended school'? The draft guidance prepared by DfES in conjunction with the Education Act 2002 gives a clue:

> As part of the Government's strategy to promote and develop extended schools, the Education Act 2002 will make it easier for governing bodies of all maintained schools to provide, or enter into contracts with others to provide, facilities or services that furthers any charitable purpose for the benefit of pupils at the school or their families or people who live or work in the locality in which the school is situated.

> This will cover the vast majority of services and activities that schools may want to provide. This will include childcare, adult and family learning, co-located health and social services, and other facilities of benefit to the local community such as credit unions or ICT access.

(DfES, 2002a: p.25)

The guidance also suggests some of the ways in which this might be achieved:

> The legislation also provides flexibility for schools by allowing the use of a variety of management structures to develop services and activities. For instance, a governing body might want to enter into an agreement with the local primary health care trust under which the trust provides health services on school premises. Further flexibility is given by allowing schools to charge for some services. This will be appropriate in some circumstances, for example if they are running a crèche or providing community education courses.

(DfES, 2002a: p.26)

The guidance makes it clear that the government is keen to extend the services provided by schools even beyond those which the most developed are already providing. Once again, the reasons are clear when the links with neighbourhood renewal are made. Research carried out by the Community Education Development Centre (CEDC) and Parentline showed that teachers are often the first port of call when parents have difficulties. This is particularly true in primary schools where parents generally take their children to school and collect them again at the end of the day. The evidence shows further that teachers are often burdened with these family difficulties and have no back-up support to deal with them. Often the agencies to which the parents might be referred are inaccessible or unavailable and it takes the teacher a considerable amount of (wasted) time if they are to access the support on behalf of the parent. Often this support is at least desirable if not essential in order that the child or children concerned can have their needs addressed to improve their learning prospects.

The extended school model provides ready access to additional support services for parents and others in the community on or from the site. Whilst it is advantageous that this might involve the physical presence of a social worker or health professional on the school site, this might not, at least in the short term, be feasible through lack of accommodation or agency staff time. One alternative is illustrated by a model such as the Medway Positive Parent Network, which provides an online access facility for parents who are able to sign up for e-mail under and without disclosing their actual identity. The parents are supported by a wide variety of local agencies (where training has been provided) in gaining access to the necessary ICT facilities in shops, banks, schools, etc. Another alternative is for school support staff to have telephone numbers which enable them to make contact on behalf of the parent with known professionals who are able to deliver the required support without the member of staff being either fobbed off or passed from pillar to post. Some schools already provide access points to health professionals for pupils and the community. At Bassett Green Primary School in Southampton, following the merger of the infant and junior schools, surplus accommodation was allocated to local health professionals who now work in the core of the estate and are readily accessible to parents and families in the area. They work alongside a pre-school facility and are also able to work with parents of younger children before they reach school age, hence providing opportunities for early intervention in cases of need.

The guidance for schools following the 2002 Act also highlights the benefits to all parties. It is known that extended activities and services:

> ... contribute to higher levels of achievement and attainment as well as improvements in children's behaviour, motivation, self-esteem and social skills.

> (DfES, 2002a: p.12)

The guidance also points to benefits for staff who are able to refer non-education needs to specialists and suggests that services for families and the wider community can attract funding for improved facilities from which the school can benefit.

There is no doubt that this vision, if implemented, will cause schools to become very different places. In the mid-1980s Peers School in Oxford made strides to open its doors more actively to the community. Among the first allies was the local health visitor who became an important community learning champion.

However, the benefits were entirely mutual since a regular weekly parent and toddler session was arranged in the school swimming pool which was actively supported by the health visitor (she would often bring clients with their children to the sessions personally). By working with families in this informal context she was able to reduce the number of visits to families, because they were all together at the same time and place, promote other learning opportunities and support a growing embryonic parent and toddler group.

There are a number of implications in these proposals for those involved in schools at all levels.

The whole welcoming nature of schools needs to be addressed. If schools are to be readily used by other professionals and the wider community, security will be of paramount importance, but this does not have to be oppressive or hostile. Banks, building societies and even social security and employment offices have proved that security can be provided without extensive physical barriers. After Dunblane, most people will accept that security locks are required to protect children from unauthorised access, but information explaining how to reach reception and a helpful staff can ensure that these do not become a deterrent. Customer care training for administrative, premises and support staff may be required in order to ensure that schools are more genuinely open and accessible to members of the community. Where this is successful, parents are led to feel that they have a stake in the school and are empowered to support it in a variety of ways – thus converging with the neighbourhood renewal agenda once again. This is well documented in the OFSTED report of Thomas Estley Community College in Leicestershire:

> On entry to the college's site one is immediately aware of its community function and its inviting atmosphere. It is a very welcoming institution. Signs for disabled access are prominently displayed at the main entrance. In the reception area posters advertising community classes and directions for the community lounge and baby changing facilities sit comfortably alongside plaques proudly displayed for a Young Enterprise award, Investor in People and National Curriculum awards. Administrative staff give calm, efficient and patient help to all age groups, and participants from the local community are made to feel that they have a stake in what goes on. The numbers attending inter-school sporting fixtures is much higher than average as being on the school site is seen as a natural occurrence rather than a special occasion.

(OFSTED, 2001: p.25)

There are other imperatives which follow from this aim. Schools may need to consider signing in arrangements for late pupils, referral systems which result in miscreants adopting the school foyer as their personal and private space, the location of pupils who are sick (often literally – with buckets held at the ready) and the nature of staff–pupil interactions which take place in their entrance foyers. The foyer of Summerbank Primary School in Stoke-on-Trent is such a stimulating area that visitors could easily spend an hour reading the displays on the wall, thumbing through the photograph albums which are displayed on the table or viewing the citations for awards accompanied by photographs which are taken and arranged by the Year 6 head boy or girl who is also the official school (digital) photographer.

Schools will also want to review (as many are already) the ways in which they include parents in their children's learning. This may have an effect on the organisation and structure of parents' consultations. There is already evidence of a good deal of innovative practice developing which ranges from longer, structured appointments with form tutors only on 'study' days to the organisation of the school into vertical tutor groups, thus limiting the number of parents to be seen by a tutor in each year group and allowing longer appointments to foster improved parent–teacher partnerships. Sparkenhoe Community Primary School in Leicester works with a wide variety of families from vastly differing backgrounds, including substantial numbers of refugees and asylum seekers. Its excellent relationships with parents have been documented by OFSTED:

> *Relationships and communication with parents are strengths of the school ... Parents have an exceptionally positive view of the school ... The school's links with parents are highly effective overall and exceptional in some areas.*

> (OFSTED, 2001: p.25)

Schools taking part in CEDC's Share Family Learning Programme have all been encouraged to work more collaboratively with parents. Although well established at Key Stages 1 and 2, the Key Stage 3 pilot prompted Thistley Hough High School to abandon homework and created 'extended study' instead. Each pupil has a brightly coloured folder and the information about the extended study contains a section which details how parents, friends and relatives can be involved in the work and how the task can achieve the highest grade. There is also a section which indicates further work along the same lines for those who wish to follow it.

The changed or changing nature of schools will require appropriate documentation when recruiting staff at all levels and it is essential that new staff are appointed to job descriptions which reflect the extended nature of the school. In some cases it may be that the pattern of working hours will change to more of a shift pattern. Stoke Park Community College in Coventry operates a three-session day with a wide variety of activities taking place outside the traditional hours. Staff work a shift pattern to enable this to occur. Mill Mead Primary School in Hertford, situated opposite the local railway station, has operated an extended school day for several years in order to support adults who work full time and especially those who travel on the train. This kind of provision will be especially important in future if the links to community regeneration and increased economic activity for local adults are to be fruitful.

Governors should notice a considerable change in their powers and scope for development as a result of the new approach. This is well catered for in the new legislation by freeing up the financial opportunities, allowing governors to reconstitute with a governing body which reflects the local need through its size and composition (subject to certain constraints) and to run or commission new activities and services through the school. The greater range of activities might put pressure on full governors' meetings which already conduct a large volume of business. Delegation of much of this work to a committee would enable governors with a particular interest in this aspect of the school to make a more substantial contribution. This committee would have the power to co-opt additional members from the community in order to involve members of other local groups in the decision-making process.

It is also increasingly important that schools take account of the balance of ethnic minorities on their governing bodies to ensure that they are truly representative of their communities. Under the Race Relations (Amendment) Act, this is no longer an option but a requirement. The successful recruitment of governors from all sections of the community is not an easy task. However, there is ample evidence, most notably in a 2002 report from The Education Network (TEN), which suggests that some LEAs have been highly successful in addressing this issue in their support for schools. However, the report also shows that there is still a long way to go before this issue is satisfactorily addressed in general:

> As all schools and local authorities, and indeed all public bodies, get to grips with their new responsibilities under the Race Relations (Amendment) Act, they can take comfort from the knowledge that LEAs, of vastly different sizes and from one end of the country to another, have managed to overcome the many problems encountered in collecting data or reaching out to their local communities. This has as much to do with community engagement as it has with school improvement. Indeed, the two are inextricably linked. Ensuring that governing bodies become and remain more representative of their school communities should also be a national priority.

(TEN, 2002)

Of course, the most dramatic change will be to the role of the head teacher. Instead of simply being concerned with the narrow focus of teaching and learning within the school, the future direction of leadership will be towards a wide range of multi-agency partnerships all of which contribute to the well-being of the core pupil group, but which thread outwards to and from the community as the school seeks to respond to the needs of families and the wider community with a particular target of encouraging learning and skill development. Heads will in future be the managers of a range of different complementary functions and partnerships as schools build learning communities around themselves.

The legislative proposals pointed to pilot projects which would be used to develop the ideas which led to the notion of 'extended schools'. During 2001–2, CEDC and Education Extra have jointly worked with DfES to pilot the Schools Plus Teams proposal detailed in the PAT11 report in six schools up and down the country. The schools were selected for their differences so that as many parameters as possible were included in the choice. There were two primary schools and four secondary. Six highly skilled consultants (team leaders) were recruited in summer 2001 to work with the schools in order to review current development plans, investigate the way in which other agencies and the community could contribute, set up action plans to take this work forward and support the schools in building increased links with their communities. The target areas were those spelled out in the *Schools Plus* report (DfEE, 2000):

- a range of Out of School Hours Learning (OSHL) activities;
- more effective work with a wider number and range of parents, including family learning;
- closer business links through, e.g. work experience, mentoring, sponsorship;
- developing the role of the community within the school, e.g. co-location of services, supplementary/mother tongue schools and outreach learning opportunities;
- enhancing the role of the school in the community by integrating school within plans for neighbourhood renewal, co-location of services, outreach work;
- increased pupil involvement, e.g. school council, citizenship.

It was originally envisaged by the report that teams of other consultants would support this work. However, practicalities (especially the establishment of a working relationship with the head and staff) soon dictated that the work of the team leader would be critical to the success of the project, although some additional expertise was provided in some cases (e.g. specialist support with breakfast clubs or the arts). In every case, team leaders found a wide range of other local agencies that were willing and able to work with the schools collaboratively. In many cases, schools were able to help the other agencies to achieve their targets and it has certainly been true that the support of other agencies will enable the schools to improve their support and the range of activities offered to pupils and their families. The schools had been unable to give the necessary time to build these partnerships and were often unaware of the potential sources of support which lay untapped but within their reach. In some cases, partners were established within the same local authority between different departments that historically did not work together, at least in the context of schools. In several cases, links were forged with Neighbourhood Renewal projects (including Local Strategic Partnerships and SRB projects).

Skinner Street Primary School in the centre of Gillingham (just off the High Street) in Medway, was one of the pilot schools. Here, an extended steering group was set up which comprised not only the local Education Action Zone (EAZ), LEA, the Early Years and Childcare Development Partnership (EYCDP), the Out of Schools Hours Learning Co-ordinator, teachers and governors, but also representatives from Medway Online, Medway First Point of Contact Centres, Medway Sports Development Team, Gillingham libraries, school nurses, the local Healthy Living Centre, the town centre manager, the local secondary school, the Education

Business Partnership, Connexions, Gillingham Football Club and the local leisure centre manager. From this group grew a new 'First Point of Contact Centre' within the school's breakfast club, a new Medway Online Centre within the school, new funding for the breakfast club and holiday provision through a joint bid, collaborative development of 'Family Sport in the Community', a tiered range of courses offering skills in peer mentoring, counselling and listening, further development of the existing strong Out of School Hours Learning provision, shared resources with the Healthy Living Centre and the local sports centre, increased links with local businesses through the town centre manager and several other potential joint bids to support joint objectives. The head teacher, although working in the area for 12 years, did not have the time and resources to go out and develop these new partnerships, but the input from a specialist consultant over nine months achieved substantial productive links with many other agencies with overlapping targets and priorities.

This is the background to the newly promoted extended schools which are explicitly contained within the government's spending plans published in mid-2002. The spending review documentation refers to opening schools wider to their communities and promoting a multi-agency approach. It details several priorities linked to increasing partnerships to support schools. These include new priorities connected to out-of-hours learning:

> *... to encourage all schools to extend their out-of-hours work with pupils and their links with the community. Formal schooling is only part of the educational process. The new comprehensive system will be built on a positive partnership with parents, the imaginative out-of-hours use of school facilities, and draw on the huge reserves of energy and commitment in the wider community to support young people's learning.*

> *There is strong evidence that out-of-school hours learning raises pupil attainment and improves behaviour and motivation, especially in the middle years of 11–14.*

(DfES, 2002b p.28)

There is also a priority to develop a multi-agency approach which highlights the fact that this is at the core of the philosophy of the 'extended school'.

> *... to provide better multi-agency support closer to schools. We will create 'extended ' schools in the most deprived areas. These schools will be able to provide a range of services for children, their families and the wider community – including childcare, study support, adult and family learning, access to modern technology, health and social care – working closely with local health and other services and voluntary bodies. We will also support local delivery of extended services in many other schools.*

> *Achieving this will help to raise standards, eradicate bad behaviour in the classroom and provide parents with a greater choice of excellent schools.*

(DfES, 2002b p.29)

Schools and community regenerators are therefore brought together by an increasingly common agenda which is now reflected in legislation and the targeting of resources. The experience of the Schools Plus Teams pilot project demonstrated that active collaboration between schools and other local agencies (including voluntary organisations) can produce a degree of synergy which benefits all parties in the achievement of their objectives. Each member of the partnership should take comfort from the realisation that they do not have to work alone in order to reach their targets. Moreover, these partnerships are the best hope of avoiding some of the regenerative failures of the past and, instead, giving local people a new autonomy with the skills to determine their own future in their own inclusive and 'learning' communities.

References

Cabinet Office (2000) *National Strategy for Neighbourhood Renewal: A Framework for Consultation.* London: Cabinet Office.

Cabinet Office (2002) *National Strategy for Neighbourhood Renewal Action Plan.* London: Cabinet Office.

Department for Education and Employment (DfEE) (2000) *School Plus, Building Learning Communities.* London: DfEE.

Department for Education and Skills (DfES) (2001) *Schools Achieving Success.* White Paper. London: DfES.

Department for Education and Skills (DfES) (2001a) *Guidance for Schools.* London: DfES.

Department for Education and Skills (DfES) (2001b) *Investment for Reform.* London: DfES.

Maslow, A. (1970) *Motivation and Personality*, 2nd edn. London: Harper & Row.

OFSTED (2002). Report on Thomas Estley Community College, Leicester, London Ofsted.

The Educational Network (TEN) (2002) *Governance Matters.* www.ten.info

17

■ ■ ■

King Alfred's Learning Village: A New Learning Solution for Oxfordshire

Bernard Clarke

Background

For many years King Alfred's was the boys' grammar school serving the small Berkshire market town of Wantage, the adjacent village of Grove, just over one mile away, and the surrounding area. Girls who passed the 11 plus exam travelled ten miles to Faringdon for their grammar school education. At each end of Wantage, nearly two miles apart, lay two secondary modern schools (Icknield and Segsbury) for all those young people who failed to make the grade.

With the 'comprehensivisation' of the 1970s, King Alfred's, Icknield and Segsbury were redesignated as all ability schools with the result that Wantage became one of very few towns of less than 10,000 people that could boast three comprehensive schools.

A boundary change took Wantage and Grove from Berkshire into Oxfordshire and it was not long before the new local education authority (LEA) concluded that the town should have just one school. So in 1984 Wantage School was created consisting of Icknield Hall, Segsbury Hall and King Alfred's Hall (the three schools renamed). In order to make it function, a fleet of buses swept through the town all day long taking students to and from their lessons.

This unusual, probably unique, solution created a fundamental problem: how to make sense of an 11–18 school of over 2,000 students on three sites each situated at least a mile from the others.

Predictably, King Alfred's, the former grammar with its large and successful sixth form, recruited strongly and maintained its tradition of high academic standards and outstanding examination results. In contrast, the two former secondary moderns, whilst retaining the fierce loyalty of many local families, were less popular, particularly amongst educationally ambitious sections of the community, and less academically successful.

A further change in 1987 created two parallel 11–16 schools at Icknield and Segsbury, each taking their students on a geographical basis, with the large sixth form located at King Alfred's. However, as neither was large enough to accommodate all the 11 to 16 year olds, it was decided that Years 10 and 11 would spend alternate days at King Alfred's. A ten-day timetable was created and over a two-week period students spent half their time at their 'home' site (re-named East and West) and half at Centre. They simply took a different journey to school every other day. This arrangement, established in those far-off days before the national curriculum and formula funding, remains in place today.

Why change?

The preceding paragraphs are probably answer enough. But King Alfred's has existed on three sites for the best part of 20 years. To the outside world there has been little apparent problem – students are happy and do well enough, parents are generally satisfied and the community is proud of its school.

For the governors, the merger of three established schools and creation of the multi-site King Alfred's had been a stressful business during which feelings ran high amongst the staff and wider community. There was no great appetite to reopen old wounds.

On the inside, however, there was a different view. About one-fifth of lessons require teachers to travel between sites in zero time, invariably arriving flustered and up to 15 minutes late for their next class. For students at Key Stage 4, the daily alternating between sites has a seriously harmful effect on their education impeding, as it does, the sort of regular daily contact and support with tutors and other staff that can be so crucial to success. For instance, homework not handed in cannot be dealt with the next day because the student is on another site and, with the best will in the world, the matter has often lost its urgency 24 hours later. Hardly surprisingly, the performance of students, very good at Key Stages 3 and 5, is much less impressive at KS4.

Staff regularly complain about the disruption, waste of resources and inconvenience. Working on three sites represents a constant, nagging preoccupation (particularly if you are dependent on colleagues for lifts) and provides a prologue for nearly every conversation. Yet, as is usually the case, despite its massive influence over every aspect of their working lives, people get on and make the best of it.

In 1998, during a broadly positive OFSTED inspection, the three-site solution was described as 'elegant', but expensive, inefficient and an impediment to educational progress. This confirmed what the governors and staff had known for many years – that the structure has an adverse effect on everything we do, from the longstanding budget deficit (and consequent underfunding of teaching and learning) to the relative underperformance of substantial numbers of students, particularly less successful learners at Key Stage 4.

The options

Shortly after the inspection, the governors embarked on a thorough consideration of the alternative courses of action open to them. Briefly, these were to make three recommendations to the LEA:

- Stay as we are.
- Consolidate three sites into two.
- Move from three sites onto a single new site because none of the existing sites is suitable to accommodate the new building.

The first course of action was rejected out of hand. Change was essential. The second would only marginally reduce the problems of inefficiency. None of the sites lent itself to the substantial adaptations that would be required and major building works would be hugely disruptive to students' education for two years at least. It was clear to the governors that neither of the first two would work. The third option, on the other hand, offered a once in a lifetime opportunity not only to remove the inefficiencies of the past 20 years, but also to create a world-class, purpose-built educational centre serving the communities of Wantage, Grove and surrounding villages.

A further option, proposed by some local parish and town councillors, was to build a new 11–16 school in Grove. Having considered the idea, the governors rejected it for a number of reasons. It would have the effect of reducing the curriculum available to local young people (year groups of over 300 make possible an exceptionally wide range of courses). In the name of 'choice' it would place an 11–16 school within a mile of an established specialist 11–18 school with one of the largest and most successful sixth forms in Oxfordshire, a county where teacher recruitment and retention presents major and growing difficulties. It would put in jeopardy King Alfred's specialist school status. It would be unlikely to generate the private funding that it was increasingly clear would be essential to move King Alfred's from its three sites. Furthermore, the governors could see no advantage to their school in the inevitable downsizing that would result.

Most important of all was the fact that they were beginning to see the possibility of a development that could bring world-class education to this community. Set against that, the proposal for a separate 11–16 school a mile away represented 'the lowest common denominator' and carried the risk of a return to the days of destructive rivalry that had existed between the Wantage schools 20 years previously.

At the annual meeting for parents in November 1999, Pam Martin, the chair, presented the governors' proposals to dispose of the current three sites and create a new, purpose-designed secondary school and community learning centre 'located near the centre of population of the growing Wantage and Grove'.

A school for the twenty-first century

The governors had already set up a strategy group to investigate the environmental, financial and educational viability of a single establishment on a new site. As their discussions progressed it became increasingly clear that our ambition represented something new and very exciting.

Late in 1998, King Alfred's had applied to the DfEE to become a specialist Sports College. When the governors learned that the application was successful, they used the opportunity to pursue with more vigour their long-cherished ambition to work more closely with the people of Wantage, Grove and the surrounding villages. As a sign of this commitment, King Alfred's was renamed 'Community and Sports College'.

Inevitably, the governors' discussions of the new project embraced this community focus, supported as it was by the national concern with lifelong learning. This in turn led them to consider the significant rural isolation that affects a great many people in this part of Oxfordshire and also the learning needs of many groups of people and small businesses in the locality.

The strategy group had been given the job of exploring ways of building a new secondary school, but it was growing into much more. The governors' proposal for a secondary school for the twenty-first century was transforming itself into a vision of an entirely new community learning centre – a rural academy.

Shaping the vision

Having an exciting idea was one thing, but being able to visualise what the new King Alfred's might actually look like and how it might function was an altogether different matter. What we were now discussing was beyond the experience of any of us and it was at this point that the governors sought expert professional guidance from a leading firm of architects with considerable experience of working in the education sector.

Two architects joined the strategy group for lengthy orientation meetings. It was essential that they be thoroughly familiar with the history and nature of the current King Alfred's. They had to understand the need for change, share the governors' enthusiasm for 'what might be', appreciate the genuine concerns of local people about such a radical proposal and anticipate and be ready to respond to the potential political issues. What the governors wanted from them was a visualisation of their mission statement – an intellectual model for the layout and composition of the new college that would create enthusiasm whilst, at the same time, anticipating and addressing concerns and anxieties within the local community.

During the following months, one of the architects and the principal met several times to identify the key issues pertinent to the project. These crystallised into a series of questions, for example:

- How do you create a place for the individual in a community of over 2,000?
- What will the college be like for children transferring into Year 7 from small, rural primary schools?
- How should the buildings facilitate the transition from dependent learning to confident, independent lifelong learners?
- How do you create a sense of place, of ownership and of community?

These and other questions led the architects to incorporate into their thinking a number of key concepts:

1 *Scale.* An overriding issue in creating a college for over 2,000 people, scale embraces the way in which an individual relates to the wider environment, from the personal space of the locker or preferred independent learning space, to the tutor group, the year group and, by extension, the wider educational community. The architectural concept should respond to these concerns both within the individual buildings and the wider campus. The buildings at the front of the college should be lower in scale, particularly the base for Year 7. Buildings can increase in scale and intensity towards the rear of the site, emphasising a more focused academic environment.

2 *Legibility.* Being able to differentiate one building from another helps to orientate people. Students, staff and visitors should be able to 'read' and understand their built environment and to find their way around with ease.

3 *Sense of place.* Defining arrival and realising a tangible sense of place are fundamental in establishing the college as an identifiable destination and a focus for its wider community.

4 *Hierarchy of circulation.* The clear circulatory strategy for the campus will differentiate between vehicular and pedestrian zones. A main entrance should define the visitor approach, augmented by additional entrance and exit points to alleviate problems associated with peak traffic periods.

5   *Community access.* The college must demonstrate in its planning and visual character that it is accessible to all. As a centre for lifelong learning, certain elements of the college will be in operation well beyond the traditional parameters of the school day. With many facilities open all day, the restaurant space should act as a core focus of activity for the community.

6   *Security.* The safety of the large population of young people receiving their statutory education will be a major priority. Unobtrusive, effective security measures must be incorporated into the design to ensure this, whilst not deterring legitimate members of the wider community.

7   *Long term adaptability.* The modern classroom is changing as part of a new educational environment. Emerging technology and the demands of lifelong learning are creating a need for new spaces for individual and group learning. New buildings must be able to adapt to changing technology and teaching methods. A blend of core facilities will be combined with more flexible space that can be adapted as the geography of the classroom changes. The entire educational environment will be underpinned by a robust ICT infrastructure.

Consideration of all these issues took place against a background of two linked and fundamental concerns. The first was the rural context. Wantage and Grove lie at the foot of the Ridgeway, one of the oldest roadways in Europe, dating back to the Bronze Age, at least. The surrounding area is characterised by small settlements separated by large tracts of farmland. Generally speaking, it is not an area of large, modern buildings and Wantage itself remains in many ways an archetypal small market town.

The other concern was with the size of the new King Alfred's. Whereas below 500 is popularly regarded as too small for a secondary school, above 1,500 is thought to be getting dangerously large. Whatever the realities of the case, it was going to be vitally important to be able to reassure local people, especially parents worried that their young children might literally or metaphorically get 'lost', that size as defined by the number of students could be managed by good design and organisation. The concept that emerged from these lengthy and absorbing deliberations was a 'learning village'.

A journey around the college

In their report to the governors, the architects take the reader on a journey around the college:

> The buildings that will form the Community and Sports College are to be arranged in the manner of a small village. Grouped around an informal square, individual buildings will house different activities and curriculum areas. Each will have its own architectural character responding to these differing roles and uses. This will help to orientate staff, students and visitors as they move around the new campus, achieving a high degree of legibility and a definable sense of place. A series of streets

will link into this central heart of the college, connecting other facilities and providing a variety of routes into the space. Composed in this way the new college will demonstrate its educational ethos through its architectural ambience. Avoiding an institutional feel, the college conveys a subtle air of authority, instilling a sense of community and responsibility.

The arrival point

A primary entrance will provide access for all members of the college community and visitors down a formal drive. Vehicles will be able to peel off and park in dedicated areas, including those solely visiting the Sports complex. At the end of the drive will be the main College Entrance, the front door used by staff, visitors and community users. This gives direct access into the heart of the college.

The student entrance

The formal entrance is counterbalanced by the main route for students into the college. This is adjacent to the coach set-down area and offers direct access into the central forum from which all the buildings can be entered.

The Year 7 centre

This building, directly adjacent to the student entrance, is a reception building for new members of the college. It provides a secure base from which to explore the wider community. It will respond in scale to the younger students, be architecturally engaging, and have familiar associations with the primary schools the children have come from. It will also acknowledge that it is the first step into a new educational environment. The single and two-storey structure will be set around a central hall and contain a variety of teaching spaces. Year 7 will spend much of their first year in the building, while attending occasional lessons in more specialist areas.

General purpose teaching areas

A series of individual, but interconnected, buildings will contain a range of different curriculum areas and teaching environments. Each block or floor will contain core spaces for each subject area. This will be the centre of activity for that department, containing learning base units, cellular classrooms, seminar space, administrative office and support space. This arrangement will allow each department to display its particular ethos, and give visual variety to the journey around the building.

Set between the main blocks will be Independent Learning Centres for both students and staff. These will be visually connected to the principal teaching areas.

Small suites of WCs and cloakroom/locker facilities are introduced at appropriate intervals to enhance the creation of a civilised environment.

The overall building group will rise in scale from the two-storey Year 7 building up to four storeys, responding to the intensified academic activity.

Art Centre and Design and Technology Centre

These two dedicated facilities are set in the landscape adjacent to the main building group. This responds to the needs of the two particular curriculum areas, for specialist teaching space and dedicated environments. Both buildings will have central display areas around which a mixture of open plan and cellular teaching space will be provided. Covered links will provide access.

Science Centre

The Science building will reflect the role of this area of the curriculum and contain a range of laboratory facilities. The laboratories will be set around an Independent Learning Centre and a dedicated area for final year GCSE students – a pre-Sixth Form common room.

Sixth Form

The Sixth Form building occupies a strategic and high profile site adjacent to the student entrance and is highly visible within the college. The building recognises the status of these students while acknowledging their role and responsibility towards younger students. It will also be directly linked to the Learning Resource centre.

Theatre

The facilities for the teaching of Drama and Music are located near to the main entrance of the college. The theatre will provide a venue for Dance, Drama and Music workshops and performances and year group assemblies, and will offer one of the main facilities for community involvement. It will be a highly adaptable space, catering for a range of performance types and having potential for flat floor use.

Central building

The arrival building will contain administration, staff facilities and reception. The entrance foyer will connect directly into the college Restaurant. This dining space is conceived as being the primary informal social gathering space in the new college. It will contain a variety of areas to facilitate different dining requirements and be a place where all members of the community can meet. It will have all necessary support accommodation and relate directly to the performance space.

Sports Centre

The Sports Centre will be highly visible on arrival at the college, reflecting its significance, while also being directly integrated in the central forum by a street.

The centre will contain a large sports hall, a 25m pool and a learners' pool, along with changing facilities, fitness suite and dance studios. Two entrances for students and visitors will meet in a central area, which will link back to the Restaurant.

Central circulation

At ground floor level, individual buildings will be linked by undercover routes. At first floor level a fully enclosed circulation loop will link all main teaching areas. Lift access will be provided in strategic locations.

Cycle strategy

The vehicular and pedestrian strategy seeks to avoid conflicts. The central forum will be a pedestrian realm. The cycle path will navigate around the edge of the main buildings and offer those students who arrive by bicycle the opportunity to gain access directly adjacent to their tutor group areas.

A learning environment for the twenty-first century

The key question, of course, concerns the process of teaching and learning inside the new King Alfred's. What can we say about education in and for the twenty-first century? Knowledge is the wealth creator and the need for education, training and learning is growing at an exponential rate. There is widespread recognition that the UK already has significant and growing skills shortages. Successful organisations will be the ones that are able to learn and develop new skills and knowledge faster and more efficiently than others.

Traditional modes of teaching and learning will be inadequate to prepare young people for that world. If that weren't reason enough to contemplate change, developments in technology certainly are. Whether or not new schools turn out to be 'networks with walls', digital technology is creating new and effective ways for people, particularly young people, to learn at a bewildering rate. The challenge for the new King Alfred's will be to harness the best of e-learning and combine it with the best of face-to-face education with the aim of developing competent, confident lifelong learners.

It is impossible to foresee the precise nature of the teaching and learning process in even five years' time. In planning an educational establishment for such an unpredictable future, therefore, we will need to rely on those central beliefs that do not change.

High quality staff

It is not sentimental to suggest that, whatever technology brings in the future, the quality of learning will continue to depend very largely on the quality of those who provide and facilitate it. At a time when there are major concerns about the supply of teachers and the effects that scarcity is having on the status, morale, ethos and quality of the profession, we are determined that the new King Alfred's will be a place where the best staff will actively want to work.

Teachers will embrace new developments in pedagogy and technology. The professional boundaries between them, teaching assistants, technicians, other adults and, indeed, students will become increasingly blurred as teams are formed that bring together the widest possible range of knowledge and expertise.

Accessibility

King Alfred's will be a centre with a physical location but also a virtual presence that will support learning in the home and workplace. The physical environment will be designed and located in such a way as to invite and welcome all comers. It will be equipped and committed to meet the learning needs of every member of this large rural community 24 hours a day, 7 days a week, 365 days a year.

Flexibility

We have the possibility to create an environment that will remove the straitjacket from learning and be based on the needs of the learner, taking account of their ages, stages, aptitudes and learning styles. It will offer an environment that will motivate all young people and attract adults back to learning. Nobody will be excluded.

Ethos

Humans are and will remain fundamentally social beings dependent for their successful development on relationships with others. In an era of unprecedented change, society will require its citizens, more than ever, to be socially and emotionally mature people, confident and adaptable in an age of transformation, sensitive to the needs of others, able to work both independently and co-operatively. Increasingly, it will be less about how we teach them and more about how we treat them. Young people will be more dependent than ever for their successful development on good role models.

Vision to reality

In some ways, the easy bit of leadership is developing and sharing a vision for the future. The really tough part, as always, is making it happen. There is widespread enthusiasm, both locally and nationally, for the proposals. It has not been difficult to engender the interest of the DfES, the Prime Minister's Policy Unit, Youth Sports Trust, Technology Colleges Trust and many other groups and organisations. A typical response runs along the following lines: 'It sounds brilliant, ground breaking. It must happen. How will you fund it? Don't let the local politicians derail it.' It goes without saying that, in order for it to happen, a number of major issues must be resolved.

Relationship between the governing body and the LEA

This lies at the heart of the notion of educational 'leadership' and raises the question of where responsibilities begin and end. The governors are of the clear view that had they not conceived the proposals for a single-site King Alfred's and developed them into the vision of a learning village serving the entire community, nothing would have happened.

Indeed, why should it? Superficially, from the LEA's point of view there is not a major problem at King Alfred's. Sure, there is the ongoing budget deficit, but they would say that can be dealt with by prudent management. If Key Stage 4 results are showing insufficient added value, the annual monitoring and target setting process will take care of that, or at least demonstrate that the officers are doing their part. In fairness, the LEA has plenty of pressing issues to deal with and, in the scheme of things, knocking down and rebuilding a school that has no obvious major problems might not appear high on its priority list.

The fact remains, though, that the vision will remain just that unless and until the LEA embraces it fully and is determined to see it become reality. The governors take the view that they must keep pressing until it does.

Funding

At first sight the issue of funding is straightforward: sell the three existing sites for development and use the proceeds to pay for the new King Alfred's. But things are never that simple. East and West sites are owned by the LEA and, notwithstanding their limited potential for housing development, could be disposed of, subject to the agreement of Sport England that we get rid of the fields. Centre site (the original King Alfred's), on the other hand, includes a number of listed buildings and stands on land owned by the King Alfred's Educational Charity. It will therefore be necessary to gain not only the trustees' agreement and support, but also that of the Charity Commissioners.

The receipts from the disposal of the three sites will not be sufficient for what we want. The learning village is not a cheap option and the shortfall could be as much as £10–15 million.

In their single-minded enthusiasm for a project they had conceived and developed, the governors sought financial backing from the business world. Given the example of the City Technology Colleges (CTCs), it seemed obvious that multinational technology companies along the M4 corridor would be queuing up to be associated with such a ground-breaking project. They quickly learned otherwise.

The only other alternative they could see (apart from a generous benefactor) was Private Finance Initiative (PFI). For various reasons, not least 15 years of 'hung council', Oxfordshire County Council has so far chosen not to pursue this route. However, with the recent reorganisation of the council into an executive structure, there are clear indications that decision making has become more clear-cut and effective and we are optimistic that the proposals will be adopted as a potential PFI project. That still leaves a number of questions to be resolved:

1 What will be the effect of PFI on the governance and ethos of King Alfred's?
2 To work as it should, the learning village must be really good – designed, built and equipped to a very high standard. How far will economic factors force us to compromise on the 'dream'?
3 Will the Learning and Skills Council have a role in the capital development of the post-16 provision?

Hearts and minds

In a part of the country steeped in tradition where many people react with suspicion to change of any sort, the plans are certainly controversial. Some local politicians have already demonstrated their unwillingness or inability to engage in a debate about the educational merits of the case. A more pressing concern to them appears to be whether the learning village will be situated on the Grove or Wantage side of the boundary and there have been the predictable newspaper headlines and correspondence about the undesirability of a 'megaschool' serving both.

Nevertheless, King Alfred's is and will remain a facility for the local community and the views of local people must have a bearing on the form it will take. In due course, if all goes well, the county council will embark on the statutory consultation process in relation to the proposals. This raises the interesting question about who will be consulted.

Meetings with parents of students currently attending King Alfred's and those likely to in the future have been positively received. Like most parents, they want their children to be safe and happy and to receive a good education. Once the initial anxieties about size and location have been addressed, they have engaged with the educational issues and seen the potential benefits for their children and their children's children.

The new King Alfred's will be a school for the twenty-first century. Many of the current staff, governors and local politicians will have moved on by the time it comes to pass. One group that will still be around is the current students – the parents of tomorrow – and it seems only right that their views should be sought.

18
■ ■ ■

If You Were Starting Again, Would You Start From Here?

Tony Hinkley

> *We cannot restructure a structure that is splintered at its roots. Adding wings to caterpillars does not create butterflies – it creates awkward and dysfunctional caterpillars. Butterflies are created through transformation.*

(Marshall, 1995: p.1)

There is a tendency to believe that state education came to England with the 1870 Education Act. In fact, the state had been involved since at least the 1830s and the debate over education for the poor had been going for many years prior to that. No progress of note was made until 1833 when parliament made its first limited grant to education. The grant itself was small and went to religious bodies which used it to build schools. Its significance was that it was the first acceptance by the government of any financial responsibility for the education of the poor.

However, it was with the Education Act of 1870 that we do have the real birth of the modern system of education in England. The Act, drafted by William Forster, included these four main points:

1 The country would be divided into about 2,500 school districts.

2 School boards were to be elected by ratepayers in each district.

3 School boards were to examine the provision of elementary education in their district, provided then by voluntary societies, and if there were not enough school places, they could build and maintain schools out of the rates.

4 School boards could make their own by-laws which would allow them to charge fees or, if they wanted, to let children in free.

These elementary Board Schools had to be non-denominational and they had to guarantee attendance for all children in their respective districts between the ages of 5 and 13.

Balfour's 1902 National State Education Act abolished all 2,568 school boards and handed over their duties to local borough or county councils. These new local education authorities (LEAs) were given powers to establish new secondary and technical schools as well as developing the existing system of elementary schools.

In the history of English education the most important piece of legislation of the twentieth century was the Education Act of 1944, also known as the Butler Act. It replaced all previous legislation. The Act raised the school-leaving age to 15 and provided universal free schooling in three different types of schools: grammar, secondary modern and technical. Butler hoped that these schools would cater for the different academic levels and other aptitudes of children. Entry to these schools was based on the 11 plus examination.

In 1965 LEAs were asked by the government to submit schemes for comprehensive secondary schooling and the debate continues. In 1972 the school leaving age was raised to 16 (readers of a certain generation will remember ROSLA – Raising Of the School Leaving Age).

The 1988 Education Reform Act has been the single most important piece of education legislation since the 1944 Education Act and it has shaped the nature of our education system for the rest of the last century and into this one. The most obvious and striking aspect of this Act was the establishment for the first time of a prescribed national curriculum for all children in state schools from the age of 5 upwards. A national assessment procedure was introduced, with testing taking place at ages 7, 11, 14 and 16. The results of schools (though not of individuals) were made available to the public in the infamous 'league tables'. Public information was a key feature of the Act and the developments that followed.

Governing bodies were given wide-ranging powers, particularly with regard to hiring and firing staff and financial management, and they had to broaden their composition to include local business people as well as a higher proportion of parents. A further shift in power away from LEAs came in the form of 'opting out' of LEA control (grant maintained schools). If a simple majority of parents wished to do so, they could remove their school from the control of the local authority in perpetuity and receive funding directly from the (then) Department of Education and Science. Daily acts of collective worship were made compulsory for all pupils in attendance at a maintained school.

Since then changes have come at what appears to have been an ever-increasing rate. These include (in no particular order) the introduction of regular school inspections by the Office for School Standards in Education (OFSTED), the results of which are made public, Special Educational Needs Code of Practice, Local Management of Schools (LMS), discontinuance of grant maintained schools, abolition of corporal punishment, changing regulations on pupil exclusion, the National Grid for Learning and so on. Now, with Tony Blair's 'education, education, education' still ringing in our ears, we have a series of White and Green Papers and the 2002 Education Act, with its promised freedoms and flexibilities arising out of 'diversity and innovation'.

So we have an education system that has evolved over many years but is still recognisable as a subject-based system with passes and failures built in – a system that values some, not all. A system that has educational exclusion as a consequence, with social unrest and disharmony following closely behind. Our education system was designed for a time and purpose that no longer exist. If you were starting again, would you start from here?

The current context

Globalisation and interconnectivity are underlying modern themes in looking at the political, environmental, societal and technical environments in education. It is becoming as easy to communicate and trade with a country on the other side of the world as with a neighbour. The world has become smaller than ever and people's expectations across the world have changed.

Educational materials and opportunities are available as never before. Too many members of society feel disengaged from learning. We must avoid the continuation of an underclass of people unwilling or unable to learn. Our future economic and societal success in a global context is dependent on the quality of our education system.

We need to develop an education system fit for society in the twenty-first century. Learning to learn for life is a prerequisite in order to cope with life's complex uncertainties. Provision of education opportunities must be truly inclusive of all members of our community and responsive to their needs. Local government agencies will need to realign their services to focus on the individual and target resources according to need. These agencies will improve their efficiency and effectiveness in delivering a comprehensive provision for our community.

How might this be achieved? Through the establishment of community learning centres (CLCs) which will be the focus of educational provision (but not the sole provider), learning opportunities will be accessible 24 hours a day, 7 days a week, either physically at community learning centres or via information communications technology (ICT); community access will be an entitlement for all and curriculum provision will be rich, varied and relevant to the needs of the learners.

If you were starting again, would you start from here?

The learning centre and the community of learners

Perhaps schools won't look like schools. Perhaps we will be using the total community as a learning environment.

(Taylor, 1993: p.41)

Imagine this. Learning activities would be based on community learning centres. Their organisation could be based on existing higher and further education centres, colleges, secondary and primary schools and libraries. Video-conferencing and e-mail would link the centres and sub-centres. Homes would also be linked to the community learning centres electronically, as would employers and higher and further education.

Community learning centres would be federated. Each federation of community learning centres would have its own governing body or management group. Each federated CLC would need a leader to ensure the most effective and economic use of the skills of those employed. Those working for the learning centres would include staff with a wide range of contractual arrangements. Flexible contracts may be an essential feature to enable deployment to meet needs.

Staff would be employed with a variety of qualifications including fully qualified teachers, PGCE students, trainee teachers, lecturers, teaching assistants and support staff. Most staff would be located at the learning centres whilst others would be available electronically, through e-mail, video or telephone link, to provide teaching, tutorial support and counselling.

Learners of any age would be able to attend physically for tutorial work and self-supported study, as well as for formal lessons or training. The centres would satisfy a range of learning needs from entry level to degree qualifications. A wide range of courses and opportunities, combining but not labelling the academic, vocational and occupational, would therefore be offered physically and electronically.

Pupils would attend the community learning centres based upon age and need rather than on calendar year. Familiar patterns of the school day and year and the nature of 'a day in school' would change. A four- or five-term year is likely for most, providing a formal academic year of even portions. For older students the concept of a term would rapidly disappear as learning is related to personal targets. Increased flexibility in the nature and timing of assessments would encourage learning flexibility. Assessments would be designed to measure what students can do when they are ready.

Students of all ages in the community would be able to access teaching programmes to gain additional qualifications or develop skills that are not age related. These would be available in and out of 'school hours'. So, for example, qualifications might be gained during holidays, at the weekend or in the evening and alongside other age groups who might be taught or be learning electronically at the community learning centres.

Funding for the centres would come from private and public sources. Public funding would come from central government, local government, and learning and skills councils. Private funding would come from those accessing the community learning centres for specific courses and also from sponsors of courses that address local needs.

Community learning centres would serve the community beyond the formal educational role. By involving the community in policy and practice, needs would have to be identified along with views from the provision of labour market intelligence.

There will be a number of important issues outstanding, including: governance regulations; financial arrangements; integration with existing national and local policy; national conditions of service for staff (including teachers and school and college leaders); national and local priorities. If education is a 'whole life' process, how do we capture and recognise learning which takes place elsewhere other than at community learning centres?

Approaches to learning

Learning is the most powerful, engaging, rewarding and enjoyable aspect of our personal and collective experience. The ability to learn about learning and become masters of the learning process is the critical issue for the next century.

(Honey, 1999)

The main role of community learning centres in the future will be to develop in all people the skills and attitudes that will enhance their natural state as learners. Children are born with an insatiable motivation to learn. It is a sadness that the systems in which they grow up slowly but steadily whittle away this motivation. These 'forces of destruction' exist in schools as much as, or even more than, elsewhere. Therefore, the approaches to learning must open up a wide range of possibilities for young people in particular and not close down potential opportunities. The barriers to learning must be identified and systematically removed if learning is to be seen as natural, valued and cherished, as well as taking place everywhere and at all times.

If learning is defined as a change in the cognitive state of the individual (e.g. skill, knowledge, attitude, behaviour), then the importance of interaction between individuals must be recognised. Learning best takes place in a communal or collaborative context and the potential tension between learning in a social context and individual learning opportunities must be reconciled. Nevertheless there needs to be a focus on the learners and their attributes and needs – individualisation of the need as opposed to the activity and a paradigm shift from the organisation to the individual learner.

On this context rests the concept of a learning society where learning is valued, encouraged and facilitated for all. This concept remains a cliché unless strategies are in place to deliver the vision. Lifelong learning is a frequently used term with few dissenters to the concept. All learning needs to be valued at whatever level and for whatever purpose.

Learning at home

We need to address what is actually happening in homes of today and in the future. Parenting skills are extremely important. CLCs will need to help develop parenting skills in order that children's learning can be enhanced at home through play, and so that they are positive about and supported in their learning at the community learning centre. Recent research indicates that early, positive and regular interaction with parents (e.g. reading, talking, playing) gives children a headstart in life – an absence of this interaction cannot be made up later.

We must also address the influence that aspects such as diet play on the cognitive development of young people. In this area we have perhaps only just begun to scratch the surface of understanding the connections between diet, health, environment and the capacity to learn.

The media will play an increasingly important role in offering learning opportunities to families and individuals in the future. Interaction and involvement with these developments will be vital for schools in order to define, capitalise on and support learning in the family situation.

Learning at community learning centres

> *Instead of a national curriculum for education, what is really needed is an individual curriculum for every child.*

(Handy, 1991: p.171)

This should not mean being taught in the traditional and narrow sense. The range of activities here should include:

1 *Teacher directed learning*: classroom activity directed by the teacher.

2 *Self-supported study*: utilising texts /internet/intranet/video conferencing, etc.

3 *Peer group activities*: social and team activities.

4 *Individualised learning programmes*: negotiated between learner and mentor.

5 *Other activities*: a broad range organised at the centres, but which are provided or led by a mixture of teachers and other adults.

In the early stages (up to, say, age 14) an agreed common core of curriculum experiences and opportunities will be needed. This would need to be designed to develop the skills and attitudes related to learning and life in general. From age 14 youngsters may learn through self-supported study/distance learning. This could be through individualised programmes with youngsters negotiating what/when/how learning should take place. We must also address the potential tension between the need to follow a prescribed curriculum and the personal motivation or desires of the learner. The delivery of the curriculum becomes an area of negotiation with each learner.

Students of all ages will need to understand better the potential of their brains. We need to investigate and incorporate the exciting work that exists and is emerging on the power of the brain, preferred learning styles, theories of 'multiple intelligences' and learning to learning strategies. The emphasis is rightly moving from teaching to learning. Again we need to investigate further what motivates people to learn and identify and remove the barriers to learning and motivation. An increased awareness of the importance of the emotional state of the learner is vital and the ability to articulate feelings in an assertive but non-threatening manner must also be developed. The concept of 'high challenge–low threat' as the most productive learning environment must be embedded in learning situations and programmes.

The use of ICT in enhancing learning and opportunities for learning needs to develop further. Resourcing to ensure entitlement for all will increasingly become an issue, but we are not talking here merely of 'schools of today with more kit', nor just of ICT and the 'virtual teacher'. ICT will be used as a tool for collaborative learning, guided and facilitated by skilful teachers who are just some of the players in the learning process in our communities.

Learning in the community

Community learning centres must see themselves as leaders of the educational and learning processes, taking the initiative in such areas as the development of family learning opportunities (more than simply learning 'schoolwork' in the family). It will be important to devise processes which will prevent (or catch) those youngsters who might 'fall through the net' of such provision. Community learning centres must take an interventionist role in ensuring all young people have an entitlement and the necessary encouragement and support to achieve their potential. Education must be inclusive of all and by this we include learners of all ages and backgrounds, of all abilities and disabilities, of all tendencies and beliefs. Community learning centres will be accessible 24 hours per day, 7 days per week, 365 days per year (physically or virtually via ICT).

We should involve adults, other than teachers, in the learning process and celebrate the achievements and enjoyment of learners, whatever the context and whatever the age. This government's scheme, Connexions, suggests one model for some of this involvement. We should utilise the media in a positive manner, both to support learning in a variety of locations and contexts and also in celebrating the achievements and enjoyment of learners.

Will encouraging children at a certain age to have more experience of the world of work (including paid employment) lead to better motivation of the learner and greater involvement from the community? Is this an area of potential for the development of some of the social and team skills that are valued? All learning, in whatever location, at whatever level and for whatever purpose must be valued and offered appropriate recognition and accreditation. The whole process of socialisation is part of this argument and a multi-agency approach is essential in order to capitalise on the potentials of young people. This will extend beyond the school and home into health, housing, social services, industry, commerce, etc.

Social and educational roles of community learning centres

We must make sure we fill the 'moral vacuum'. It will be important not to overlook the social, moral and ethical contribution that CLCs will continue to make to society. Currently many schools provide the 'social glue', giving structure and certainties to many young people and their families, whereas life is often lacking such structure and full of uncertainties (but also full of information and, increasingly, access to information without controls). With the increasing spread of dysfunction in family life, for many students school is the only stable environment. This contribution needs on-site contact with others. For many communities the extended family has all but disappeared; for some pupils, schools provide the only stable societal experience they may have. Therefore, parenting skills should be at the forefront. These might include how parents could help their children to learn, supporting literacy, numeracy and information communications technology (ICT), the impact of diet and exercise on learning and behaviour, managing time, personal finance and maximising opportunities.

Many schools provide necessary child-care facility whilst also delivering the core purposes of education. Community learning centres will have to become more flexible to make best use of specialist buildings and facilities, whilst capitalising on the resources and contexts in the various communities in which schools are located. Students will not keep regular hours since such flexibilities will not be compatible with the 8.45–3.30 school day. The 'welfare dependency' aspect of 'free' school meals etc. will also need to considered further.

There is an increasing sense in which schools (and, by definition, teachers) are taking on those complex roles, and the sense that the expectations on schools and on teachers are becoming untenable unless something changes. If successful learning is to be the prime purpose of the community learning centre, then these issues must be addressed. Models which exist in other countries (such as teacher as subject specialist, counsellor as social development specialist) might warrant further investigation to ascertain the desirability and transferability of such practices. One solution may be for the community learning centre to be part of what is, in effect, a multi-agency approach; i.e. the physical site of the institution contains a range of professionals all working in concert to meet the needs of the young person. This would also suggest a radical review of the tutorial function in schools and a much broader perspective on what are currently teaching perspectives on careers education and guidance, personal, social and health education and citizenship.

There is currently a clear tension between the roles of schools as experts in curriculum pedagogy and the social roles that schools have to play (both implicitly and explicitly). It is part of the business of schools to 'teach' aspects of citizenship and how to cope in modern society. But citizenship should be lived rather than taught. What better way for ensuring that young people play their full role in adult democratic processes than through their engagement in real democracy and citizenship activities during their formative years?

Students will need to be encouraged and helped to become active citizens rather than passive subjects. They should be engaged in discussion that recognises their own experiences and extends their comprehension and involvement, debating citizenship on a wider platform – locally, nationally and globally. Ensuring the provision of an educational 'bill of rights' for students will be a fundamental part of the social development role of community learning centres. With rights go obligations, and the exercise of these is essential to the development of active citizens.

Community learning centres will have a clear responsibility to work with their own communities and agencies within them in order to develop students' capacity to contribute to society at a number of levels. Their role will involve developing in students some appreciation that there may be many sides to these concepts, each representing a particular ideological viewpoint. This approach raises critical faculties and awareness of society's origins and perspectives; thus preparing students for the challenges of adulthood in an uncertain world. Living (safely) with uncertainty helps facilitate the capacity to develop alternatives and innovation.

Part of the social and educational role of community learning centres involves the development of the autonomous individual. Therefore they will have to consider how to provide learners with the authority to make choices about content, form and direction of their own learning. Learners having more influence and control over their own destiny and mode of operation will inevitably mean teachers having less control than at present. This is a challenge not to be taken lightly. It will require courage and courageous leadership.

Leadership roles and teachers

Where there is genuine vision, people excel and learn, not because they are told to, but because they want to.

(Senge, 1990: 9)

Vision – a key aspect of leadership – and education leaders must provide the inspiration for others to achieve what they might not have imagined possible. As well as leading learning, we must be the leading learners in our organisations and communities and set the necessary personal example to others. There will be leadership requirements for setting and maintaining moral and ethical stances and an appropriate ethos, as well as leading the management of the interface between the community learning centres and the community, and continually seeking opportunities for improvement.

The role of the head teacher

Community learning centres will still have the parent-substitute and socialising role up to, say, 14 years of age, and there will be leadership requirements for setting and maintaining moral and ethical stances and maintaining an appropriate ethos. These are skills similar to those needed today, though their application may vary for students of different ages and in different contexts. The role of the leader (what new title will be more appropriate than 'head teacher'?) will therefore require an ability to maintain a cohesive overall view. The ability to have a 'presence' for students and staff in such a diverse arrangement will require advanced skills of communication including a facility for using developing technologies.

Many of the current expectations will, of course, remain. These include leading the management of the interface between the community learning centre and the community, and continually seeking opportunities for improvement, as well as the more mundane aspects currently found in job descriptions. Some of these skills will also be important in developing and maintaining an international aspect to education to ensure adoption of best practice on a global scale.

Role of the teacher

Teacher workload is increasingly recognised as a problem and the issue of 'teacher as parent-substitute' as opposed to 'teacher as learning director' must be resolved. Skills will need to become more focused and time more effectively used. There may be different specialists for different roles, and these specialists may not always be teachers. Either way there will be a need for flexibility due to the diversity of opportunity provided by the education system.

Again enhanced communication skills will be needed together with a facility for using advanced technology. An ability to work in isolation and as part of a team, both remote and at close quarters, may be needed. Initiative to be self-sufficient in acquiring the skills and traits for particular aspects of the job may be a greater advantage than at present. Knowledge of the world of work will be required as part of an integrated aspect of learning and/or as part of the more closely linked subsequent stage after 'standard education' but sand-wiched between or alongside further education.

Teachers will not lose their responsibility for curriculum pedagogy. They will need to develop further their professional expertise in the newer areas of lead-ing learning rather than the management of teaching. The management of increasing numbers of 'para-professionals' (e.g. learning support assistants) will become the norm. Development of assessment strategies that are compe-tence based and management of groups that are not necessarily age related provide other examples of the changes and challenges.

Governance as community leadership

Schools are subject both to an overall professional supervision by an LEA and to lay governance through a board of governors. To assist both groups in their functions there is external scrutiny by OFSTED. The role of the governors in ensuring that the system works is likely to be enhanced, but will they continue to be lay appointees or should a more professional (paid) dimension develop?

The nature of the school as a centre for community learning (providing leader-ship, vision, expertise and resources) will need an enhanced role for governors, possibly with increased financial implications. Community learning centres that are completely porous, i.e. which operate as 24-hour, 365-day a year schools, will not be communities in the sense that schools are now. Clearly they will need a different approach to governance in order to fulfil this different role in the community. Schools must become more community focused – communities must become more involved in the support of their schools.

Specific desired outcomes

The transformation of our education system is at the heart of the government's reform agenda. It is a challenge that is great, necessary and possible. It also has profound moral depth as it addresses directly the learning needs of our students, the professional growth of our teachers and enhances the role of the school as an agent of social change.

(Hopkins, 2002: p.1)

What might we see that is different? Surely we would expect to see improved results in public assessments and exams, at least meeting and hopefully exceeding government expectations. In addition increased uptake of learning opportunities and raised self-esteem in learners of all ages would be evident, leading to a better qualified population and improved employment opportunities for the people. A significant improvement in morale and sense of community well-being and pride in residents and employees nationwide would ensue as well as increased participation in social and economic prosperity.

The time is ripe to agree a new set of principles, plan for the changes needed and act to create the education system our children deserve to inherit.

Acknowledgements

The author is grateful for the contributions of the following SHA Council members and allies in the production of this chapter. SHA: Bernadette Barnes, Richard Bird, Carolyn Brawn, Marsha Elms, Richard Fawcett, Terry Gibson, Barbara Peck, Chris Wade.

Others: Valerie Bayliss, RSA; Dr Paul Clarke, Leeds Metropolitan University; Toby Greany, Campaign for Learning; Tony Hutchinson, Suffolk LEA; Professor John West-Burnham, Hull University.

References

Handy C. (1991) *The Age of Unreason*. Cambridge, MA: Harvard Business School Press.

Honey, P. (1999) http://www.peterhoney.com/main/declaration

Hopkins, D. (2002) 'ZONEin' *EAZ Newsletter*, summer 2002.

Marshall, S.P. (1995) http://www.21learn.org/publ/synthesis/synthesis_four.htm

Schools Plus (2000) *Building Learning Communities: Report from the Schools Plus Policy Action Team*. London: DfES. pp. 18–19.

Scottish Office (1988) *Communities: Change Through Learning; Report of a Working Group on the Future of Community Education*. Edinburgh: Scottish Office. p. 6.

Senge, P. (1990) *The Fifth Discipline*. New York: Currency Doubleday.

Taylor, A. (1993) 'How schools are redesigning their space', *Educational Leadership*, 51 (1).

Index

■ ■ ■